Authors and Publishers

Authors and Publishers

Agreements and Legal Aspects of Publishing

Second Edition

Lazar Sarna

of the Quebec Bar

Butterworths

Toronto and Vancouver

Authors and Publishers, 2nd ed.

Printed and bound in Canada.

The Butterworth Group of Companies

Canada
Butterworths, Toronto and Vancouver

United Kingdom
Butterworth & Co. (Publishers) Ltd., London and Edinburgh

Australia
Butterworths Pty Ltd., Sydney, Melbourne, Brisbane, Adelaide and Perth

New Zealand
Butterworths (New Zealand) Ltd., Wellington and Auckland

Singapore
Butterworth & Co. (Asia) Pte. Ltd., Singapore

South Africa
Butterworth Publishers (SA) (Pty) Ltd., Durban and Pretoria

United States
Butterworth Legal Publishers, Boston, Seattle, Austin and St. Paul
D & S Publishers, Clearwater

Canadian Cataloguing in Publication Data

Sarna, Lazar, 1948-
Authors and publishers

Bibliography: p.
Includes index.
ISBN 0-409-80628-5

1. Authors and publishers - Canada. 2. Contracts - Canada. I. Title.

KE2825.S37 1987 343.71'0780705 C87-093371-X

Executive Editor (P. & A.) - L. Hines
Sponsoring Editor - D. Lundy
Managing Editor - L. Kee
Supervisory Editor - M. Graham
Editor/Cover Design - M. Posner
Production - J. Thomson

TO MY JEWEL

Table of Contents

Table of Cases

Table of Statutes

Canada

Bankruptcy Act, R.S.C. 1970, c. B-3
Canada Council Act, R.S.C. 1970, c. C-2, as amended
Canadian Bill of Rights, 1960 (Can.), c. 44 (R.S.C. 1970, App., III)
Copyright Act, R.S.C. 1970, c. C-30
Criminal Code, R.S.C. 1970, c. C-34
Income Tax Act, 1970-71-72 (Can.), c. 63, as amended
National Library Act, R.S.C. 1970, c. N-11

Alberta

Defamation Act, R.S.A. 1970, c. 87
Libraries Act, R.S.A. 1970, c. 206

British Columbia

British Columbia Cultural Fund Act, 1967 (B.C.), c. 7, as amended
Funds Control Act, R.S.B.C. 1979, c. 146
Libel and Slander Act, R.S.B.C. 1979, c. 234

Manitoba

Arts Council Act, R.S.M. 1970, c. A140
Defamation Act, R.S.M. 1970, c. D20
Public Libraries Act, R.S.M. 1970, c. P220

Ontario

Arts Council Act, S.O. 1984, c. 57
Libel and Slander Act, R.S.O. 1980, c. 237, as amended
Paperback and Periodical Distributors Act, R.S.O. 1980, c. 366
Public Libraries Act, R.S.O. 1970, c. 381

Prince Edward Island

Defamation Act, R.S.P.E.I. 1974, c. D-3

Quebec

Act respecting the guarantee of certain loans to publishers and booksellers and to amend the Québec Industrial Development Assistance Act, 1975 (Que.), c. 15
National Library Act, R.S.Q. 1977, c. B-2
Newspaper Declaration Act, R.S.Q. 1964, c. 49
Press Act, R.S.Q. 1977, c. P-19, as amended
Public Libraries Act, R.S.Q. 1964, c. 59

Publication and Public Morals Act, R.S.Q. 1964, c. 50, as amended
Publishers Loss Insurance Act, R.S.Q. 1977, c. A-27, as amended

Saskatchewan

Arts Board Act, R.S.S. 1978, c. A-28
Libel and Slander Act, R.S.S. 1978, c. L-14
Public Libraries Act, R.S.S. 1978, c. P-39

Introduction

The basic purpose of a publishing agreement between an author and publisher is to permit the latter to publish and distribute, under certain terms and conditions, the author's work, and to provide to the author a right to remuneration often contingent upon publication. The author in the circumstances may be the creator, editor, compiler or translator of a manuscript; the publisher may desire to reproduce the manuscript in the form of a book, brochure, newspaper or magazine article. Depending on the nature of the manuscript and type of publication, the agreement between the author and publisher will vary in form, explicitness and scope: it is a common occurrence in the book trade that an author enters into a written agreement with the publisher following acceptance of the manuscript but prior to publication; depending on the size and content of the work, publishers of newspapers and periodicals often rely on mere cross-letters for the constitution of their contractual arrangements with the author.

As mentioned, the more sophisticated agreement may be found in common use within the book trade; consequently, the present analysis will in great measure deal with author-publisher agreements contingent upon the publication of a work in book form. Book trade agreements usually set out an exhaustive list of rights and obligations imposed upon both parties with perhaps greater economic concern displayed toward the interests of the publisher. The publisher after all is in most cases not funded by the author and must incur the ordinary business risks involved in printing, marketing, selling and distributing the work in a profitable manner. While the author may receive the social honour attendant upon having a work printed and circulated as well as financial remuneration for services rendered in creating or compiling manuscripts, it is ultimately the publisher who assumes the greater financial burden; he therefore attempts to limit his business risks by assuming as much control as necessary over the work. Accordingly, many book trade agreements are standard form documents drafted by the publisher depending on his relative bargaining strength, the author may or may not accede to all contractual issues, including such points as assignment of copyright, minimal royalty schedules, and conferral of all subsidiary rights which prove to be of great value to the publisher if the publication turns out to be a highly marketable product.

Agreements generally provide to the publisher the following rights: the right to print, distribute, translate, reprint in cheaper editions, arrange serialization and reproduction of the work in other forms. On the other hand, the obligations incurred by the publisher include the obligation to publish, pay royalties and account for profits. The author takes benefit of the obligations just mentioned and often incurs the obligations of warranting originality, assuming responsibility for libel, and even proofreading and modifying the manuscript for subsequent editions.

There is little guidance to be found in existing statutory law respecting the drafting, content and interpretation of author-publisher agreements. The Copyright Act[1] certainly provides a basis for determining the extent to which rights to reproduce have been given or transferred to the publisher by the author. Nevertheless, many of the obligations contained in the contractual arrangements between the parties must be defined by the existing common or civil law on contract insofar as the form, substance and execution are concerned. Where contract law itself is not explicit, reference must be made to trade practice and common business usage if difficulties arise in applying the agreement to particular situations. At the present stage, the Canadian case law on the subject is minimal and finds its basis for the most part in the statutory copyright provisions as well as the English judicial experience in the matter.

The present study will contain a clause-by-clause treatment of the most fundamental provisions of current author-publisher agreements and, in this regard, will discuss within the framework of the book publishing industry the obligations and rights involved in the undertaking to publish, distribute, pay royalties and effect re-editions. The study will also discuss the form of agreements, as well as the relationship of the parties as far as literary agency and subsidiary rights are concerned.

---

[1] R.S.C. 1970, c. C-30.

Chapter 1

The Publishing Industry

Statutory Background

The publishing industry is not regarded by statute law as a utility. Unlike services provided by gas, water and electrical service corporations, publishing is not subject to intense regulation with respect to licensing to operate, royalty tariffs, authorization to publish individual works and distribution. This is not to say that various jurisdictions have not enacted legislation specifically governing the publishing industry. It is however intended to indicate that for the most part publishers are free to operate their industry with little more legislative control than that governing other commercial enterprises in Canada. The current copyright legislation[1] certainly affects the publisher in that it defines to a degree the nature and extent of copyright to materials produced. The legislation purports to fix royalties in limited non-conventional situations[2] and to prescribe the nature of the publication of a specific work under ministerial licence.[3] The law furthermore limits the importation practices of publishers insofar as copyright infringement is concerned.[4] Nevertheless, even recent proposals for a revision of the existing copyright law[5] do not aim at a system of regulation of the publishing industry in all its aspects, save insofar as the proposed modified notion of copyright is affected. Although the recent legislative proposals are supportive of the regulation of collective authors' societies as far as contract and

[1] Copyright Act, R.S.C. 1970, c. C-30.

[2] *Ibid.*, ss. 7(1), 14(8).

[3] *Ibid.*, s. 14.

[4] *Ibid.*, s. 27.

[5] Keyes, A. A., and Brunet, C., *Copyright in Canada — Proposals for a Revision of the Law, Consumer and Corporate Affairs Canada*, Ottawa, 1977, pp. 45-53; to some extent, see recommendations 110-113 of the *Charter of Rights for Creators*, Appendix C below. See generally, *Bishop v. Tele-Metropole* (1985), 4 C.P.R. (3d) 349.

royalty disputes are concerned,[6] there is certainly no contemplated tendency toward treating the publishing industry as a utility.

The publishing industry *per se* receives no special tax treatment under the federal income tax law, but rather is entitled to benefit from schemes of exemptions or reductions available to all other enterprises. The Income Tax Act[7] does provide that reasonable advertising expenses are deductible from income as expenses incurred for the purpose of gaining or producing income from a business, although such expenses are limited in respect of amounts expended by a taxpayer for advertising in an issue of a non-Canadian newspaper or periodical. While this tax scheme is more directly beneficial to the advertiser, it is designed as a limited incentive for the promotion of the use of Canadian published newspapers and periodicals.

Various jurisdictions have enacted legislation respecting the direct or indirect distribution of publications for the purposes of censorship or regulation of commercial competition. In the Province of Quebec the Publication and Public Morals Act[8] requires the filing of a declaration by a publisher and/or his agent who seek to distribute within the province, for the purpose of regulating the moral content of these publications. It is however to be noted that books are excluded from the definition of publication contained in s. 1(d). By comparison, in the Province of Ontario the Paperback and Periodical Distributors Act,[9] provides that no person shall carry on business as a distributor or seller of paperbacks or periodicals unless registered under the provisions of the statute. While the Act does purport to regulate the marketing of books, nevertheless, those books appearing in hard cover are excluded from the operation of the statute.[10] Operation of a distributorship is contingent upon prescribed residency qualifications, and retention of the status of distributor is subject to continued compliance with the requirements set out in the Act.

In the same vein, several jurisdictions have enacted laws having an indirect effect on publication and distribution by way of regulating defamation and corruption of morals. In this regard, the Criminal Code provides sanctions for publications proven to be obscene[11] or to contain blasphemous or defamatory libel.[12] Many provinces have as well enacted legislation for the purpose of regulating defamatory and libellous publications.[13] A typical statute respecting libel may be seen in the Ontario Libel and Slander Act. It provides that

---

[6] *Ibid.*, p. 222.

[7] 1970-71-72 (Can.), c. 63, s. 19, as amended.

[8] R.S.Q. 1964, c. 50.

[9] R.S.O. 1980, c. 366.

[10] *Ibid*, s. 1(h).

[11] Section 159.

[12] *Ibid*, ss. 260, 261 and following.

[13] Ontario: Libel and Slander Act, R.S.O. 1980, c. 237; Quebec: Press Act, R.S.Q. c. P-19; Saskatchewan: Libel and Slander Act, R.S.S. 1978, c. L-14; British Columbia: Libel and Slander Act, R.S.B.C. 1979, c. 234; Manitoba: Defamation Act, R.S.M. 1970, c. D20; Prince Edward Island: Defamation Act, R.S.P.E.I. 1974, c. D-3; Alberta: Defamation Act, R.S.A. 1980, c. D-6.

defamatory words in a newspaper are deemed to be published and to constitute libel. No action for libel lies unless the plaintiff has, from the date of learning of the libel, within six weeks given notice and within three months sued the defendant. Damages are recoverable only if:

(*a*) the alleged libel was published in good faith;

(*b*) the alleged libel did not involve a criminal charge;

(*c*) the publication of the alleged libel took place in mistake or misapprehension of the facts; and

(*d*) a full and fair retraction of any matter therein alleged to be erroneous,

(i) was published either in the next regular issue of the newspaper or in any regular issue thereof published within three days after the receipt of the notice mentioned in subsection (1) and was so published in as conspicuous a place and type as was the alleged libel, or

(ii) was broadcast either within a reasonable time or within three days after the receipt of the notice to defendant and was so broadcast as conspicuously as was the alleged libel.

The damages claimed must be actual. It is further to be noted that a fair and accurate report in a newspaper or in a broadcast of certain public proceedings (such as legislative proceedings) are privileged, unless there is proof of malice.

It may be noted there are various statutes establishing central libraries for the purpose of acquiring, collecting, cataloguing and making available for research and consultation a copy of every book published within the territory of the jurisdiction. The foremost statute, the National Library Act,[14] provides for the mandatory deposit of copies at the National Library in Ottawa at the expense of the publisher, in default of which fines may be levied by way of summary proceedings. Although it has been argued that the Act establishes a system of indirect taxation of the publisher, or expropriation without compensation, the wider aim of the legislation is to provide an ongoing archive for the works published within the jurisdiction. In Quebec, compulsory deposit to the Bibliothèque Nationale du Québec is sanctionable by nominal fines. Deposit is imposed upon the following terms:

> Every publisher of a document published in Québec shall, within thirty days from the date of publication of such document and at his own expense deliver two copies thereof to the National Library; but where the retail value of the two copies to be delivered exceeds in the aggregate twenty-five dollars, or where not more than fifty copies of such document are printed, one copy only shall be required.
>
> Failing a publisher domiciled or having a place of business in Québec, the obligation imposed by this section shall devolve upon the following persons domiciled or having a place of business in Québec:

[14] R.S.C. 1970, c. N-11. Similarly, in Quebec, an Act respecting the Bibliothèque Nationale du Québec, R.S.Q. c. B-2, s. 8.

(*a*) the printer of the document or the person who reproduces it by a graphic process other than printing or, failing them,

(*b*) the person having the exclusive right to distribute the document in Québec or, failing him,

(*c*) the author of the document, in the case of a printed document.

Documents are defined as any publication of any kind reproduced by printing or any other graphic process.

Most publishing enterprises are privately owned and depend upon sales and agency distributions for income. Various governments do operate printing and publishing institutions although output is limited in large measure to the issuance of books, pamphlets and portfolios containing statutes, government reports, maps and general information concerning government services. Although there is little direct competition between the state and private publishing concerns, this is not to say that the governments at various jurisdictional levels have not assumed both a mildly regulatory and supportive function with respect to private publishers. As already implied, the purpose of state regulation is not primarily to prefer the Queen's printer but to create a certain order in the free market. As to the supportive function, mention may now be made of the diverse public funding schemes incorporated in statute and other legislative instruments. Support of the publishing industry takes the form of guarantees of loans by government bodies as well as subsidization of individual works, and outright grants for research and operational costs. The most well-known body involved in the field is the Canada Council established under the Canada Council Act.[15] The objects of the Council are to foster and promote the study, enjoyment and production of works in the arts by sponsoring publications of works and providing grants, scholarships or loans to persons in Canada for study or research.[16] Many provinces have established provincial arts council bodies patterned on the Canada Council program, but have otherwise preferred to treat the publishing industry in a manner no different than other industries with respect to subsidies and loans.[17]

In the Province of Quebec, a person who claimed publishing to be among his principal activities could take benefit of a provincial government guarantee of loans provided he met the domiciliary requirements set out in the Act respecting the guarantee of certain loans to publishers and booksellers and to amend the Québec Industrial Development Assistance Act.[18] Publishers of non-periodical printed publications having not less than 49 pages of text or illustrations could

---

[15] R.S.C. 1970, c. C-2.

[16] *Ibid*, s. 8 as amended 1976-77, c. 24, s. 23.

[17] With respect to Ontario: Arts Council Act, S.O. 1984, c. 57; Manitoba: Arts Council Act, R.S.M. 1970, c. A140; British Columbia Cultural Fund Act, 1967 (B.C.), c. 7 continued by Funds Control Act, R.S.B.C. 1979, c. 146; Saskatchewan: Arts Board Act, R.S.S. 1978, c. A-28.

[18] 1975 (Que.), c. 15, s. 6, now repealed.

receive a guarantee for a sum not exceeding the sum of $5,000,000 for loans used by the publishers for the purposes of their business. While the Act did not restrict the operations of the publishers to the Province, the regulations provided that the loan which is the object of the guarantee must be used only for book selling or publishing operations carried on in Quebec. The provincial government by order-in-council as well provided non-statutory grants for publication and distribution of books to companies and individuals meeting certain Quebec residence requirements.[19] Currently, the Act respecting the Societé de Developpement des Industries de la Culture et des Communications[20] establishes a government corporation SODICC to promote the creation and development of book publishing communication services, and other cultural endeavors. While the corporation does not have the power to grant subsidies, it may grant loans at lower than market interest rates. Under regulations, SODICC may lend up to $250,000 to a single applicant under prescribed conditions. Finally, the provincial government provides publishers' loss insurance which is an undertaking by the Minister of Cultural Affairs to purchase from the publisher at cost price a fixed percentage of the issued copies of an insured work, or in certain circumstances to purchase all unsold copies at cost price plus 25 percent, and to pay to the author twelve and one-half percent of the cost price. Upon acceptance of a manuscript for insurance by the Minister and following payment of a premium, the publisher may obtain loss insurance not exceeding $100,000 in each fiscal year.[21]

Economic Background

During the course of recent years, a series of studies affecting the publishing industry has been issued by royal commissions and public bodies with the

---

[19] See also regulations under the Act respecting the guarantee of certain loans to publishers and booksellers, O.C. 3952-75, August 27, 1975, Reg. 75-454, August 28, 1975, s. 8.01, now repealed and replaced by the Reglement sur l'aide financière, s. 18.3, r-2. Order-in-council respecting assistance for the publication and distribution of books, O.C. 352-72, February 2, 1972, *Official Gazette*, February 19, 1972, p. 1721.

[20] R.S.Q. c. S-10.01.

[21] Publishers Loss Insurance Act, R.S.Q., c. A-27:

> **2.** Publishers loss insurance is an undertaking by the Minister on behalf of the Gouvernement du Québec:
>
> (*a*) to purchase from the publisher at the cost price of one-third of the issued copies of an insured work, if he has not sold more than two-thirds thereof within the prescribed delay or, if he has sold more, to purchase all unsold copies at the cost price plus twenty-five per cent, without however exceeding the cost price of one-third of the copies;
>
> (*b*) to pay to the author of an insured work an amount equal to twelve and one-half per cent of the cost price of the copies purchased by the Minister.

principal view of reforming the existing law insofar as the concept of intellectual property is concerned. In April 1977, the Ministry of Consumer and Corporate Affairs of the Federal Government issued a report entitled *Copyright in Canada: Proposals for a Revision of the Law* the main purpose of which was to provoke public discussion on a revision of the Copyright Act. The Proposals were not written by its authors[22] in a vacuum; the document continued an analysis begun in two earlier reports, one issued in 1957 by the Royal Commission on Patents, Copyright, Trade Marks and Industrial Design (Ilsley Commission),[23] and one in 1971 by the Economic Council of Canada.[24] The Proposals recognized that Canada is a net importer of books and other published materials, and that revised legislation must balance low cost, availability of sufficient creative efforts to meet cultural objectives, and the public interest at large. The authors of the document made several recommendations affecting the protection of Canadian publishers and authors in the face of foreign competition, such as the term of copyright protection,[25] limitation of Canada's international copyright commitments to the status quo,[26] abolition of manufacturing or printing clauses[27] and adoption of a modified form of public lending right within a separate legislative framework.[28] The Proposals however gave little direct guidance for the rationalization and stimulation of the publishing industry, although the authors suggested that the problems of buying around, dumping and unauthorized importation were best considered within the framework of other legislation.

Approximately six years earlier, the Economic Council of Canada issued its *Report on Intellectual and Industrial Property*[29] based on terms of reference much wider than those given to the authors of the Proposals. The Economic Council demonstrated that one of its basic concerns in recommending modification to the existing copyright legislation was the economic impact of such revision. In summary, the recommendations for revision included the development of the copyright registration system, provision for the use and regulation of copyright collectives and the performing-rights-society approach to copyright enforcement, the removal from the present legislation of the import barriers, as well as the provision of new broadcast and typography rights. In the words of the Report,[30]

> Most of these recommendations would, if implemented, tend to have a positive

---

[22] A.A. Keyes and C. Brunet.
[23] *Report on Copyright*, Ottawa, 1957.
[24] *Report on Intellectual and Industrial Property*, Information Canada, Ottawa, January 1971.
[25] *Ibid.*, p. 63.
[26] *Ibid.*, p. 46.
[27] *Ibid.*, p. 77.
[28] *Ibid.*, p. 123.
[29] Information Canada, Ottawa 1971.
[30] *Ibid.*, p. 178.

> impact on the incomes of authors, artists, publishers, broadcasters and other producers. The removal of import barriers would have its main direct impact (the negative one) on the incomes of distributors of foreign books in Canada, but there would be benefits to Canadian consumers.

The guidelines proposed by the Economic Council demonstrate a concern for the low cost distribution of published materials to Canadian consumers, protection of the various participants in the production process of creative works and the availability to Canadians of information and publications ordinarily available in their countries. In a brief discussion of author-publisher agreements, the Report notes that the use of copyright legislation to increase protection of authors may be easily offset or frustrated by a compensating adjustment in various aspects of a contract such as a reduction of royalties; the Economic Council was accordingly driven to recommend the increase of bargaining power on the side of the author or creator by favouring the growth of copyright collectives.

The guidelines suggested by the Economic Council were in some measure influenced by the Report on Copyright issued by the Ilsley Commission in 1957.[31] The Ilsley Report considered many aspects of the existing copyright legislation and recommended important revisions respecting the term of copyright of published and unpublished works, the creation of a broadcaster's right of copyright, the modification of printing clauses in current legislation and the re-definition of copyright in original works. For the most part, the Report focused little emphasis on the publisher-author relationship and had little to recommend with respect to the economic reality of the publishing industry in Canada. Nevertheless, contained in its discussion on the import restrictions mentioned in s. 27 of the Copyright Act, the Report provides the following insight:[32]

> Section 27 was the subject of sustained vigorous representations by a number of book publishers and organizations representing book publishers. Their concern was not only to have the section retained but to have it immensely strengthened from their point of view. The book publishing companies of Canada are, generally speaking, mainly importers of books. They say that if they are to remain in a financial position to carry on the original publishing of Canadian books and thus assist in the development of Canadian literature, they must not be unduly hampered in carrying on their importing and distribution activities. For the most part, they are not the owners of the Canadian copyright in the books they import, but are exclusive selling or distributing agents of the copyright owners. The great bulk of the books they handle are imported by them from publishers in Great Britain, the United States and France.

---

[31] *Royal Commission on Patents, Copyright, Trade marks and Industrial Designs*, Ottawa, Queen's Printer, 1957. Reproduced with permission of the Minister of Supply and Services Canada.

[32] Page 91.

The Ontario Royal Commission report on book publishing issued in 1972[33] provides by far the most extensive examination of the Canadian publishing industry. The authors of the Report reviewed the questions of ownership of Ontario and Canadian publishers, copyright and book publishing, marketing, educational use of published materials and the vital role of publishing in establishing a Canadian identity. The recommendations of the authors include administrative centralization of government policy and organized government incentive programs for authors and publishers, the creation of a system of insurance for the purpose of guaranteeing to authors their earned royalties, as well as a broad incentive program for the export of books manufactured, produced and created in Canada. With respect to copyright revisions, the Report suggested that publication in Canada should carry with it no disabilities for the author regardless of his country of citizenship or domicile that would not attach to publication in the other principal publishing countries of the world. Aside from other changes to the existing legislation, the Report urged that the Federal Government be requested to keep under continuing review the possibility of embedding a public lending right in the copyright law at some future date.[34] In reviewing the question of author and publisher agreements, the Commission noted:

> One of the most important incentives that an author can have, of course, is the assurance of competent and reasonably prompt publication on fair and just terms, and of effective marketing by the publisher thereafter. This is not to be achieved merely by legislating a doubling of royalties or an increase in advances to authors or by requiring that books be kept in print when they will not sell in sufficient quantity to repay the cost of doing so. On the other hand, it is too easy to take the view that if Canadian publishers are looked after, Canadian authors will be able to look after themselves.[35]

The Report continued to criticize various portions of standard form author-publisher agreements and specifically dealt with clauses respecting royalty payments, division of income from subsidiary rights, termination clauses and the right of first refusal. According to the Report, some publishing practices under review displayed a tendency for publishers to overload their programs and to make commitments beyond their editorial and financial capacity to implement. The Report noted that some authors are unjustly exploited by having to wait inordinate periods of time in order to see their work published and distributed.

The authors considered in detail the Economic Council *Report on Intellectual and Industrial Property* and disagreed with several of its recommendations, including the removal of copyright as an import restricting

---

[33] *Royal Commission on Book Publishing*, Government of Ontario, 1972.
[34] *Ibid.*, pp. 256-79.
[35] *Ibid.*, p. 45.

device, as well as its failure to recommend specific incentive programs for authors and publishers by increasing the existing levels of protection.

The concerns and recommendations of the several reports mentioned above are surprisingly fresh and relevant even years after their initial expression. In an overall statistical review of the publishing industry, Statistics Canada has recently noted[36] that the general Canadian domestic book market for the year 1976 was approximately half a billion dollars, 15 percent of which resulted from the sales of books in the French language. Approximately 84 percent of the surveyed net book sales came from publishers located in Ontario, although Canadian controlled publishers accounted for 46 percent of the surveyed sales. Only 13 percent of reported sales were attributable to exports and most of the Canadian book exports were English and destined for sale in the United States. The major customers of publishers for the base year were elementary and secondary educational institutions and retail stores. It may be noted of particular interest that sales of books produced domestically accounted for only $145,000,000 of the estimated total value of the Canadian book market evaluated at $533,000,000. Finally, it is to be noted that publishers as well as producing their own books acted as exclusive agents for foreign publishers as an essential ingredient in their overall sales campaign; sales of imports by publishers acting as exclusive agents yielded approximately $127,000,000, being almost equivalent to revenue generated from books domestically produced. Sales of books imported by other entrepreneurs produced revenue at a level more than one and one half times greater than that from sales of "Canadian" books.

More recent years have seen a greater focus on the need to seriously reverse the existing copyright legislation. In 1984, a report issued through the federal Ministry of Communications and Corporate Affairs, *From Gutenberg to Telidon*, suggested extensive amendments which would bring copyright into the technological age and expand the horizons of copyright subject matter. That white paper was soon followed by the Report of the Sub-Committee on the Revision of Copyright (Standing Committee on Communications and Culture) entitled *A Charter of Rights for Creators* in October 1985; the *Government Response* to the *Charter* issued in February 1986. The recommendations of the *Charter*, and the *Response* are wide-ranging and may have a major impact on the way publishers conduct their business, and commercially relate to authors: the more salient features are reproduced in Appendix C of this volume.

Conclusions

It may be seen from a review of the reports and analyses of the publishing industry that in large measure Canadian publishers are dependent on domestic

[36] Culture Statistics, *Book Publishing and Industry Analyses*, The Minister of Industry, Trade and Commerce, Ottawa, December, 1978.

sales for revenue, and that these sales mainly involve material published in a country other than Canada. Foreign controlled firms report greater sales overall than Canadian controlled firms and it is generally the foreign controlled publishers which are the giants in the industry. The Canadian author is obviously not only in competition with native writers but also with foreign authors. Canadian publishers attack the market not only as native publishers but also exclusive agents for foreign publishers whose material is ostensibly more saleable.

Chapter 2

Form Of Author-Publishing Agreements

The form of author-publisher agreements varies with the nature of the work, and the relationship between the parties. The most common form of agreement is a single written document[1] providing for the assumption of risks of publication and distribution by the publisher in return for a right to publish; the author is compensated for his services of creation by extending to him a right to royalties based upon a percentage of retail sales. The details of this arrangement may vary where the work has been commissioned or accepted prior to completion by the publisher in that letters of committal will be sent prior to the signing of a formal agreement and remuneration will be made on the basis either of an advance lump sum payment upon publication of the manuscript, or of a lump sum payment with a continuing right to royalties on the basis of sales performance. A letter of commission from the publisher, the author's letter of formal acceptance or delivery of manuscript, and a memorandum of agreement may constitute the contract between the parties. In many cases, the commission to deliver a work is contained within the memorandum of agreement which also

---

[1] The agreement itself is not required to be in written form although the Statute of Frauds may cause certain problems if the agreement is not to be performed within the period of one year: for example, see *Canada Law Book Co. Ltd. v. Butterworth* (1913), 9 D.L.R. 321; revd 12 D.L.R. 143 (Man. C.A.); affd 16 D.L.R. 61 (P.C.) In Quebec, Article 1233(1) C.C. permits oral testimony to prove facts relating to commercial matters which in the present circumstance would cover author-publisher agreements. As to the non-opposability of an oral assignment or contract of publishing rights in the United States of America, see Rotherberg, Stanley, "Oral Copyright Contracts and Statutes of Frauds" (1977), Bulletin of the Copyright Society, Volume 25, p. 159. A contract, of course, may be implied from the acts of the parties or partial performance: Hirst, A.J. "Contractual Freedom in English Copyright", in *Copyright Contracts,* Jehoram, H.C., ed., 1977, p. 146.

provides all other terms respecting the proposed publication conditional upon the delivery of an acceptable manuscript prior to a stipulated date.

An example of a commission arrangement is found in a decision of the Federal Court in *Breen v. Hancock House.*[2] In that case, a commissioned author was found to have included portions of an unpublished thesis in his own manuscript; the publisher, unaware of the plagiarism, published several thousand copies of the work, only to be sued in damages for infringement by the author of the thesis.

In the words of the court, the defendant Gould, (the "writer"), a professional writer on the West Coast, entered into an agreement with the defendants Hancock House Publishers Ltd. and David Hancock (the "publisher") to write a book on ranching. The work was to be part of a series of books on the history of Canadian Western resource activities. The writer had already authored books on the timber industry, the oil industry, the trucking industry and on other subjects of historical interest. In both character and format, these books were targeted towards the average reader, with special emphasis on the high school student. The writer had been a newspaperman for many years and his style lent itself to easy reading without too many academic overtones. In this series of books, the publisher had acted throughout as the publisher and distributor for the writer.

In the case of a work which has been submitted by the author following its completion to the publisher on the mere hope that the latter will publish, the contractual arrangements may consist of an initial letter of enquiry from the author to the publisher requesting to know whether the latter would be interested in considering for publication a manuscript on the relevant topic, followed by a non-committal letter of interest from the publisher. Upon actual submission of the manuscript, the author usually forwards a covering letter indicating he offers the work for consideration and eventual publication, which letter may be followed by a publisher's letter of acceptance and a form memorandum of agreement covering publishing terms. Whether the work is commissioned, pre-accepted or unsolicited, the content and commitments contained in the cross-letters sent prior to the execution of the memorandum of agreement will constitute part of the contractual arrangements between the parties. It often occurs that a covering letter accompanying the delivery of the manuscript and a letter of acceptance to publish constitute the entirety of the formal arrangements between the author and publisher; notwithstanding the absence of formal expression of such essential provisions as assignment of copyright, the nature of publication and schedule of royalties, the courts are prepared to interpret the contractual arrangements in light of implied conditions and industry practice where no express term exists, as well as on the basis of previous contracts between the parties.[3]

---

[2] (1986), 6 C.I.P.R. 129.

[3] *Morang & Co. v. LeSueur* (1911), 45 S.C.R. 95 at p. 103; *Lucas v. Moncrieff* (1905), 21 T.L.R. 683 at p. 684: "Mr. Justice Warrington in the course of his judgment said the question for his decision mainly turned on the proper construction on the two letters of November 11 and 14, 1898 which constituted the contract between the plaintiff and Mr. Grant Richards. In his Lordship's opinion these letters amounted to nothing

The relationship between author and publisher may call for a contribution to the costs of printing and distribution by the author in the form of a subsidy to the publisher, subject to the author's right of recouping his contribution from royalties or a share in profits. In such circumstances, the parties usually execute a form of agreement common to those relationships mentioned above accompanied with an addendum imposing upon the author the obligation to make a financial contribution. On the other hand, a subsidy publishing agreement may in fact be a profit-sharing agreement, or a partnership, or a joint venture by the parties for the purposes of printing and marketing a manuscript, the rights of which are held by the author or his assignee.

The importance of categorizing the relationship of the parties lies in the resulting interpretation of the various provisions of the contractual arrangements. Suffice it to say for the moment that author-publisher agreements may consist of cross-letters, letters and memoranda of agreement, or may be entirely verbal in form. Agreements which provide for the assignment or licence of copyright must ostensibly comply with the provisions of s. 12(4) of the Copyright Act which declares that no such assignment or licence grant is valid unless it is in writing signed by the owner of the right in respect of which the assignment or grant is made or by his agent. The Act further provides in s. 40(1) that any grant of an interest in a copyright, either by assignment or licence may be registered in the Register of Copyright at the Copyright Office upon production of the original instrument, which is presumably in written form. Nevertheless, an author may be precluded from exercising his statutory right against a publisher who has published and distributed the work in question where there has been a mere verbal or implied transfer of rights or an indication of such transfer from the conduct of the parties.[4] On the other hand, there is no statutory requirement as to the actual form of writing of the assignment or transfer itself and consequently, a single letter or series of letters, as well as a written receipt for the price of the transfer of copyright interest will amount to compliance with the legislation.

Where the assignment or grant is not in writing, the equitable owner may still proceed to suit in his own name but must implead the legal owner as a party for the maintenance of his action.[5] However, in *Downing v. General Synod of the Church of England et al.*,[6] plaintiff's action for damages and injunction resulting

---

more than an agreement between an intending author who had not yet written the book and a publisher for the publication of the book when written on certain terms. . . ".

[4] *Drabble Ltd. v. Hycolite Manufacturing Company* (1928), 44 T.L.R. 264 (Ch.D.) where the court held that there is a presumption the intentions of an advertiser and his advertising agent are to vest the copyright to an advertisement in the former if the agent prepares the advertisement on the instructions and information given to him by the advertiser.

[5] *McClelland and Stewart Ltd. v. Coles Book Stores Ltd.* (1976), 21 C.P.R. (2d) 270 (Fed. Ct.) notwithstanding s. 20(3) of the Copyright Act which provides for an action by a person deriving a right of copyright by assignment or grant in writing.

[6] [1943] 3 D.L.R. 553 (Ont. C.A.).

from infringement of copyright allegedly assigned in writing was dismissed for lack of evidence that such writing had been accepted by the author or that such document had been lost, or had ever indeed existed.

Author-publisher agreements may be categorized under the following general headings: printing or publishing contracts with commission; profit-sharing agreements; sales of the work for a lump sum payment, which may include franchise and employment agreements; and term licences in return for royalties.

"Vanity" Printing Contracts

With respect to printing contracts with commission, it is evident that simple instructions to a printer to set type and to effect distribution of works does not vest in the printer any right respecting copyright in the work. The printer merely acts as an independent contractor performing a service contract on behalf of the author and receives payment of a lump sum plus a percentage of sales, if any, in order to provide incentive to the printer to perform his services with greater diligence and attention. This form of agreement highlights what is called "vanity publishing" in which the entire liability and risk for the expenses of publishing fall in many cases upon the author, the publisher or printer being guaranteed, in advance, recoupment of all costs plus the promise of added profit in the event of sales at a certain level.

Profit-Sharing Agreements

Distinct from the agreement to print on commission is the profit-sharing agreement which assumes several forms. The purpose of the agreement is to consolidate a joint venture or *ad hoc* partnership respecting publication and marketing of a work, created by one of the parties, at the joint risk of both. The agreement often provides that the author shall contribute a manuscript, and the publisher shall assume initially all costs of publication subject to repayment out of proceeds of the sale. Although the author is entitled to remuneration, his remuneration is in the form of a portion of profits and not in "royalties".

One form of joint venture agreement appears in *Crépeau v. Minister of National Revenue*.[7] In that decision, an author undertook to provide a manuscript to a co-operative association which in turn obliged itself by way of advances repayable by the author to make the necessary disbursements for the preliminary printing of a certain manual to be used by an educational institution. The author, out of the proceeds received from the sale of his work, undertook to reimburse the association for the advances made toward the printing of the work, including his share of the overhead expenses apportioned

---

[7] (1966), 31 Fox Pat. C. 93 (T.A.B.).

annually *pro rata* to the sales of each work published by the association. Furthermore, the author undertook to contribute to the reserves of the association and for this purpose, the latter was entitled to make a deduction from the net proceeds of the sale of the work in accordance with a specified table of percentages. However, in the event of a resulting deficit from the sale of the work, the author was not obliged to reimburse the association except out of the net proceeds of one or other of his works published by the association. In reviewing the tax liability of a taxpayer who collaborated with the author in the production of the manual, the Board held:

> In the case in point the publisher, the author and the collaborator joined themselves together to undertake a certain venture. Now, taking a risk is the very essence of a venture. Who is not aware of the expression "to risk a venture". . . .
>
> There is no doubt that the appellant carried out intellectual activity for the purpose of deriving a profit therefrom. . . .
>
> This was done on February 17, 1960. The author and the appellant signed an agreement which was handed to the publishing syndicate. Thus it has been proved that the appellant became a member of the syndicate which undertook to edit, publish, sell the book — the instruction manual — in which the appellant's name is given as a collaborator.[8]

On the other hand, a profit-sharing agreement may limit the right of the publisher to the role of acting merely as an exclusive agent for distribution or as an importer of the work for distribution based upon a commission schedule contained in the memorandum of agreement.[9] In the same vein, the agreement may constitute the giving of a franchise of copyright material and stipulate a participation in profits by both parties and an assumption of initial outlays by only one of the contracting parties.[10]

The most comprehensive discussion of a joint venture publishing agreement appears in *Reade v. Bentley*.[11] The facts of the case are analogous to the circumstances existing between the parties in the *Crépeau* case, namely that the publisher undertook to publish at his own expense certain works in which the plaintiff was the author and after deducting the proceeds of sale, the charges of printing, paper and advertisements, including a commission of ten percent, the profits remaining on every edition were to be divided in two equal parts for the benefit of the parties. The court held that the agreement constituted a license to publish and a joint venture which plaintiff was entitled to terminate at any time following the publication of a given edition upon notice to the publisher. Sir Page Wood V.-C. indicated that the agreement did not amount to an assignment of the

---

[8] *Ibid.*, at p. 98.

[9] *Maison du Livre Français de Montréal Inc. v. Institut Littéraire du Québec Limitée and Minister of National Revenue* (1959), 31 C.P.R. 69 (Que.).

[10] By analogy, see *Peat Business Systems Ltd. v. Minister of National Revenue* (1951), 12 Fox Pat. C. 36 (T.A.B.).

[11] (1858), 4 K. & J. 656.

copyright but on the contrary created no more than a joint venture. Insofar as a licence was granted, such licence was to be interpreted as extending only so far as would be necessary for carrying out the joint venture between the parties:

> Agreements between authors and publishers assume a variety of forms. Some are so clear and explicit that no doubt can arise upon them. Thus, where an author assigns his copyright, the transaction is one which every person understands and which leaves no room for uncertainty as to the rights of the parties. Again, where as in *Sweet v. Cater,*[12] the author assigns a particular edition, the rights of himself and the publisher are equally clear; and although in that case the point did not require determination — the Court observed, and justly observed, that where an author has sold an edition of a given number of copies to one publisher, he is not at liberty, before they are sold, to publish the same work himself or through another publisher, in such a manner as to compete with the edition he has sold, but is bound to afford to the purchaser a full opportunity of realizing the benefit of his contract.
>
> The case now before me, like that of *Stevens v. Benning,*[13] is of an intermediate description. Here as there, the author does not sell or purport to sell any interest whatever in the copyright. It was contended, and very strongly, in *Stevens v. Benning,* that the author had done so; but I held that he had not and my view was affirmed by the Lord Justices. Here also, as there, the publisher was to publish at his own risk. Nevertheless, in *Stevens v. Benning,* the agreement contained other provisions considerably more definite than any in this case. It pointed to a series of editions to be published for the author by the same publisher as to every one of which the author himself stipulated as part of the contract that he would assist in the publication. . . .
>
> It has been contended by the plaintiff, that the case is one of simple agency; that, by the effect of the agreement, the defendant became a mere agent of the plaintiff. But it is clear that he became more than that. A mere agent may be paid, as the defendant was to be paid, by a share of the profits; but a mere agent never embarks in the risk of the undertaking; and here the defendant took upon himself the whole expense and risk of bringing out the work. Clearly, therefore, the case is something more than one of simple agency.
>
> On the other hand, it was contended for the defendant, that, if the effect of the agreement was not an assignment of the copyright (which it is now clearly decided

[12] (1841), 11 Sim. 572, where the publisher of a legal text undertook to print 2,500 copies of a new edition at its sole cost, in three volumes and to pay to the author royalties on a fixed-sum installment basis in return for the right to publish; the court held the publisher was entitled to protect the new edition from infringement by injunction in equity without registration of the author-publisher agreement. But see *Warne v. Routledge* (1874), L.R. 18 Eq. 497 where the publisher undertook to publish in consideration for a royalty of 1d per copy sold; the court held the publisher had obtained no assignment of copyright and no right to restrain the authors from publishing a second edition of the work even while the printed stock remained unsold.

[13] (1855), 6 De G. M. & G. 223, where the court refused to grant injunctive relief on a finding that the publisher obtained no assignment of copyright: the agreement merely recited the usual obligations and rights respecting delivery of the manuscript, printing at the expense of the publisher, issuance of subsequent editions, and payment to the author of a portion of profits without mention of the interest of the parties in the copyright.

> that it could not be), it resulted in a joint adventure, in which the defendant was to have a license to publish the work; and that, from the nature of the case, and by the terms of the agreement, that license was irrevocable . . .
>
> Community of risk did not appear to me to be by our law, any more than it was by the civil law, essential to constitute a partnership; one partner being at liberty to contract with another that he will take all the losses of the concern upon himself.[14]

In summary, the points indicative of the existence of a joint venture agreement include the contribution by both parties of skill and funding to the pursuit of the publishing venture, the assumption of risks by one or both of the parties for disbursements and losses and, the payment of royalties as a distribution of profits, if any, and not as a charge upon the publisher alone. As a result of the existence of a profit-sharing agreement, the parties stand in a fiduciary relationship, and are prohibited from placing themselves in situations involving conflicts of interest. The parties must furthermore furnish an accounting of activities and make available all books and agreements related thereto.[15]

By contrast, joint authors between themselves may enter into a shared-royalty arrangement on the basis of their respective contribution to a manuscript, either by way of text or illustration. While the publisher is not in contract bound by an inter-author agreement, a joint author who finds himself unacknowledged in the printed text may enjoin the publisher from distribution until his name is added. In one recent decision, the unacknowledged joint author who was responsible for revising and completing a story line and text was held to be entitled to thirty per cent of royalties received by the sole acknowledged author.[16]

Sale of the Work

An outright sale of the work entails the divesting of all rights on the part of the author to the publisher respecting the published work. The sale of the copyright is usually expressed in the agreement as being an assignment of copyright by the author to the publisher. A readily imaginable agreement involves a situation similar to that contained in *Larue v. Minister of National Revenue.*[17] In that case,

---

[14] At p. 661 and following.

[15] Fox, *The Canadian Law of Copyright and Industrial Designs,* 2nd ed. (Toronto: Carswell Company Limited, 1967) at p. 575.

[16] *Courtenay v. Polkosnik* (1984), 77 C.P.R. (2d) 140, at p. 143:

> What return is the plaintiff entitled to for his writing of the story?
>
> As stated, I find a contract struck by the parties to this action to the effect they would share the royalties. Normally, where parties do not agree to so fundamental a term as compensation a contract is void for uncertainty. However, where the contract is actually performed as here where the writing was done, it behooves me to hold that it is a valid and binding contract and to determine the proper rate of compensation for the plaintiff's work.

[17] (1963), 25 Fox Pat. C. 20 (T.A.B.).

a university professor signed several contracts with his university whereby the latter obtained the copyright in and the right to publish the works of the professor. At a later date, the parties entered into a further contract whereby the university purchased all the rights of the professor under the previous contracts for a lump sum in the amount of $75,000. In dismissing the contention by the professor that the amount of $75,000 was a capital receipt, the Board found that the appellant wrote treatises under prior agreements with the university not so much with the idea of acquiring copyrights as with that of placing on the market texts suited for modern teaching. The Board held the agreement constituted a business venture in which the professor did not acquire the ownership of the copyright; in effect, the professor sold his services as a writer for cash remuneration based on the number of volumes to be sold by the university. The Board took a similar view in another matter involving a lawyer who compiled an encyclopaedia of legal forms in consideration for a stipulated lump sum payment payable in advances over the period of time required to prepare and complete the work.[18]

Although neither case just mentioned involved a situation where the author was the employee of the publisher, there are publishers of specialized texts which do engage on a part or fulltime basis, authors for the purpose of producing manuscripts or compiling works with the eventual aim of publication. In these situations, the employment agreement itself may provide and confirm that copyright in works to be produced is sold, assigned or vested in the publisher.[19] The publisher is not entitled to damages for breach of contract against the author simply because the work ultimately produced is not marketable or unsuitable for publication; after all, the employer has taken and accepted the risk that the skills of the author will under suitable supervision produce a manuscript adequate for publication.[20] Nevertheless, since the employer is the absolute owner of the copyright, he is at liberty to make changes necessary to render the manuscript fit for publication subject to certain rights of the author which will be discussed in a later chapter.

As to the position of journalists it has been suggested[21] that the contract between newspaper publisher and writer, whether salaried or not, should implicitly recognize the right of free disclosure of the work (without substantive editorial interference), the right to object to alteration, the right to a public declaration of authorship of the work, and a right to reconsider or retract the work in the event the journalist no longer subscribes to the views expressed. To say the least, these suggestions are more idealistic than extant. The contract of employment of a journalist is usually seen in its traditional sense, namely an express consent to a transfer of copyright, with moral rights attached, to the

[18] *No. 682 v. M.N.R.* (1961), 20 Fox Pat. C. 126.

[19] In confirmation of the presumption contained in s. 12(3) of the Copyright Act.

[20] Copinger and Skone James on *Copyright*, 11th ed. (London: Sweet & Maxwell 1971), para. 1002, p. 394.

[21] "Le droit d'auteur des journalistes" (1984), 119 R.I.D.A. 123.

publisher. Non-salaried journalists paid by the article suffer the presumptions mentioned above.

There is a generally accepted legal proposition that transfer of title in a physical object does not transfer the separate intangible property right of copyright associated with that object. It has accordingly been held that no absolute assignment of copyright is contemplated with respect to the delivery of prior fire insurance plans and rating schedules,[22] plans and architectural documents relating to a proposed civic centre[23] and engineers' structural design plans.[24] The presumption, however, against a transfer of copyright is rebuttable on the submission of "slight" evidence to prove that with the passing of the tangible property there was also an equitable assignment of the copyright. This rule is substantially based on the observation that the natural intention of the parties to an agreement is not to separate the intangible property right from the transfer of title to that property.[25]

Although the contract may specifically declare the assignment of copyright by the author to the publisher, this is not to say that the assignment is unconditional. Depending upon the drafting of the relevant clause, the courts have held that the assignment or transfer of proprietary interests in the manuscript falls in the event of the failure of the publisher to respect an implicit obligation to publish a manuscript even though it has been adjudged by the publisher to be unsuitable.[26]

---

[22] *Massie & Renwick Ltd. v. Underwriters' Survey Bureau Ltd.*, [1940] S.C.R. 218 citing *Re Dickens*, [1935] Ch. 267. Generally, *Meikle v. Maufe*, [1941] 3 All E.R. 144.

[23] *Webb and Knapp (Canada) Ltd. et al. v. City of Edmonton* (1970), 63 C.P.R. 21 (S.C.C.).

[24] *Netupsky et al. v. Dominion Bridge Co. Ltd.* (1969), 58 C.P.R. 7 (B.C. C.A.); revd 3 C.P.R. (2d) 1 (S.C.C.); *Koch v. Continental Steel* (1985), 82 C.P.R. (2d) 156. As to what constitutes a literary work, see *Bullman Group v. Alpha One-Write Systems* (1981), 54 C.P.R. (2d) 171 at 177 per Addy J.:

> It is of some importance to note that not only in s. 4 but throughout the Act, "literary works" are linked with dramatic, musical and artistic works. It is settled law that the literary merit of a work need not be high and indeed might be minimal or, to all intents and purposes, non-existent, especially in the case of a compilation. There still remains, however, the essential element of conveying special information of some kind. The work must of itself possess either aesthetic or informative value. In other words, to be the subject of copyright it is not always necessary that the work have literary quality or merit in the sense of aesthetic quality or virtue. It might be a trade director (*Lamb v. Evans*, [1893] 1 Ch. 218) or a compilation of some sort as long as some original skill and judgment is required in its preparation. But, it is essential, however, that of itself, it be informative and not merely part of a system which permits someone else to gather, insert and convey information more efficiently.

See also *Slumber Magic v. Sleep King* (1985), 3 C.P.R. (3d) 81; *Royal Doulton v. Cassidy's* (1984), 1 C.P.R. (3d) 214.

[25] Fox, *op. cit.*, p. 287.

[26] *Morang & Co. v. LeSueur* (1911), 45 S.C.R. 95 at p. 102-103, *per* Davies, J.:

> "I think the argument submitted . . . is sound, namely, that in effect the contract provided that LeSueur should write a manuscript life of Mackenzie . . .

Licences

A licence to publish is merely an authorization given to the publisher to print and distribute the manuscript within a specified territory and for a given period of time without any control over copyright in the work. The licence according to its terms may be exclusive but on the other hand, may in the absence of a stipulation that it is a sole licence, permit the author to grant a competing licence to another publisher.[27] A recurring difficulty arising out of ambiguous wording in an author-publisher agreement is to determine whether or not the intention of the parties as confirmed by the agreement is to confer an assignment or a mere licence with respect to copyright in the work. The Copyright Act is of aid in resolving the ambiguity by creating a presumption in one limited respect: copyright is deemed to vest in an employer where the author created the work while in the employment of the latter and in the course of the fulfillment of his contract of service.[28] Further presumptions have arisen as a result of judicial interpretation: for example, the stipulation in an agreement to the effect that the author is entitled to a large fixed sum as remuneration for contribution to the work is indicative that the parties intended that copyright vest in the publisher by way of assignment.[29] Similarly, copyright in works published in a serial publication is deemed to be assigned to the publisher where the author is engaged by the latter to prepare a book for such publication.[30] Where the grant of authority to publish given by the author to the publisher is exclusive, absolute and without duration, the courts are inclined to interpret the agreement as constituting or containing an assignment of copyright and not a mere licence.[31] However, even where the authority to publish is limited as to duration, the court is entitled to find that an equitable right to the copyright has vested in the

---

with the hope that it would be accepted and published by the company in their series of books . . . that until acceptance the author was at all the risks of suitability or unsuitability of the manuscript; that if accepted the property passed and the company was bound to complete the money payments if incomplete and publish the manuscript as part of the series, while if rejected no property in the manuscript passed no right to retain the rejected manuscript remained after the tender or return of the money consideration paid by them. . . .

"The whole question rests upon the construction of the contract and not upon any special rights of either authors or publishers apart from contract."

27 *Warne v. Routledge* (1874), L.R. 18 Eq. 497.

28 Section 12(4). See also *Sweet v. Benning* (1855), 16 C.B. 459; *Lamb v. Evans*, [1893] 1 Ch. 218 at p. 233.

29 *Lawrence and Bullen v. Aflalo and Cook*, [1904] A.C. 17 at p. 24, *per* Davey, J.: "The circumstances here are that the publisher is minded for his own profit to publish an encyclopedia of sport; he is prepared to spend, and does spend, a very large sum of money amounting to some thousands of pounds upon the enterprize . . . In my judgment, he could not adequately protect the articles which he had purchased . . . without having the right to prevent an invasion of the copyright in those articles."

30 *Morang & Co. v. LeSueur* (1911), 45 S.C.R. 95 at p. 121.

31 *Stevens v. Benning* (1855), 6 De G. M. & G. 223.

publisher until the expiry of the term or until the number of copies stipulated in the agreement have been disposed of or sold.[32]

The courts are more inclined to find the agreement provides for a conferral of a licence and not of an assignment where some provision is made for the payments of remuneration to the author on the basis of royalties per copy or share of profits which indicate a continuing interest by the author in the publication and sales of the printed work.[33] However, it goes without saying that copyright in the work resides in the party who is expressly declared by the agreement to have all rights pertaining to the enforcement of the copyright, or who has reserved such rights, even though the agreement provides a remuneration to the author in the form of a lump sum.[34]

The practical distinction between an assignment and a licence is multifold: we have discussed or will later see that rights to royalties from assigns, to make alterations, or to act following the publisher's bankruptcy vary depending on the nature of the agreement as an assignment or licence of copyright. The courts have however in one respect restricted the distinction. It has been argued that where an alleged case of copyright infringement occurs, an assignee, grantee or licencee entitled under the provisions of the Copyright Act[35] to protect and enforce his rights may do so not by commencing an action in his own name, but by becoming a party to an existing action instituted by the author or owner of the copyright. It has recently been held by the Trial Division of the Federal Court that the existing copyright legislation is broad enough to permit a licencee of the rights to reproduce certain printing material to institute proceedings in his own name without having to participate in an action instituted by the copyright owner or implead the latter. In *Ashton-Potter Ltd. v. White Rose Nurseries Ltd.*[36] the court ruled that while the point is not free from doubt a licencee may initiate proceedings to remedy an infringement, assuming that the licencee agreement is duly executed by the author or other owner of the copyright.

---

32 *Sweet v. Cater* (1841), 11 Sim. 572.

33 *Hole v. Bradbury* (1879), 12 Ch. D. 886.

34 *Imperial Book Co. v. Black* (1905), 35 S.C.R. 488; affg 8 O.L.R. 9 (C.A.); *Canadian Performing Right Society Ltd. v. Famous Players Can. Corp. Ltd.*, [1927] 2 D.L.R. 928 (Ont.); [1927] 3 D.L.R. 931 (C.A.); affd [1929] 2 D.L.R. 1 (P.C.). There is no implied term that copyright will pass to the publisher where the manuscript has been accepted by the latter upon submission in a literary contest in which the author has participated: *Ketelby v. Maggett*, [1911] Macg. Cop. Cas. 9.

35 Section 20(5).

36 (1972), 7 C.P.R. (2d) 29; revd 9 C.P.R. (2d) 112 (Fed. C.A.).

Chapter 3

Publication

The principal object of an author-publisher agreement is to convey to the publisher authority to publish the work in return for some valuable consideration to the author. The drafting of the authority to the publisher to proceed with printing and publication varies in form. In some agreements, the grant is expressed in the following manner:

> The author hereby grants to the publisher, subject to the terms of the present agreement and during the term of copyright, the exclusive right to print, produce and publish in book form in the English language a work entitled ——— in North America.

In other agreements, authority to publish is conveyed in the following manner:

> The author hereby grants and assigns to the publisher world copyright to print and publish first and subsequent editions of the work in volume form.

Finally, short form agreements containing little more than an acknowledgment of acceptance of manuscript with an agreement to pay a certain schedule of royalties make no express conveyance or grant for the purpose of authorizing the publisher to proceed with printing and distribution.

Authors are often counselled to avoid executing an agreement which effects an outright sale of the work.[1] In order to limit the nature and scope of the grants, the author is advised to stipulate the granting of an exclusive right to publish in

[1] For example, see Authors Guild Bulletin 13 (Oct.-Nov. 1963); Shapiro, Andrew O. "The Standard Author Contract: A Survey of Current Draftsmanship" in ASCA, Copyright Law Symposium No. 18, Columbia University Press, New York, 1970, p. 135.

one language for a determined period of time in book form only within the domestic market. The effect of such limitation is to reserve to the author all subsidiary rights which must thereafter be enumerated exhaustively in order to give to the publisher full control over the accessory rights attached to the work. As is evident, an outright disposal of all rights attached to the work will render superfluous the clause dealing with subsidiary rights such as publication in translation, dramatization, abridgment and other forms.

Notwithstanding the expression used in the grant clause, the obligation to publish must arise out of an independent stipulation. Many contracts in common use permit the publisher a large degree of discretion in deciding when the act of publication will occur following the submission of the manuscript in satisfactory form. Where the agreement does provide a specific period of time or even "a reasonable period", the publisher also stipulates the possibility of an extension of the period as a result of *cas fortuit,* labour problems and other factors beyond the control of the publisher. Publication may also be suspended indefinitely by stipulation to the effect that the publisher may refuse to proceed with printing and distribution if he is of the opinion that the work, if published, would constitute an infringement of copyright or of the laws relating to libel and obscenity.

As is apparent, the obligation to print and publish by way of assignment or licence constitutes one of the most essential undertakings in the agreement. The legal query which immediately comes to mind relates to the nature of the recourse, if any, available to the author in the event of the publisher's failure to publish. A further query may be made as to what constitutes satisfactory fulfillment of the obligation to publish: does, for example, undue delay in proceeding with printing and issuance of the work constitute a breach of the basic obligation sufficient to entitle the author to exercise his recourses?

The various remedies available to the author upon the failure of the publisher to publish include rescission of the author-publisher agreement, the return to the author of the manuscript by the publisher, reimbursement to the author of sums expended by him toward the course of publication, specific performance, as well as damages usually evaluated on the basis of loss of royalties on the projected sale of a reasonable number of copies of the work.

An agreement between the parties whereby the author is commissioned to write for publication a work in return for lump sum royalty payments implies a tacit agreement to publish the manuscript, if accepted. In the event the manuscript is rejected as unsuitable for the purpose for which it was intended, no property in the manuscript is passed and the author is entitled to the return of the manuscript upon reimbursement of any consideration which he has received.[2]

---

[2] *Morang & Co. v. LeSueur* (1911), 45 S.C.R. 95 at pp. 98-99, *per* Fitzpatrick C.J.: "The majority of French writers, and among them some of the most eminent, such as Pardessus, held that the obligation to publish is always to be considered as an

Damages against the publisher for breach of the agreement are in principle available where the author demonstrates the latter's failure to execute and there is no proveable defence of frustration caused by the author. In the case of *Barrow v. Chappell and Co. Ltd.*,[3] the publisher undertook to publish a musical work composed by the plaintiff who had executed a written assignment in favour of the latter. The author had indicated he required publication to be effected as soon as possible, and, in fact, to be made in a certain issue of the publisher's music journal. As a result of certain objections made by the author respecting the publisher's editing of the work, the publication was delayed for several months. Nevertheless, even after having withdrawn his objections, publication was not proceeded with in due course following a demand made by the author's attorneys. The court held that the publisher was in breach of its obligations to effect publication for inclusion in the issue of the journal mentioned, but that the author was entitled to specific performance and not rescission because damages were difficult to assess and would not be an adequate remedy. The court however did award a nominal sum in damages upon certain proof of losses resulting from delay in the publication.

In deciding the quantum of damages, the court will consider several elements including how the publisher would have exercised his discretion in issuing the published work, the number of copies which the publisher might have published, the number of editions which would be reasonable in the circumstances, the reasonable expectation of sales, the reputation of the author and the available market for the work.[4]

The question of the availability of specific performance against the publisher is more difficult. An order for specific performance will not issue unless the order is capable of enforcement. Inappropriateness of the remedy is often the case with respect to a contract of personal service, although the court will not hesitate to restrain acts done by the parties in contravention of such personal contract.[5] Accordingly, a court will not force an author to complete a work in progress,[6] nor will a publisher be compelled to publish a manuscript, unless no

---

implied term in every contract for the purchase of the manuscript of a book; but admitting with the minority that a contract might be drawn which would transfer the whole property in the manuscript to the purchaser so that it would be in his power to retain it in his possession for his own personal use, all the French authorities admit that where, as in the present case, the parties have chosen to leave so much to intendment and implication, the court should give to the contract a construction wide enough to include the obligation to publish, that being, generally speaking, the more probable intention of the parties, as it was in this case their admitted intention at the inception of their negotiations."

[3] [1976] R.P.C. 355 (Ch. D) reprinted from (1952) LXII The Author, No. 2, p. 38.

[4] *Abrahams et al. v. Reiach Ltd.*, [1922] 1 K.B. 477 at p. 480.

[5] Spry, *Equitable Remedies*, 1971, p. 52.

[6] *Gibson v. Carruthers* (1841), 8 M. & W. 321 at p. 344:

"Sir Walter Scott suggested several grounds to show that the credit, the skill, the judgment, integrity and personal character and reputation of a publisher were

other adequate remedies are available and specific performance may in the circumstances be reasonably expected from the publisher.

Nevertheless, publishers are often in default to proceed with publication purely for monetary purposes unrelated to the quality of the manuscript. In many cases, an order to proceed with specific performance may result in forcing upon the publisher the publishing project at a time when his economic priorities dictate that project be held in reserve. A publisher of books who is ordered by the court to proceed with a sizeable investment in a work which has no immediately foreseeable economic return is not in the same position as a publisher of a periodical who is merely forced to make inclusion in a forthcoming issue of a certain manuscript. Even if the publisher under economic constraint does manage to print the work, the author in practice may suffer the fate of second-rate distribution and marketing efforts and little co-operation from the publisher during the progress of the publication project.

While in certain circumstances a publisher has an implied obligation to publish, the extent of the obligation is limited to one edition, unless there is express provision in the agreement to the contrary. The publication itself must be effected within a reasonable time following the delivery and preparation of the manuscript which in daily practice may vary from one month to more than one year.[7]

---

matters of great importance to an author on which the success and reputation of his works might greatly depend and therefore insisted . . . he was by their bankruptcy discharged from his contract. I must own that his reasoning appeared satisfactory to me; but a more obvious illustration of the principle on which it rested would have been afforded by reversing the case, and supposing that Sir Walter Scott had been the bankrupt and his publishers solvent, would they have been content to pay their 4,000 £., and take the risk of publishing a novel written by the assignees of the novelist?"

[7] *Abrahams et al. v. Reiach Ltd.*, [1922] 1 K.B. 477.

Chapter 4

Distribution Of Publications

Agreements between authors and publishers rarely make extensive reference to the manner of distribution of the published work. It is assumed that the publisher has an intense economic interest in seeing to the rapid and most expedient manner of distribution once constituted in printed form. It is therefore understandable that contracts usually declare that all details as to the manner and time of distribution and advertisement of printed copies shall be left to the sole discretion of the publisher. The parties nevertheless stipulate an obligation on the part of the publisher to distribute six to ten free copies of the printed work to the author and to effect a free distribution to editors and book reviewers as the publisher deems necessary. Before further discussion of the legal ramifications of the obligation to distribute, reference may be made to the systems of distribution available to the publisher in the market place.

Distribution entails the placement of printed materials into the hands of consumers, usually through direct mail shipment or through bookstores. The publisher himself may have a staff and facilities equipped to distribute publications by mail order, or by transport to a number of participating retail outlets. On the other hand, the publisher may have a contractual relationship with an independent distributing organization: the independent distributor deals in the publications of a number of publishers and effects the placement of books into the hands of consumers often through the agency of wholesalers who in turn deal with numerous retail outlets in their territory. The chain from the publisher to the consumer therefore appears in three basic forms:

(a) distribution directly from the publisher to the retail outlet or consumer,
(b) distribution by the publisher through the independent distributor directly to the retailer,
(c) distribution by the publisher through an independent distributor through a wholesaler to the retailer.

A detailed analysis of one highly effective system of distribution has been reviewed by the court for the more narrow purpose of determining whether an anticipated debt due to a distributor by a publisher for the return of unsold books constituted an allowable deduction from income. Although the tax problem will not be considered in this chapter, the system of distribution as reviewed by the court is worthy of note. As appears from the facts giving rise to the case of *Harlequin Enterprises Ltd. v. Minister of National Revenue*[1] the publisher Harlequin published paperback novels of a light romantic nature for marketing in Canada and the United States through distributors and wholesalers (wholesale market) and through distributors to retailers (direct market). Distribution in Canada to both the wholesale and direct markets was done by Curtis Distributing Company Limited in accordance with a written agreement which provided:

> 2. . . . The number of titles and amount of copies of books to be shipped in any one month hereunder will be determined by mutual agreement. Shipment of titles in the quantities so agreed upon shall be made by publisher f.o.b. such wholesaler destination points as shall be specified by Curtis. Title to books and risk of loss thereof shall remain in publisher until delivery to wholesalers.
>
> 3. Books which are considered unsaleable shall be fully returnable. Curtis and publisher shall, from time to time, determine what books are unsaleable, but in any event, books which have been on sale for twelve months shall be conclusively presumed to be unsaleable, and shall be fully returnable at the option, of Curtis . . . All returns shall be shipped, return transportation collect, to such points as publisher shall designate. Curtis shall be entitled to credit on its monthly statements for all returns, at the price charged Curtis for books hereunder.
>
> 4. . . . Settlement shall be made hereunder by Curtis by the 10th of the month for books shipped during the second preceding month.

Shipment of the books was made not from the publisher's head office but from the office of the printer in another city. Unsold books returned by the distributor were not physically returned; the retailer stripped the front title covers which were returned as evidence of destruction of unsold books and credit notes were issued by the distributor. Distribution in the United States of America to the wholesale market only was done by Curtis Circulation Company ("Curtis U.S.") under a written agreement which provided:

> (3) Harlequin agrees to sell and Curtis agrees to purchase the books for resale in accordance with this Agreement . . . The purchase price shall become due and payable by Curtis sixty days after shipment by Harlequin and Harlequin shall invoice Curtis monthly. Books shall be shipped and delivered by Harlequin or its agent to the wholesaler or other outlets as directed by Curtis . . . Curtis shall become the owner of the books purchased on delivery of the same to such delivery points specified by Curtis.

[1] (1977), 15 N.R. 28 (Fed. C.A.); confirming 74 D.T.C. 6634.

(4) Curtis shall sell Books to Customers subject to full return privileges as hereinafter described. Books shall always be fully returnable by Curtis to Harlequin for full credit. Curtis will initiate computation of the Customer's credit for returns for unsold Books via return authorizations issued by Curtis . . . Curtis shall give return credit to Customers upon receipt of authorizations from Customers and shall receive credit from Harlequin upon the giving of such credit to customers . . .

(6) Curtis shall pay Harlequin for shipments of books to Curtis or to Customers within sixty days after shipment is made by Harlequin. This payment shall be adjusted for return credits (issued in accordance with paragraph 4 hereof) for previously uncredited returns.

Distribution in the direct market in the United States was however governed by an agreement in writing between Harlequin and Simon & Schuster, Inc., therein designated "Publisher". Under that arrangement Harlequin provided the Publisher with plates and negatives permitting the Publisher to print in the United States titles Harlequin had or proposed to distribute in Canada. The Publisher undertook to cause a minimum number of copies of each title to be printed within a specified time of the provision of the plates and negatives and to pay Harlequin royalties on net sales.

The facts of the case are of extreme interest in that they demonstrate an economic reality which requires the publisher to maintain a certain leeway or freedom in determining the type and scope of distribution of individual works. New published works are born into a pre-arranged system of distribution governed by ongoing distributor and sub-agent agreements. While each author is convinced of the uniqueness of his work and may consequently feel entitled to a unique or special distribution treatment, there is little doubt that the publisher may feel more inclined to rely on and utilize existing distributor contracts than to engage in original marketing ventures with each new publication. This may certainly not be the case where the publication, made exceptional by virtue of the reputation of its author or subject matter, is forecast to surpass normal sales expectations; in such unusual circumstances, the profit incentive will dictate that extraordinary distribution measures be taken to meet expected demand. The legal problem in drafting and interpreting author-publisher agreements arises in delineating the scope of the publisher's obligation to distribute and the right of the author to see his work made available to the ultimate consumer.

There is of course an additional level of distribution which calls into play subsidiary distributors. Distributors sub-delegate to subordinate distributors the problem of placing published material in specialty stores, custom clients or foreign regions. In one recent case,[2] Benjamin Distribution found its rights of distribution to Flammarion's "J'ai Lu" book line terminated.

According to the court, between 1977 until 1981, Benjamin had been one of the Canadian distributors of the "J'ai Lu" collection. The terms of such

---

[2] *Benjamin Distribution v. Les Éditions Flammarion* (1983), 68 C.P.R. (2d) 251 where the Quebec Court of Appeal maintained an injunction against the distributor from importing Flammarion books directly from France.

distribution were fixed by an exchange of letters between Flammarion and Benjamin and details were subject to renegotiation each year. In its initial letter, Flammarion referred to the "J'ai Lu" collection as something "dont nous assurons pour le Canada la diffusion exclusive". The same letter provided that Benjamin would deal with "la Socadis, notre organe de distribution".

There was a contract between Flammarion and an affiliated company, Les Editions J'ai Lu, S.A., whereby the latter confirmed that it had transferred to the former "l'ensemble de ses droits, titres et intérêts pour le territoire du Canada dans les oeuvres faisant partie de la collection J'ai Lu". The contract included a declaration and warranty by Les Editions that it was "le titulaire des droits d'édition littéraire en livre de poche des oeuvres cédées pour les avoir acquis les titulaires en vertu de contrats d'édition et ce, en conformité avec les dispositions concernant la Loi sur le droit d'auteur en France".

Compulsory Distribution: Legal Deposits

The obligation of and right to distribution is in one confined area determined by statute: this area deals with compulsory distribution in the form of legal deposits in designated libraries. Some legislative jurisdictions in Canada have created by statute, national or provincial libraries, the purpose of which is to provide a depository and archive for matter published within the jurisdiction. These libraries do not serve the same function as that of public or private lending libraries;[3] on the contrary, they serve as a home for the cultural heritage of the jurisdiction as expressed through books, documents, records and tapes issued by a publisher. The libraries as well provide book lending and exchange facilities, bibliographical and research services, and programs to facilitate cataloguing, retrieval and acquisition of material. In order to achieve these ends, a statutory obligation is imposed upon publishers to effect a deposit of one or several copies of an edition of each book published within a stipulated delay following the date of publication; publishers who fail to effect a legal deposit are subject to a fine.

The National Library Act specifically provides[4] that a publisher must deposit two copies of each book published in Canada at his own expense unless the retail value of the book exceeds $50 in which case one copy is deemed sufficient. "Book" is defined by the Act[5] as library matter of every kind including any document, paper, record, or tape published by a publisher or in which

---

[3] See for example, Public Libraries Act of Ontario, S.O. 1984, c. 57; of Quebec, R.S.Q. c. B-3; of Manitoba, R.S.M. 1970, c. P220; of Alberta, R.S.A. 1980, c. L-12; of Saskatchewan, R.S.S. 1978, c. P-39.

[4] R.S.C. 1970, c. N-11, s. 11; National Library Book Deposit Regulations, C.R.C. 1978, c. 1109.

[5] Section 2 definition of "book".

information is written, recorded, stored or re-produced. While publishers have been inclined to be forgetful or hesitant with respect to their obligation to deposit the National Librarian has suggested that the legal deposit has definite advantages for the publisher: deposit creates a permanent center for preservation of books; and items deposited are listed in bibliographical publications which are distributed to various libraries.[6] Nevertheless, it has been argued that s. 11 of the Act requiring compulsory deposit of copies is *ultra vires* the Parliament of Canada in that it provides for a system of expropriation of property without compensation thereby contravening s. 92(13) of the British North America Act, dealing with "Property and Civil Rights in the Province". This argument has been successfully rebutted in *R. v. Appleby (No. 2)*[7] where the court held s. 11 of the Act falls within the legislative competence of Parliament to provide library facilities to the Government and people of Canada under the residual legislative jurisdiction in s. 91 of the British North America Act, and furthermore, does not infringe upon the right to enjoyment of property and due process provided under the Canadian Bill of Rights.[8]

It would as well appear that failure to effect a legal deposit does not affect copyright, the right of the copyright owner to institute and maintain infringement proceedings,[9] or the validity of all contracts accessory to the publication.

Although the Quebec legislature has followed the scheme and content of the National Library Act with some fidelity, the Quebec National Library Act[10] has in many respects made legal deposit a more onerous obligation. Section 8 of the provincial legislation imposes the obligation of deposit upon the publisher of a document in Quebec, "document" being defined as any publication reproduced by printing or graphic process, including phonographic and photographic processes.[11] Where the publisher has no domicile or place of business in the Province of Quebec, the obligation to deposit is imposed upon the printer or reproducer, or the exclusive distributor in the Province, and failing them, the author of a printed document. Furthermore, the existing regulations enacted under s. 10(d) of the Act require that the quarter and year of deposit as well as the words "Legal Deposit" appear on all documents.[12] On constitutional grounds, it is doubtful that failure to conform to the requirements of the provincial legislation can affect copyright, even if express provision to that effect were made in the statute.

---

[6] "The National Library" (1953), 18 C.P.R. 105.

[7] (1976), 76 D.L.R. (3d) 110 (N.B.C.A.).

[8] 1960 (Can.), c. 44, ss. 1(a), 2 (R.S.C. 1970, App. III)

[9] *Griffin et al. v. Kingston and Pembroke R. Co.* (1889), 17 O.R. 660. The present Copyright Act, R.S.C. 1970, c. C-30 makes no reference to legal deposit similar to that contained in former s. 52 of the Copyright Act, R.S.C. 1952, c. 55, repealed 1968-69, c. 47, s. 15.

[10] R.S.Q. 1977, c. B-2.

[11] *Ibid.*, s. 1(c).

[12] Regulation Respecting Legal Deposit, s. 5, O.C. January 7, 1968, *Official Gazette* January 20, 1968, p. 452.

Both federal and Quebec statutes respecting the National Library may be said to impose the obligation of deposit upon books and documents which are and are not copyrighted. Although the material must be published within the relevant legislative jurisdiction, the statutes purport to demand deposit regardless of the jurisdiction of creation, first publication, copyright registration, or domicile of author or publisher.[13]

Scope Of The Obligation To Distribute

The obligation to distribute flows directly from the obligation to publish. The statutory definition of publication contained in the current copyright and criminal legislation[14] relates to the issuance, exhibition, or delivery of the work to a third party or the public. An undertaking by a publisher to publish a work therefore necessarily implies he will distribute the work, although the extent of the obligation to distribute is not thereby defined. Within the context of an author-publisher agreement, it may hardly be argued that a distribution of free copies to the author, or to reviewers constitutes a full execution of the obligation to distribute. On the other hand, an advertisement to the public regarding the availability of a work or a placement of books in a retail book outlet with or without subsequent sales does not constitute a distribution made in accordance with the agreement. Depending on the wording of the agreement, it may generally be said that a publisher has an obligation to print works given to him under contract and to make them available for sale.[15] This however does not necessarily mean that a book with a limited market or outdated subject matter must be distributed continually until a purchaser is found. It is uncertain whether this obligation in the absence of the publisher's contractual discretion, entitles the author to require adequate inventories and efficient distribution where public demand for the work is clearly evident on a short or long-term basis. On this matter, one would expect the courts to hold that a contract, which does not explicitly oblige the publisher to effect an adequate distribution of published works, does nevertheless implicitly impose an obligation to issue the work to the public in accordance with the standard commercial practice in the industry.[16]

---

[13] The origins of the legal deposit have been traced to the French Ordonnance of December 1537, which prohibited the sale of all "livres, volumes ou cahiers" prior to the deposit of a copy of the publication at the library of François Premier. Similar decrees and laws in Europe had the double effect of preserving the literary output for posterity as well as providing a mechanism of surveillance. *Le dépôt légal,* Institut International de Coopération Intellectuelle, Paris, 1938.

[14] Copyright Act, R.S.C. 1970, c. C-30, s. 3(2); Criminal Code, R.S.C. 1970, c. C-34, s. 263.

[15] *Société des Editions du Trident v. Genet,* R.I.D.A. No. LIII, 1967, p. 58; *Société Anonyme des Editions Nagel v. Beer,* R.I.D.A. No. XIV, 1957, p. 210.

[16] *Société d'Editions Musicales Grande Avenue, et al. v. Quenehen (PEC)* R.I.D.A., No. XXXXVI, 1965, p. 208.

Accordingly, acts by the publisher indicative of underprinting, neglect to fill received orders, refusal to undertake shipment of inventory, undue delay in complying with stock orders resulting in loss of sales and failure to reprint in the same or cheaper edition, may constitute a breach of the author-publisher agreement entitling the author to claim damages and rescission.[17] In reviewing the issue, the courts would necessarily consider evidence respecting the advertising, printing and sales performance of other publishers of similar works, and would evaluate damages on the basis of lost royalties on projected sales.

The primary defences of a publisher may certainly include allegations of impossibility of performance due to strikes, default of the independent distributor to ship, absolute contractual discretion respecting distribution and defects in the work in the nature of error, defamation or plagiarism.

The right of the author to compel the publisher to distribute cannot extend to the distribution of the work in a territory where the publisher, by his activity, infringes the copyright of third parties. An author who has given to a publisher an exclusive right to print and publish his work in Canada, and has at the same time conferred similar rights to another publisher to cover the territory of the United States of America, cannot require his publishers to export into the territory of the other thereby causing an infringement of rights conferred by the author himself.[18]

Another important factor involved in distribution is the setting of a price for the published work. It may be said that the author has an intimate interest in seeing that the price fixed upon copies of the works are not below ordinary market prices for the simple reason that his royalties are fixed as a percentage of the retail sales price. On the other hand, the author may be wary of an inordinately high retail price attached to the edition insofar as an excessively priced edition may prevent a large number of sales. Author-publisher agreements usually stipulate that the publisher shall have the sole discretion to fix the price of the published work for the obvious reason that the publisher must assure that proceeds from the sale will be sufficient to recoup advances made for the cost of printing, overhead and the payment of royalties. If the agreement is silent in this respect, the jurisprudence has held that the publisher is entitled to fix the price of the work, except in the event that the publisher is

---

17 *A v. Société des Editions B et C,* R.I.D.A., No. XXXXIV, 1964, p. 245; *Héritiers Gounod v. Société Heugel et Cie* R.I.D.A., No. XIV, 1957, p. 215.

18 See by analogy, Sharp, R.C., "*Import Restrictions in the Canadian Copyright Act*" (1975), 17 C.P.R. (2d) 20 respecting criticism of suggested legislature amendments that importation of existing Canadian copyright where the author consents to importation, even when a Canadian licence is held by someone other than the author. See also, Noel, W., "The Importation Provisions of the Canadian Copyright Act" (1977), 9 Ottawa L.R. 156; *Clarke, Irwin & Co. Ltd. v. C. Cole & Co. Ltd.* (1960), 33 C.P.R. 173 (Ont.); *Godfrey, MacSkimming & Bacque Ltd. et al. v. Coles Book Stores Ltd.* (1974), 13 C.P.R. (2d) 89 (Ont.); *McClelland and Stewart Ltd. v. Coles Book Stores Ltd.* (1976), 21 C.P.R. (2d) 266 (Ont.); *Simon & Schuster Inc. et al. v. Coles Book Stores Ltd.* (1976), 23 C.P.R. (2d) 43 (Ont.).

merely a printer executing as an independent contractor a contract given to him by the author to issue the work for a stipulated sum with or without a commission.[19]

[19] *Reade v. Bentley* (1858), 4 K. & J. 656; *Abrahams et al. v. Reiach,* (1922) 1 K.B. 477.

Chapter 5

Royalties

A royalty is the main pecuniary remuneration which the author receives in consideration for permitting the publisher to print and distribute his work. It is common practice to set out a schedule of royalty payments based on or varying with the number of copies sold and the nature of the edition distributed. One might often expect to find royalties expressed as a percentage of the retail selling price of a book up to a certain amount of copies with an increment in percentage points as the number of copies sold increases; for example, a basic minimum royalty may be ten percent on the first 5,000 copies, 12 1/2 percent on the next 5,000 copies and 15 percent on all copies sold thereafter. Nevertheless, the parties may agree to a different royalty schedule as the nature of the edition varies; accordingly, basic royalty percentages will differ where the copies are sold at a clearance or remainder price, where the work is sold in the form of sheets or bound copies for export, and where the publisher has issued under his imprint a cheaper edition. The parties may also stipulate that no royalties are payable on copies given to the author or to editors and reviewers for promotion purposes, or for lost or damaged copies which are unsaleable or remain unsold. If the publisher is interested in marketing the subsidiary rights, the agreement may provide that the author shall be entitled to a major portion of the proceeds on such rights as dramatic, cinematographic, translation, serial broadcasting, anthology and book club rights.

In anticipation of sales, the agreement may provide for a payment of a certain sum of money as an advance upon royalties. Unless payment is made to the author in one lump sum in full and final payment of all royalties due, the publisher will undertake an obligation to account to the author on a periodic basis and to reveal to him the number of copies printed, the number bound, the number distributed and sold, as well as the relevant retail or wholesale prices of the printed work.

In law, a royalty is a tariff or toll payable to the author based on and fixed as a percentage of publisher's actual or projected income from the sale of the printed work.[1] The use of the word "royalties" in an agreement will be given its usual publishing-industry meaning even though one of the parties may have intended to denote some other meaning, such as sale price or commission.[2] On the other hand, the use of the word "royalties" does not prevent third parties, particularly the tax authorities, from considering the payments as being in reality a premium, price or payment for services rendered.[3] The usual industry meaning includes the notion of remuneration made by way of payment of a percentage of profits periodically or in one lump sum. There has been an attempt to distinguish "royalties" from "lump sum payments", especially for tax purposes,[4] although lump sum payment may be regarded as a mere commutation of minimum royalties otherwise payable.[5]

Royalties Upon Bankruptcy

Many agreements contain a termination clause which provides among other things that upon the bankruptcy of the publisher the agreement shall *ipso facto* terminate and all rights granted to the publisher shall revert to the author. Nevertheless, by consent, the trustee in bankruptcy may be entitled to melt the plates and sell copies of sheets remaining on hand as inventory; and this may be done subject only to payment to the author of the royalties as stipulated in the event that the author fails to exercise an option to purchase the plates which he must exercise in a specified period of time. In practice, however, the insolvency or bankruptcy of a publisher may be accompanied or immediately followed by a purchase of all assets by a competing publisher who will have an interest in directly contacting the author for the purpose of renewing or extending the contracts.

In the absence of a purchase of assets by a new publisher, the author must fall back upon the remedy provided in current bankruptcy legislation in the event of the demise of the publisher. Section 61 of the Bankruptcy Act[6] provides that the

---

[1] *Composers, Authors and Publishers Assoc. of Canada Ltd. v. Maple Leaf Broadcasting Co. Ltd.* (1952), 13 Fox Pat. C. 101 (Ex. Ct.); affd 14 Fox Pat. C. 152 (S.C.C.).

[2] *M.N.R. v. Wain-Town Gas & Oil Co. Ltd.* (1952), 13 Fox Pat. C. 5 (S.C.C.); *Frontenac Shoe Ltée v. M.N.R.* (1963), 24 Fox Pat. C. 190 (Ex. Ct.); conf. in part 23 Fox Pat. C. 4 (T.A.B.); see also *Gingras v. M.N.R.* (1961), 23 Fox Pat. C. 14 (T.A.B.); conf. in part 24 Fox Pat. C. 176 (Ex. Ct.).

[3] *No. 682 v. M.N.R.* (1961), 20 Fox Pat. C. 126 (T.A.B.).

[4] *Hould v. M.N.R.* (1965), 31 Fox Pat. C. 89 (T.A.B.); *Peat Business Systems Ltd. v. M.N.R.* (1951), 12 Fox Pat. C. 36 (T.A.B.); *Crépeau v. M.N.R.* (1964), 31 Fox Pat. C. 93 (T.A.B.); *Larue v. M.N.R.* (1963), 25 Fox Pat. C. 20 (T.A.B.).

[5] *No. 442 v. M.N.R.* (1957), 17 Fox Pat. C. 23 (I.T.A.B.).

[6] R.S.C. 1970, c. B-3.

author's manuscript and any copyrights assigned to a publisher or printer which becomes bankrupt shall revert and be delivered to the author; any contracts between the author and the bankrupt shall then terminate in the event the work covered by such copyright remains unpublished and has not been put on the market at the time of the bankruptcy and no expenses have been incurred in that connection. On the contrary, if expenses have been incurred by the bankrupt and if the work has been put in type even in part, the manuscript and copyright shall revert and be delivered to the author only upon payment of the expenses incurred although the product of the expenses shall be delivered to the author. Payment by the author in this respect is considered optional and in the event of failure of the author to exercise his option within six months of the date of the bankruptcy, the trustee may carry out the original contract which would otherwise be considered terminated. Furthermore, if the trustee fails to carry out the contracts following six months from the date of the bankruptcy, manuscript and copyright revert without expense to the author and the contract is then considered terminated and void.

The bankruptcy legislation furthermore indicates that in the event the bankruptcy occurs when the work has already been published and put on the market, the trustee is entitled to sell copies of the published work and the author is entitled to royalties in accordance with the terms of the agreement. The trustee, however, is not entitled to assign the copyright or transfer the interest of the bankrupt by licence or otherwise without the written consent of the author except upon terms which will guarantee to the author payment of royalties or a share of the profits at a rate at least equivalent to that which the publisher was obliged to pay; the author-publisher agreement is then considered terminated and void except with respect to the disposal of the copies of the work published and placed on the market before the bankruptcy. Where the work has been published, the trustee must offer in writing to the author the right to purchase the manufactured or marketable copies of the work in the estate of the bankrupt at a price and in a condition which the trustee deems fair and proper before disposing of the copies in the manner mentioned above.

In summary, the author has little to fear in the event that bankruptcy intervenes prior to the commencement of printing and publication of the work; the manuscript will be returned to him and he will be left free to seek publication through another publishing vehicle. On the other hand, the trustee in bankruptcy is entitled to proceed with the execution of the contract simply by the fact that expenses have been incurred in the preparation of the manuscript for publication. The concern of the author at this stage will relate to the distinct possibility that the distribution aspect of the publishing venture will not be executed as expeditiously as it would have been had the enterprise been solvent and operated by a person other than an official appointed in a statutory capacity. The necessary bureaucracy required to administer a venture in conformity with statutory restrictions may have a dilatory or deleterious effect upon the ultimate success of the published work in the market place. It is the intention of the legislator enacting the legislative provision to protect copyright owners from being deprived of their interest in the copyright and represents a textual reproduction of an analagous section in the English bankruptcy legislation. Prior to the enactment of the provision it was generally held that an author was only entitled to damages for breach of contract in the event of the bankruptcy of a publisher who is the assignee of the author's copyright on terms of being paid royalties on sales.[7]

It is to be noted that where the publisher is under an obligation to pay royalties to the author, but no interest in copyright has been assigned by the author to the publisher, the bankruptcy of the latter will cause the termination of the agreement and the trustee in bankruptcy is not permitted to proceed with publication.[8] Although the bankruptcy legislation does make special provision for authors in accordance with the scheme set out above, the Bankruptcy Act does not consider an author, being a creditor of unpaid royalties, as a secured creditor nor is the latter entitled to any priority of claim on the basis of the royalties due.[9]

While there is a special mechanism permitting the author to obtain royalties from the trustee in bankruptcy, there is no legislation establishing a vendor's lien or fixing a charge upon the copyright assigned for royalties to a publisher who subsequently re-assigns to a stranger the original contract. Due to a lack of privity, the author cannot successfully claim payment of royalties from the second assignee unless there is consent, even though the latter was aware of the existence of the initial author-publisher agreement.[10]

Public Lending Right

On the federal governmental level, there now exists a limited scheme by which authors receive automatic but not full compensation for library use of their books. The scheme, administered by the Public Lending Right Commission, recognizes the loss of royalties suffered by authors as a result of public and university use of books through library systems. The author does not receive compensation if his published work is wholly or mainly a musical score, a newspaper, magazine or periodical, a calendar, diary, agenda or coloring book, a directory, index compilation or bibliography of minimum critical content, or the catalogue of an exhibition. The work is excluded if it was written by more than four authors or contributors whose names appear on the title page, was written for an employer under a contract for service, was intended primarily as a

---

[7] *In Re Grant Richards, ex p. Deeping,* [1907] 2 K.B. 33; Duncan and Honsberger, *Bankruptcy in Canada,* 3rd ed., 1961 at p. 436.
[8] *Lucas v. Moncrieff* (1905), 21 T.L.R. 683.
[9] Bankruptcy Act, R.S.C. 1970, c. B-3, s. 107.
[10] *Barker v. Stickney,* [1919] 1 K.B. 121 at p. 133, *per* Scrutton, L.J.

textbook, is a purely instructional "how-to" book, is a work containing fewer than forty-nine pages, or a childrens' work containing fewer than twenty-four pages.

Compensation is calculated on the following basis: the original, eligible author of an eligible title is entitled to 100% of a payment, but only if no other contributors, such as co-authors, illustrators, or photographers, are involved. Illustrators or photographers, if eligible, will share the applicable PLR payment with the writer of the work. In this case, claimants must come to an agreement between or among themselves as to the percentage share for which each will apply. The original author of a translated and eligible title is entitled to 60% of the payment; the *translator* is entitled to 40%.

For edited titles, provided an eligible edited title also contains significant Canadian content, an editor whose name appears on the title page is entitled to 20% of the payment for that title. If multiple editors share copyright, they must divided this 20% between or among themselves.

Due to the prohibitive cost of determining payments on the basis of actual library borrowings the calculation of payment will be based on a sampling of the holdings of a representative number of public and university libraries: the larger the number of libraries in which an eligible title is found, the larger the payment. Any titles not found in a certain minimum number of libraries will not receive a payment.

Chapter 6

Delivery And Warranty Of The Work

One of the fundamental obligations of the author is to deliver the manuscript not later than a specific time stipulated in the agreement in a form and content suitable for publication. The author-publisher agreements often stipulate that time being of the essence the author shall deliver to the publisher within a fixed period one or several complete, double-spaced typewritten copies of the work in form and content satisfactory to the publisher, and in the event of the failure of the former to deliver, the publisher shall be entitled to terminate the agreement. The publisher as well usually stipulates that the author is under the obligation to furnish as part of the work a title page, a preface, table of contents, photographs, illustrations, and artwork, if any, as well as an index. Failure on the part of the author to supply any of the above entitles the publisher to provide the same and charge the costs to the author by making deduction from royalties. The author is as well called upon to revise and return proof sheets within a reasonable delay in order to permit the mechanics of publishing to proceed on schedule. The apparent purpose of these provisions is to impose upon the author the complete task of preparing the work in publishable form. Since the author is the master of his work, it is apparent that the latter has a greater facility and expertise in preparing all technical aspects related to the work, including a table of contents and index which ultimately make the work more accessible and useful to the reader.

It has been held that the failure of an author to deliver the manuscript or a portion thereof which he has contracted to write and forward for delivery entitles the publisher to seek damages which are appreciated or quantified with regard to the profit which would have been forthcoming from the publication.[1]

---

[1] *Gale v. Leckie* (1871), 2 Stark. 107, where the author refused to supply the manuscript to be published at the publisher's sole expense subject to a division of

The publisher is furthermore entitled to recover expenses incurred in reliance on the contract. However, as previously discussed, the court will not force by way of injunction the author to write the manuscript and to effect delivery, although such may not be the case where the work is in complete manuscript form and unlawfully retained by the author in anticipation of submission to other publishers.

Most widely used agreements provide that the publisher requires the author to maintain a copy of the manuscript delivered; or provide simply that the publishers are not insurers of manuscripts delivered or submitted, and are not liable for the loss, destruction or damage to the same. Some forms of agreement provide that the publisher shall be responsible for the safety of the manuscript from fire, water or loss only to an amount limited to the cost of retyping the manuscript. There is little doubt that the law upholds the validity of clauses of non-responsibility or stipulations in limitation of liability, save in the event of gross or willful negligence. Nevertheless, even in the event that loss of manuscript is caused by gross negligence of the publisher, it is difficult to see how the author may rightfully claim more than simple nominal damages. Surely, it is incumbent upon him, unless he wishes to invite trouble, to retain a copy of the manuscript unless invaluable and original artwork is involved. Accordingly, a claim for damages by the author may be limited to the simple technical replacement costs of the manuscript.

It has been suggested that in the absence of an express stipulation, the degree of care required of the publisher varies with the nature of the submission: if the manuscript is submitted on an unsolicited basis, the publisher is not responsible for imprudent or negligent handling leading to loss; where the manuscript is solicited, the standard care is that of the prudent man of business with respect to his own property.[2]

The distinction as to the origin of the original submission assumes great relevance in present day industrial conditions, which see a daily inpour of unsolicited manuscripts to book publishers and periodicals by far outnumbering submissions made on the basis of invitation. An author of an unsolicited manuscript cannot unilaterally impose an obligation of safekeeping upon a publisher who happens to receive his manuscripts simply because post office officials have left the work at his doorstep. On the other hand, the increasing deluge of unsolicited material has driven many publishers of books and periodicals to announce that unsolicited manuscripts will not be returned unless accompanied by return postage and packaging. It is suggested that such an undertaking to return may have the undesirable effect of creating an obligation to safeguard the unsolicited material submitted and to take all prudent steps necessary to effect return.

---

profits upon sales. The court suggested that a good defence to the action in damages would be that the intended publication was of an illegal nature, although in the instance, the author failed to demonstrate illegality.

[2] Fox, *Canadian Law of Copyright and Industrial Designs,* p. 584.

Warranty By The Author

As a form of limited and often illusory protection the publisher generally exacts from the author a written warranty covering one or all of the following elements: a warranty that the work submitted for publication is original; that the author is the proprietor and creator of the work and has full unrestricted power to enter into a contract of publication with the publisher; that publication of the work will not give rise to any infringement of a proprietary right or copyright; that the work has not been previously published in book form; and that the work contains no matter which is libellous, obscene, blasphemous or otherwise contrary to law. Breach of such warranties require the author to indemnify the publisher for all costs incurred as a result of defending actions and claims or recouping losses and expenses incurred toward publication.

By reading together the clause assigning or granting a licence with respect to the author's copyright, with the clause warrantying originality, it may be said that the author furthermore warrants that the work is subject to copyright protection. While this interpretation of the agreement may appear strained, it must be presumed that the intention of the parties is to favour the existence of a right for the benefit of the publisher to take maximum advantage of the work in return for the payment of royalties; the publisher is presumably given the implicit right to restrain competition from a substantially similar work in the market place. In the event that the publisher discovers the author's work is in fact a property in the public domain or does not fall within the definition of works protected by copyright, the publisher will not be entitled by law to restrain competition and should therefore be entitled to a recourse born of contract against the author.[3]

Notwithstanding the insertion of a warranty of originality in a standard form agreement, it may occur that the publisher is fully apprised of the fact that a work to be published may be the subject of copyright protection for a copyright holder whose authorization has not been obtained prior to publication. Aside from the situations of outright fraud, there are numerous instances especially within the realm of scholarly publication where authors in their capacity as editors submit for publication an unpublished work of a deceased author in an

[3] The warranty of originality must be construed in relation to the use of the word originality in the prevailing copyright law. Accordingly, the author is under the obligation to warrant the originality of the expression of his ideas and not of the ideas themselves. As to the definition of "originality" see Fox, pp. 41-47; *Underwriters' Survey Bureau Ltd. et al. v. American Home Fire Assurance Co. et al.*, [1939] 4 D.L.R. 89 (Ex. Ct.); *Latour v. Cyr* (1951), 15 C.P.R. 21 (Ex. Ct.); *Goldner v. Canadian Broadcasting Corp.* (1972), 7 C.P.R. (2d) 158 (Fed. Ct.); *Collins et al v. Rosenthal et al.* (1974), 14 C.P.R. (2d) 143 (Fed. Ct.); *Formules Municipales Ltée v. Pineault et al.* (1975), 19 C.P.R. (2d) 139 (Fed. Ct.). As to unauthorized previous use, see *Dickson v. Venue Publishing* (1985), 4 C.P.R. (3d) 279.

edited and annotated form.[4] The manuscript is usually found by the editor during his research in a public or university archive and notwithstanding *bona fide* inquiries, the editor is unable to locate the heirs of the author for the purpose of obtaining authorization to publish. Although the publisher in the circumstances exacts an obligation of warranty of originality or indemnification in the event of breach of copyright, it is suggested that such terms may in particular circumstances be deemed to have been waived by the publisher, if he has been advised of the difficulties involved in obtaining and the absence of due authorization.

The warranty in practice proves illusory in view of the often scant resources of the author for the purpose of making good any cost incurred by the publisher. On the other hand, where the publication has proven successful and royalties are payable on a large scale, the publisher may decide to set off against royalties costs incurred related to the objects of the author's warranty. A quick review of the elements of warranty just mentioned will reveal that only one factor may be independently verifiable *a priori* by the publisher, namely the obscenity and illegal nature of the content of the work. Unless the publisher has at his command extraordinary research facilities, the other elements mentioned are not readily ascertainable, except in the rare event of prior publication of the same work under the same title. Nevertheless, the factors warranted are of overwhelming importance: false representation by the author in any respect may see the abrupt termination of the publication, and distribution of the work at the instance of a third party unknown to the publisher at the time of commencement of the venture.

Although a stipulation of warranty on the part of the author is not objectionable, one might take issue with the accompanying indemnification clause requiring the author to indemnify and hold harmless the publisher from all expenses, costs, charges and damages resulting from suits and claims asserted against the publisher arising out of the representations warranted. Even where the rights and claims asserted by third parties are ill founded, frivolous or unproven, the author in many standard form agreements binds himself to compensate the publisher for expenses incurred. One would surely have thought more equitable a formula by which the publisher assumes all costs of litigation where the author's representations prove truthful. One would also find more favour with a proposal that authors be given some right to assume the course of the defence or litigation where one of his representations comes under attack by third parties.

Many form agreements as well contain a representation misdescribed as a warranty requiring the author not to publish any other edition of the work in a form revised, corrected or abridged, or to publish any other work which might

[4] Dryden, Jean E., "Copyright in Manuscript Sources" Archivaria, Vol. 1, No. 1, Winter 1975-1976, p. 39.

interfere with sales of the original work. Restrictive covenants of this nature are discussed elsewhere in the present work.

Finally, it may be noted that it is not general practice to include in the warranties provision a clause providing for joint action or the option to bring joint suit where the work to be published is infringed. It is usually assumed by the parties that the one who retains or has been assigned copyright is entitled to the exclusive initiative in prosecuting possible acts of infringement by third parties. From the point of view of legal procedure, it is perhaps wise at least to stipulate that the party who is given the right or burden to bring suit in the event of infringement is entitled to proceed either in the name of the other or with the latter's consent.

In certain circumstances, a warranty of title or of interest in copyright may be implied from the representations made by the author or his representatives. For example, in *Sims v. Marryat*[5] the court held that certain letters emanating from the executor of the deceased author to the publisher referring to an offer to treat respecting the copyright of the author, as well as an "exclusive right of publishing" constituted a representation that the executor had a copyright interest in the manuscripts in question.

---

[5] (1851), 85 R.R. 462 at p. 469, *per* Lord Campbell Ch. J.:

> "Here is an acknowledgement of a contract whereby the defendant sold 'the exclusive right of publishing'. How could he do so unless he had it? If we were confined to the words of the receipt alone, I think they would of themselves amount to an express promise that plaintiffs were to have the exclusive right so long as the copyright should endure; and is not that promise broken if the defendant had not the exclusive right to give them?"

See also *Downing v. General Synod of the Church of England in Canada et al.*, [1943] 1 D.L.R. 446; revd [1943] 3 D.L.R. 553 (Ont. C.A.).

Chapter 7

Re-editions And Revisions

The value of a book or published work is in most cases directly related to its relevance and currency of subject matter. Texts in the scientific or legal field are easily rendered out of date and perhaps unsaleable due to new discoveries or revolutionary developments which have not been covered or envisaged by the author at the time of publication. It is in the interest of the publisher to retain a right or option permitting him to bring up to date a published work; at the same time, it may be in the author's interest to seek to revise his work and produce a new edition notwithstanding the cession or licencing of rights to the original publication.

A new edition of a work which includes substantive changes by way of condensation, addition, correction or re-arrangement, is to be treated in law as a new work subject to a copyright different from that of the old.[1] In making a special stipulation regarding re-editions, the parties may not contemplate a simple reprinting of the first edition which is otherwise covered by the initial obligation to print mentioned in the agreement. What may be contemplated is the creation of a new text which contains sufficient modification to the original publication so as to constitute a new book which is susceptible of an independent existence and separate copyright. Nevertheless, it is generally accepted that the word "edition" means any issue or publication of a work; the simple undertaking to effect a re-edition may therefore not encompass an obligation on the part of the publisher to issue a revised text or edition of the work. It is not necessary that new type be set or even that more copies be printed for a new edition, since the essential definition of the word relates to the issuance of copies of the work to the public, whether from existing stock or fresh from the

[1] *Sweet v. Cater* (1841), 11 Sim. 572, respecting copyright infringement by the same author through a subsequent edition.

press.[2] However, in stipulating the option to issue a new edition, the parties may contemplate both a new printing and a revised printing; the unfortunate ambiguity of the term re-edition remains to be interpreted from the tenor of the remainder of the agreement.

Some standard form agreements make the following provisions respecting re-editions:

> In the event of further editions of the book being required, of which the publisher shall be the judge, this agreement is to remain in force except that should the publisher be unable or unwilling to produce a further edition within five (5) years of publication of the first, then this agreement is to be at an end and all rights and privileges embodied hereunder will revert to the author, his heirs, devisees and assignees.

As is evident, the clause favours the publisher in that it permits him to extend the duration of the agreement to cover the publication of new editions regardless of the extent, if any, of revisions made to the new publication; this is not to say that the stipulation is inequitable, for the publisher does require at least a few years of sales experience with the original publication prior to being competent to make an economic decision as to whether or not the printing of a new edition is warranted. The author on the other hand is entitled to treat the agreement as terminated either by the simple expiry of the period of time stipulated, or by the expression of firm intent by the publisher that he is unable or unwilling to produce a further edition in accordance with the clause. In *Cartwright & Sons Ltd. v. The Carswell Co. Ltd.*[3] the publisher advised the author several months prior to the expiry of the delay that no publication of a revised edition was contemplated for at least two or three years. The court held that the author was entitled to treat the agreement as terminated and that he was free to publish a revised edition otherwise than through the original publisher.

As indicated, an undertaking to effect a re-edition may not involve the issuance of a revised edition. The reason is evident: unless the writing or compilation of the work involves a minimum amount of skill, it is usually the author alone who is sufficiently conversant with the subject and style of the work and can effect textual modifications. Furthermore, agreements rarely grant to the publisher the right to make substantial textual changes without the consent of the author. In other words, the author plays an important role in determining the availability of a revised text for the purposes of re-edition, and consequently a simple undertaking by the publisher to effect a re-edition may not involve revisions to the work. However, in this regard, many agreements do provide that the author undertakes to effect revisions for the purpose of further editions, in default of which the publisher may engage another author to do the same. There are also provisions which declare that the publisher shall have the

---

[2] 30 *Halsbury's Laws of England,* 3rd ed., p. 546; *Reade v. Bentley* (1858), 4 K. & J. 656, *per* Page Wood V.-C.; *Blackwood v. Brewster* (1860), 23 Sess. Cas. (2nd Ser.) 142.

[3] (1946), 5 Fox Pat. C. 49 (Ont.).

right to make such editorial changes in the manuscript as it deems desirable, but the author shall have the right to pass upon such changes as are made; this stipulation has the effect of mitigating the unilateral power of the publisher to appreciably alter the content of the manuscript for marketing purposes, and to provide a mechanism of co-operation in adjusting the content of the publication for the purpose of increasing sales.

In the event of an ambiguity in the text, the court will imply a right to publish with alterations even though substantial where the agreement confers a licence to publish, although the court at the same time will limit the right to alter.[4] Notwithstanding the nature of the agreement and in the absence of an express clause to the contrary, the publisher is entitled to make spelling, grammatical and other mechanical corrections and alterations to the text.

Where the publisher does proceed to the publication of a new edition without the participation of the author, it may occur that the work is so altered and modified as to no longer reflect adequately or justly the ideas, intentions or thinking of the author as contained in the original edition. If the agreement is so worded as to totally extinguish any continuing right in the work for the benefit of the author, the latter is without apparent recourse to prevent publication. In the absence of such a specific and far-reaching provision, the author may invoke his *droit moral* as codified in statute, or base an action in damages or an injunction upon an allegation of libel or passing off.[5]

Apart from the content of the work, the author has an interest in seeing to the proper representation of his work on the physical cover of the publication, as well as in advertising and marketing projects issued by the publisher. A book jacket or poster which misrepresents the nature of the work either by way of graphics or false attribution of authorship or publisher will entitle the author to an injunction prohibiting the continuation of the misrepresentation. The

---

[4] *Frisby v. B.B.C.*, [1967] 2 All E.R. 106.

[5] Section 12(7) of the Copyright Act, R.S.C. 1970, c. C-30:

> "Independently of the author's copyright, and even after the assignment, either wholly or partially, of the said copyright, the author has the right to claim authorship of the work, as well as the right to restrain any distortion, mutilation or other modification of the work that would be prejudicial to his honor or reputation."

See, for example, *Angers v. Leprohon* (1899), Que. S.C. 170 at p. 173, *per* Doherty, J.:

> "Considering that insofar as her susceptibilities as an author may have been wounded by said change of title not having taken the means provided by law for retaining her property in and the control of said story and having in effect allowed the same to become public property, she cannot legally claim protection against the consequences, unpleasant though they may be to her, resulting from the exercise by other persons of the right become common to all of re-publishing said story in the exercise of which right the persons so exercising it are under no legal obligation to conform to her taste or preferences in the matter of the title under which said story should be published."

Frisby v. B.B.C., [1967] 2 All E.R. 106; *Joseph v. National Magazine Co. Ltd.*, [1958] 3 All E.R. 52.

remedy of the author in the instance would appear to be based more on the laws of libel and contract rather than on the strict provisions of the copyright statute.[6]

An author who has sold an edition or a certain amount of copies to one publisher may not prior to the extinction of the stock authorize another publisher to issue a new edition in such a manner as to compete with the first edition; he is bound to give to the first publisher the full opportunity of realizing the benefit of his contract.[7] Nevertheless, if the new edition is substantially different from the original work so as to constitute a separate work, the author may proceed with publication through another publisher in the absence of any stipulation to the contrary. Furthermore, where the agreement does not constitute an assignment of copyright, or provide that the authorization to be published is exclusive, and in effect merely provides a right to publish in consideration for a royalty based on a percentage of sales, the publisher may not restrain the author from publishing another edition of the same work even though the stock of the first publisher remains unsold.[8]

---

[6] *Le Nordet Inc. et al. v. 82558 Canada Ltd.*, [1978] Que. S.C. 904 at p. 908.

[7] *Reade v. Bentley* (1858), 4 K. & J. 656.

[8] *Warne v. Routledge* (1874), L.R. 18 Eq. 497; but see *Educational Co. of Ireland Ltd. v. Fallon and Getz,* [1919] 1 Ir. R. 62 respecting an assignment of copyright.

Chapter 8

Subsidiary And Subsequent Rights

In addition to the grant of permission to publish a work in book form, author-publisher agreements usually contain a supplementary grant of rights relating to the exploitation of the work in the following forms: abridgment, anthology, digest, reproduction on radio and television, phonograph records, magnetic tapes, microfilming, motion pictures, drama, reprint or cheap editions, book clubs, serialization in periodicals or newspapers and in translations. As previously indicated in the discussion on royalties, the publisher may stipulate a right to compensation or consideration for the sale of the subsidiary rights expressed as a percentage of proceeds received upon the sale. Payment to the publisher on account of the sale of subsidiary rights may be justified both as compensation for the publisher's role as agent in seeking out potential customers for reproduction rights, as well as added remuneration for risks inherent in the reproduction of the work in the initial book form. In the latter regard, it has been noted that the successful exploitation of subsidiary rights is a real necessity to the publisher in view of the increasing difficulty in publishing a book profitably merely on its trade sales.[1] For this reason, the agreements in common use rarely grant to the author a right of refusal or veto over the exploitation of enumerated subsidiary rights.

A brief definition of various subsidiary rights and forms is now in order. First, serial rights refer to the publication of the entirety or a portion of a work in the form of a magazine or newspaper article prior to or concurrent with publication in book form. The serial reproduction may be in the form of a verbatim extract from the work or may be a summary or condensation of the book prepared by the publisher of the periodical or newspaper. Serial reproduction may be said to

[1] Marks, Joseph, "Subsidiary Rights and Permissions", in Grannis, C.B. (ed.), *What Happens in Book Publishing*, Columbia University Press, 1957, p. 213.

have a double-edged effect, namely to publicize widely the nature and content of the book thereby stimulating sales; and on the other hand, making known to the public the essence of the book thereby detracting from the sales of the work in book form.

Secondly, serial rights refer to serialization, mainly through the forum of newspapers and usually takes place following and not before the publication of the work in book form. The sale is made by the publisher to feature syndicates affiliated with newspaper publishers which in turn seek to resell the items to newspaper organizations.

Book club rights refer to the sale of the work to associations whose subscribers undertake as a condition of their membership to purchase a minimum number of books per year in return for reduced prices and discounts on editions of the work. The book club may purchase the proofs or copies of the plates executed by the publisher and undertake the manufacture of an edition of the work through to its own resources. The distribution of the club edition is in some circumstances made simultaneously and in others subsequent to the issuance of the trade edition. The advantage of selling to book clubs is, of course, the prospect of possible sales of large amounts of copies of the work through the highly organized distribution network which the club operates.

Rights respecting translation refer to the sale to or licensing of publishers within or outside the country for the purpose of permitting the latter to publish and distribute the work in translated form. The cost of translation is borne by the purchaser or licensee and the transaction may confer upon the latter the right to distribute the work in the specific language on a territorial or worldwide basis. Usually joined with a transfer of translation rights are foreign publication rights permitting foreign publishers to reproduce or distribute the work in the foreign language within the specified territory outside the country of original publication.

The conveyance of reprint rights involves an authorization to another publisher to issue a less expensive or cheap edition of the work. Upon conveyance, the new publisher reprints the work in his own form and effects distribution through channels not otherwise covered by the publisher of the original edition. Reprint rights usually result in the issuance of the work in mass paper back form or may involve soft bound reprints of a higher technical quality.

Finally, a conveyance of performing rights involves the granting of authorization to radio, television, motion picture and dramatic enterprises to use the book, its story or ideas and title as a basis for programs and projects within the respective media. Although the conveyance of these rights pre-supposes the initial publication of the book, recent practices and contractual arrangements have provided for the simultaneous issuance of motion pictures and books or of the motion picture followed by the publication of the book as a form of mutual promotion.

Where the subject matter involves an illustration, comic character or symbol, the contract may call for a perpetual right of use in relation to a specific field of activity, for example, a cartoon animal to be used by the publisher in relation to an educational service.[2]

---

[2] In *Kerr v. The Queen* (1982), 66 C.P.R. (2d) 165, the court found on the basis of the following contract that the creator had given his consent to use of his cartoon character in relation to the metric system campaign, even though he retained copyright:

> 1.
> The contractor shall, during the period commencing on the 1st day of October, 1974, and ending on the 31st day of March 1975, provide the following services to the Minister:
> (as per terms of reference attached)
> (hereinafter referred to as the "said services").
>
> . . . . .
>
> 3.
> (1) This Agreement shall remain in force until the 31st day of March 1975 unless sooner terminated in the manner described in subsection (2) or (3).
> (2) This Agreement may be terminated by either party giving at least one week's notice thereof in writing to the other party.
> (3) Notwithstanding subsection (2), this Agreement may be terminated by the Minister without prior notice to the Contractor if, in the opinion of the Minister, there is sufficient cause for so doing.
>
> TERMS OF REFERENCE ATTACHED TO AND FORMING PART OF CONTRACT 93/810-689 DATED SEPTEMBER 27, 1974
>
> (1) To provide artwork of a cartoon character known as "METRIX" for various posters, pamphlets, brochures, booklets, animated cartoon story boards and other special drawings on a time-to-time basis, as requested by the Metric Commission. This artwork should be provided (a) in a rough draft form for approval, with changes to be made to rough drafts as required; (b) to provide finished, camera-ready artwork of the approved drawings:
>
> (2) Her Majesty will pay the Contractor the amount of any outstanding fees due to him under subsection (1) after presentation by the Contractor to the Minister of a statement, certified correct by the appropriate officer of the Department of Industry, Trade and Commerce, showing:
>
> (a) Professional Fees not exceeding two hundred dollars ($200.00) per hour.
>
> . . . . .
>
> 6(1) All research, reports, papers, material and information forming part of or produced in the performance of the said services and all patents and trade marks arising therefrom are the property of Her Majesty with the exception of the cartoon character "Metrix", the copyright to which said cartoon shall belong to the contractor.
>
> (a) It is further agreed that Her Majesty shall use or allow to be used the cartoon character "Metrix" in perpetuity in relation to the Metric System only, without any further remuneration to the contractor;
>
> (b) It is further agreed that the cartoon character "Metrix" can be changed, altered or modified to suit the publicity medium to be used;
>
> (c) It is further agreed that the contractor shall not use, nor allow others with his permission to use, the cartoon character "Metrix" in Canada for a period of five years commencing April 1, 1975 and terminating March 31, 1980.

Options On Future Works

The publisher may wish to spread his risks on a specific publishing venture, not only by acquiring subsidiary rights and printing subsequent editions; he may also look to possible return from subsequent works produced by the same author. To this end, a publisher may require an author to agree to a clause giving the publisher the right of first refusal, including the first opportunity to review for publication the next or subsequent work of the author. In this regard, the parties usually stipulate that new terms and conditions will be negotiated for the purpose of effecting publicaton of the new work. The right of first refusal entitles the publisher to first receipt of the manuscript for a review period usually of one month during which the publisher is given sufficient time to evaluate the quality and marketability of the work. Upon the expiry of the review period, the author is at liberty to contract with another publisher with respect to the work in the event the initial publisher has either refused or has not responded regarding publication.

On the other hand, the publisher may seek to obtain from the author an assignment of copyright in all future works to be produced by him within a given period of time, often five years. The effect of such an assignment at first glance appears to be more restrictive than a simple option especially with respect to the time element. The publisher is furthermore given a real interest in the copyright itself. Nevertheless, it often occurs that the assignment of future works is drafted in the form of an option providing for an assignment of copyright to be exercised upon a certain number of works to be written by the author in the future upon notification by the publisher of his willingness or decision to proceed with publication of those works. It has been held in situations where the author has made such agreement but chosen in contravention to proceed with publication through the facilities of another publisher that the new publisher having notice of the assignment-option clause is subject to a judicial order of restraint from publication of the work. It has as

---

(d) It is further agreed that after March 31, 1980 the contractor shall not use the cartoon character "Metrix" or allow other with his permission to use the cartoon character "Metrix" without first having obtained the written permission of the Minister.

(2) Subject to subsection 6(1), neither the contractor nor any officer, servant or agent of the contractor shall divulge, release or publish any such research, reports, papers, material or information without having obtained the written permission of the Minister.

(3) Her Majesty reserves the right to publish in whole or in part, or not to publish at all, or with the consent of the contractor to publish any amended version, as the Minister may deem fit, any research, reports, papers, materials or information produced in the performance of the said services.

well been held that while an action in damages lies against the author in the event of contravention, no remedy is available against the innocent second publisher in that only upon the exercise of the option does the initial publisher obtain an interest in copyright.[3]

Non-competition Clauses

Another form of restraint upon the future activities of the author may be found in a non-competition clause which often provides that an author undertakes not to use the material in the work as the basis for another publication and not to publish otherwise or with another publisher a work susceptible of competing in the market place with the work projected for publication or actually published. The purpose of the restriction is to permit the distribution and sale of the published work without threat of injury from competition with similar works by the same author. While the publisher has little if no control over other works by third parties on the same subject in the market place, he does have by means of the author-publisher agreement at least the power to restrain the same author from acts which may prove injurious to the publication project and sales.

As a general rule, contracts deemed to be in restraint of trade are void if they prevent or restrain the supply of goods or services. Nevertheless, freedom to compete is not absolute and the courts are prepared to enforce a restrictive covenant where it is accessory to the sale of a business, sale and lease of land, collective agreements, exclusive distributorships as well as employment agreements; there is a further proviso that the restrictions on freedom of movement and the right to effectively deal in the market place be reasonable with respect to time, territory and nature of activity contemplated.

It is rare that an author-publisher agreement will contain an undertaking by a publisher not to publish similar works; the evident reason is that the publisher, in assuming the entire risks of the publication venture, wishes to be free to enlist whichever works he feels should be published by his enterprise in order to maintain his going concern, even though he may be thereby competing with himself with respect to books of similar subject matter. Although it has been said that an undertaking by a publisher not to publish a conflicting publication may be

---

3 The option to obtain an assignment of copyright reflects an inchoate interest being a mere right to acquire an interest in the copyright upon signification of the publisher's decision to do so: *MacDonald Ltd. v. Eyles,* [1921] 1 Ch. 631 at p. 639, *per* Peterson, J.: "Until they exercise their option they will not be assignees of the copyright wholly or partially . . . for it is only the exercise of their option that converts their option to become proprietors or owners of a part of the copyright into equitable ownership of part of the copyright or an interest in the copyright."

implied,[4] the circumstances giving rise to such implication may be limited to an exclusive right given by contract to the author to edit or write a work containing the subject of the original publication.

On the other hand, covenants imposing restrictions on the author are much more common. The court will not imply a term in a contract having the effect of preventing the author from publishing competing works through another publisher. The courts have even held that there is no implied agreement on the part of an author restraining him from publishing a second edition of a work with another publisher notwithstanding that the entire first edition has not yet been sold.[5]

In recent times, the courts have tended to reduce the author's restrictions, especially where the author is obligated not to produce any work, similar or otherwise, for a competing publisher. For example, in the case of *Schroeder Music Publishing Co. Ltd. v. Macaulay*[6] a 21-year-old song writer entered into an agreement with a music publishing company whereby the latter engaged his exclusive services for a period of five years. The author assigned to the publisher full copyright for the whole world in every musical composition composed, created or conceived by him, alone or in collaboration with any other person during a period of five years or possibly longer. The author was to receive no payment except for an original nominal advance, unless the work was published, although the publisher was under no obligation to effect publication. Failure of the publisher to publish did not entitle the author to terminate the agreement or to have any copyrights re-assigned. Upon an action for declaration that the agreement was contrary to public policy as being an unreasonable restraint of trade and void, the House of Lords held the contractual restrictions contained in the agreement were unnecessary, or reasonably capable of enforcement in an oppressive manner and were consequently void. In the course of argument, counsel for the publishers suggested that the contract was in a standard form in common use between music publishers and song writers, and that the restraints the agreement sought to impose on the liberty of the author must be presumed to be fair and reasonable. Lord Diplock noted that standard form author-publisher agreements are of comparatively modern origin and result from a concentration of a particular kind of business in relatively few hands; the terms of this standard form of contract have not been the subject of negotiation between the parties to it nor approved by any organization representing the interests of the weaker party.

---

[4] Fox, pp. 579-80 citing *Gollancz v. Dent* (1903), 88 L.T. 358, where the court considered the interpretation of the following clause: " 'In the event of a cheaper or other form of edition of any or either of the plays being thought advisable by the publisher, it shall form the subject of an agreement with the author on similar *pro rata* terms to those embodied therein.' "

[5] *Warne v. Routledge* (1874), L.R. 18 Eq. 497; *Blackie etc. & Co. v. Aikman* (1827), 5 Sess.Cas. 719; *contra Educational Co. of Ireland Ltd. v. Fallon and Getz,* [1919] 1 Ir.R. 62 and *Kamala Book Depot Ltd. v. Soureendranath Mukherji,* [1934] I.L.R. 62 Calc. 57 cited in Fox, at p. 583.

[6] [1974] 3 All E.R. 616.

The fact that the bargaining power of the publisher vis-à-vis the author was strong enough to enable the former to adopt a take-it-or-leave-it attitude raised no presumption that the publisher used it to drive an unconscionable bargain with it; but in the field of restraint of trade, it called for vigilance on the part of the court to see that the publisher did not.[7]

Within a week of the judgment, the Court of Appeal considered a similar contractual restriction, and refused to grant to the publisher an interim injunction seeking to restrain the alleged infringement of copyright in certain songs and the distribution of a record album.[8] The Court found that the undertaking by composers of a work to assign copyright in present and future works for a period of five and possibly ten years without a reciprocal obligation on the part of the publisher to publish was onerous and unconscionable; and in view of the inequality of bargaining power, it was suggested that the agreement should not be enforced and the assignment of copyright be deemed to be invalid and set aside.[9]

Notwithstanding the considerations mentioned by the Court, it appears evident that clauses which restrain the trade of the author are nevertheless fully enforceable where the author is apprised of his rights, has independent counsel and voluntarily signs away his rights, even though he may be motivated by the fear that he will find no other publisher who is prepared to assume risks of publication of the work. At the same time, it is suggested that the courts may be less inclined to set aside such restrictions where the author is merely a part-time writer and earns the major proportion of his income in a vocation other than writing.[10]

Assignment Of Contract

While an author-publisher agreement may entail the sale of a manuscript, it has been noted that the transaction is not subject to the same rules as the sale of ordinary objects of commerce.[11] The author or vendor maintains a continuing

---

[7] *Ibid.*, at p. 624.

[8] *Clifford Davis Management Ltd. v. W.E.A. Records Ltd. et al.*, [1975] 1 All E.R. 237.

[9] At p. 241, *per* Lord Denning M.R.: "They were cyclostyled and hence came from a stock of forms. They were very long and full of legal terms and phrases. Hence they were drawn up by lawyers. Some spaces have been filled in by typewriters, others left blank. Hence done by clerks in the office. Both the composer and the publisher signed in the presence of the same witness. It may be inferred that the manager took a stock form, got the blanks filled in and asked the composer to sign it without reading it through or explaining it."

[10] In Quebec, the considerations of public policy and the desirability of promoting the freedom of contract parallel those in the common law jurisdictions. Contracts in restraint of employment are not on their face illegal as being contrary to public order and good morals unless unreasonable with respect to duration and territory: *Cameron v. Canadian Factors Corp. Ltd.*, [1971] S.C.R. 148.

[11] *Morang & Co. v. LeSueur* (1911), 45 S.C.R. 95.

''interest'' in the property and the agreement taken as a whole is construed as a personal contract. Although commercial contracts are ordinarily assignable, an author-publisher agreement cannot be assigned except by mutual consent owing to the personal nature of the agreement. Many standard forms of agreement contain clauses prohibiting the assignment of the rights mentioned on the part of the author. On the other hand, some provision is usually made granting to the publisher the right to make an assignment. The practical reason for permitting the publisher to make a subsequent assignment lies in the internal organization of the corporate publisher. A publisher may maintain several incorporated divisions which are responsible individually for the publication of books according to specialization of market and subject. Where an agreement must be signed with the publisher, the holding company or mother corporation will sign the agreement but later distribute the tasks of publishing, distributing and marketing to one of its corporate arms. On the other hand, a prohibition on the part of the author to make an assignment may be justified as a means of maintaining his personal skill, reputation and commitment to the work. The prohibition however may effectively prevent the author from transferring the rights contained in the agreement to a ''personal'' corporation which he has established for the purpose of dividing income and creating tax savings.

To avoid this problem, the parties often issue cross-letters confirming the right of the personal corporations to maintain and exercise the rights in order to satisfy the requirements of the tax authorities.

Rights Upon Termination

Author-publisher agreements rarely contain clauses having the effect of absolutely terminating the contract upon the expiry of a fixed delay. It is far more common to discover unilateral termination clauses or "out of print" provisions which entitle the publisher to notify the author in writing that the work is declared out of print upon a determination that public demand or changes in market conditions do not justify continued publication. Although the common law has determined that an author may terminate his contract in the absence of a specific stipulation only at the end of each edition provided the publisher has incurred no expense toward a further edition,[12] it is extremely rare that contracts currently in use omit this vital power in favour of the publisher. Upon notification of termination, agreements commonly provide to the author the right within a 60 to 90-day period to request the return of all rights assigned, if any, and to purchase plates, type or film which the publisher may possess and which have been used for the production of the work. For the publisher, the plates and type used in producing work which is no longer in demand has no or negative value and will be destroyed unless otherwise claimed by the author. On the other hand, aside from sentimental value, it is rare that the author has any

---

[12] Fox, p. 575.

interest or contemplated utility for the publication hardware and will rarely exercise the option to purchase.

The use of the term "out of print" in many form agreements is misleading in that reference is not being made to the absolute exhaustion of stock or inventory of the work, but rather to withdrawal from sale or decline in public demand to about zero. A publisher may therefore have or maintain a large inventory of a book which has been declared out of print due to the lack of meaningful sales over a reasonable period of time. Where stocks do exist, the author is often given the right to purchase the publisher's stocks at one-half to less than the list price of the book. The definition of "out-of-print" is expanded in some agreements to include the absence of royalty earnings over two consecutive payment periods, the lack of exploitation of any subsidiary rights and exceptionally, the withdrawal of demand for the work by the main purchaser such as an educational institution or organization.

In the event of the failure of the publisher to publish the first edition of the work for reasons imputable to himself or the author, the contract will lapse and all rights revert to the respective parties if so stipulated. While in rare circumstances the agreement may set out a right of reversion of advances, copyright, manuscript and other elements, it is more common to discover total silence on the issue. Where the agreement is silent, the court is often the ultimate resort in seeking to determine upon an interpretation of the agreement whether in law such rights as copyright and possession of the manuscript do revert.

Following termination and a reversion of rights, a chance occurrence may see a sudden renewed public interest in the work. The publisher, of course, is not entitled to issue a new edition or to demand renewed execution of the original contract which has now lapsed. The publisher must execute a new agreement with the author if he is so willing. The publisher is as well fully entitled to sell whatever existing inventory of the work it currently warehouses even following the termination of the agreement.

In *Howitt v. Hall*[13] the author contracted with a publisher for the publication of a book which was printed in three consecutive editions. The course of the agreement was stipulated to last for four years; and following the expiry of the time period, the author sought to restrain the publisher from selling stock printed during the term. The courts held that the publisher had acquired the right to print the book lawfully and was consequently at liberty to sell it at any time. Although the author argued that the effect of such a position would be to destroy the copyright in the author altogether insofar as the publisher might hypothetically during the term of such agreement run off enough copies to last forever, the court concluded the publisher was not likely to incur the useless expense of printing. The author was furthermore advised to guard against such contingency by stipulating a limit to the number of copies which should be permitted under an agreement respecting a right to publish.

---

13 (1862), 6 L.T. 348.

Chapter 9

Translator-publisher Agreements

Unlike the creation of an original manuscript, a translation is usually solicited by a publisher from a translator; the solicitation is based on the previous performance of the original manuscript in terms of sales in the original language, as well as upon the potential market for the work in the other language. The identity of the translator will often vary with the nature of the work: reference texts, works containing technical language, and poetry and fiction will require translators of varying qualifications. The publisher will only proceed with the publication of a translation if so authorized by the copyright holder or if he himself is entitled to make a translation as a result of the grant of full copyright or of subsidiary rights owned by the author.

The translation itself is subject to protection under copyright legislation as an original work, the translator being considered in relation to the translation in the same position as the author to the initial work.[1] In exceptional circumstances, especially in the field of translation of poetry and fiction, the translator retains copyright to the translation. The court is however more inclined to view the translator-publisher agreement as an employment or service agreement having the effect of vesting copyright in the publisher. The agreement therefore between the publisher and translator must contain for the purpose of mutual protection many of the elements contained in the author-publisher agreements already discussed.

Translator-publisher agreements usually oblige a translator to produce a

[1] *Pasickniak v. Dojacek,* [1928] 2 D.L.R. 545 (Man. C.A.). An unauthorized translation of a work constitutes an infringement of copyright: Copyright Act, s. 3 (1) (a). Some authors submit that an unauthorized translation, even though constituting an infringement of copyright, is itself protected from infringement: Copinger and Skone James on Copyright, 1971, no. 145, p. 64.

typed manuscript in the language chosen for translation containing all of the elements found in the original work, including the index, preface, main text, titles, captions, dedications, and possibly cover blurb and footnotes. The translator must not simply transpose words from one language to another, but must as well capture the essence of the thoughts of the author in adapting the text to a new language. In view of the fact that the editors and printers of the publisher will have little familiarity with the translated text once completed, the translator must as well undertake to review and revise the printed proofs and to aid in the technical preparation of the book, especially insofar as the placement of captions, illustrations and notes are concerned. Where the work is a reference, technical or professional text, the translator may also be called upon to add to the work by including an index which is not simply a translation of the words of the initial index, and even to supply a bibliography.

Aside from the quality of the translation, the main concern of the publisher is the speed with which the translator prepares his text. In view of a common apprehension that translators are rarely capable of completing their work within a reasonable period of time, translater-publisher agreements provide strict deadline clauses requiring submission of the work in chapters or portions on a monthly or other periodic bases until full completion of the work; furthermore, payment for services rendered is made conditional upon the submission of portions of the translation at the stipulated periodic deadlines.

While some agreements do provide for payment of remuneration to the translator based on a percentage of retail sales price of the published work, it is far more common practice for a publisher to pay a translator a lump sum fee for professional services rendered varying with the length of the work and degree of difficulty involved in effecting a translation. The translator as well is usually given a credit on the title page of the published work.

The warranty of the translator should make reference to the fact that the translation is original, and that authorization from the copyright holder has been secured prior to publication if the publisher has no interest in the copyright. Prior to proceeding with publication, the publisher must assure himself that he holds a grant or licence both from the translator respecting the translation as well as from the author of the original text.

Chapter 10

Literary Agency

The primary purpose of a literary agent is to obtain a publisher for the work of the author and in some circumstances, to negotiate a contract on the author's behalf. It is fair to say that literary agency in Canada is not as well developed as in other jurisdictions, notably, the United States of America and Europe. In those jurisdictions, the literary agent also plays an essential role in reviewing the manuscript submitted by the author, suggesting changes and in effect, acting as an intermediary or screening agent on behalf of or for the benefit of the publisher. The publishers, of course, would prefer to review those manuscripts which have already been analyzed for readability and marketability by independent parties upon whose skill and literary integrity they come to rely, and will give much more attention to an unsolicited manuscript recommended by literary agents than to one received directly by the publisher. Many literary agents charge a fee for review and analysis of the manuscript and as well exact a percentage of royalties received by the author once the work has been accepted for publication or actually published. In many circumstances, literary agents demand a written undertaking by the author to grant to them an exclusive agency for a stipulated period of time for the negotiation and sale of rights of publication of a work.

Agency agreements are not unlike mandates given for similar purposes in the commercial and real estate fields. The agent undertakes to negotiate the sale of rights and to obtain the best possible conditions for publication. The author undertakes to accept all reasonable offers to purchase the rights and to pay a stipulated commission, usually in the range of ten percent of any sums received by him under a publishing agreement.

Aside from the existence of independent literary agents, publishers themselves act as agents on behalf of the author for the marketing of subsidiary rights where the publishing agreement provides for such agency. In certain cases, the publisher is entitled on behalf of the author to licence the right to translate and publish the work in book form in other languages, and to licence first serial rights, publication by book clubs, re-issuance in paperback editions by other publishers, publication in the form of condensations, anthologies and newspaper articles. In consideration for the negotiation of such agency activities, the publisher is entitled to a percentage of proceeds ranging from 25 percent upward, in notable contrast to the basic ten percent commission commonly charged by independent literary agents for the negotiation of the original publishing rights.

In *Chappell & Co. v. Redwood Music*,[1] the House of Lords reviewed the question of entitlement to copyright in certain songs. The facts reveal a beneficial agency practice with respect to collection of royalties:

> On 16th July 1934 the author of the words and the author of the music of this song assigned their copyrights to publishers in New York and transferred to them 'the right to secure copyright therein throughout the entire world' and to hold the copyright. Under an agreement made in the United States on 1st July 1948, Mrs. Pollack as administratrix of the estate of Lewis Pollack and her two sons sold to the publishers the United States renewal copyright in the music of which Lewis Pollack was the author 'together with all their and each of their right, title and interest, vested and contingent, therein and thereto'. Clause 1 of the agreement which provided for this also provided that if the term of the copyright in the USA was extended the copyright was assigned for the extended term. Clause 2 provided for the payment of royalties by the publishers 'until the expiration of the term of said renewal copyright' and also 'until the expiration of the term of the respective copyrights thereof in all countries outside of the United States and Canada' for the payment of 'fifty percent (50%) of all receipts from sales and uses (subject to the deduction of foreign income taxes, if any)'. It was contended that the terms of this agreement were wide enough to cover the assignment of the copyright in the music of the song which had, if the song was not a collective work, on the expiry of 25 years from Lewis Pollack's death reverted to his legal personal representatives.
>
> An American lady, a Miss Stern, learnt of the curious limitation imposed by s. 5(2) of the 1911 Act and not repeated in the 1956 Act on the power of authors to dispose of their copyright. Having learnt of it, she believed that reliance on the proviso might lead to an increase in the royalties and assist widows and children of dead authors to obtain a fairer share of the profits made on the songs. She formed a corporation called the Miriam Rose Stern Agency. When these actions were fought, the agency represented 177 estates of dead authors and the number of songs involved was between thirty and forty thousand. It was proposed that the publishers pay to the estates which the agency represented 50% of the royalties they had received during the past six years and that, broadly speaking, they should keep 50% of the earnings from the songs for the next ten years but no longer. The agency was to get a commission not exceeding 30% of the increase in royalties which it secured. This proposal was not accepted by the publishers, and a company, Redwood Music Ltd., the respondent, was formed and assignments made to it of copyrights alleged to have reverted to legal personal representatives of deceased authors so that it might start actions to test the validity of the contentions advanced by Miss Stern.

[1] [1980] 2 All E.R. 817 (H.L.)

Another form of literary agency occurs where the author uses a "personal" corporation to hold copyright in his works and receive income accruing upon publication. In *McClelland and Stewart Ltd. v. Coles Book Stores Ltd.*[1] the facts reveal that a certain author named Farley Mowat entered into an agreement with Farley Mowat Limited which provided that all works thereafter produced by the author would be the property of the corporation. The corporation, and not the author, entered into agreements with publishers granting exclusive rights to printing and publication in book form of certain works. Although the particular case does not elaborate, it may be generally seen that personal corporations are established by authors for the purpose of avoidance of personal income tax liability arising upon the receipt of royalties.[2] A secondary purpose of such corporations is to delegate to the employees of the corporation, if other than the author, the role of negotiating and concluding contracts on behalf of the creator of the manuscript. Where the publisher is dealing with a one-man company, he is not in reality, but is in law dealing with an independent agent of the author. While the tax authorities may not regard the corporation as a sham, it is evident that the publisher cannot treat an agent, which deals exclusively in the manuscripts written by its own majority shareholder, as any other independent literary agent.

[2] (1974), 21 C.P.R. (2d) 266 (Ont.).

[3] See a review of jurisprudence in Matheson, D.J., "Service Corporations" (1976), 24 Can. Tax J. 329; Graschuk, H.S., "The Professional Corporation in Alberta" (1977), 25 Can. Tax J. 109.

Chapter 11

Periodical Publication

Passing reference may now be made to the relationship between authors and publishers of periodicals and newspapers. Generally speaking, the previous discussion respecting publishers of books has equal application to the publishers of works which are contained in a one-shot or serial fashion in a periodical or newspaper, referred to hereafter as "periodical".

Mention has already been made respecting the effect of statute law on the operations of publishers of both books and periodicals. Legislative and regulatory provisions do attempt in a limited manner to control the distribution of publications, but as well to provide a stimulus to the publishing field. It will suffice in the context of the present discussion to deal with those various legislative provisions which directly encompass the circulation of periodicals. In the Province of Quebec, the Newspaper Declaration Act[1] provides at s.1 that no person may print or publish in the province any newspaper, pamphlet or paper containing public news until a sworn declaration has been made and deposited with the Clerk of the Peace for the district in which the publication is printed. The Act further provides that the sworn declaration must set forth the title of the publication, the real name, style, description and residence of the printer or publisher and other incidental information respecting ownership. The effect of the deposit of the statement is to provide a public document which may be admitted as conclusive evidence of the truth of all matters set forth therein. However, the value to the newspaper publisher of the deposit of the statement is to permit the latter to avail himself of the benefit of certain immunities created under the Press Act.[2] The latter legislation provides for a short prescriptive delay for bringing action in the event of libel and sets out

[1] R.S.Q. c. J-1.
[2] R.S.Q. c. P-19.

provisions for retraction and qualified privilege for certain reports made accurately and in good faith.

Unlike the statutory scheme of deposit in the Province of Quebec, the Libel and Slander Act of Ontario[3] permits the publisher of a newspaper to benefit from certain statutory immunities and privileges if the names of the proprietor and publisher and address of publication are stated either at the head of the editorials or on the front page of the newspaper. The production of a printed copy of a newspaper is admissible in evidence as *prima facie* proof of the publication of the printed copy and the truth of the statements as to ownership and place of publication.

As previously discussed, various provincial jurisdictions do have legislation regulating the distribution of the publications other than books. The purpose of these provisions is basically two-fold: to provide for some order in the market place, and to permit administrative officials to assert a right of moral censorship upon periodicals circulated in public.[4]

Works published in periodical form differ vastly from those published in book form with respect to content, length, market distribution, readership, price and subsequent disposal. Authors of works appearing in periodicals, more often referred to as contributors, are in many circumstances employees of the publisher of the periodical, either on a full or part-time basis. It is extremely rare that the author is required to support economically the publication of his work in a periodical, or bound to review proofs, or in any other way interfere with the publication process. Unlike the field of book publishing, the publication of periodicals is in large measure supported by proceeds from advertisers, as well as retail sales revenues. The periodical publisher is concerned with the issuance of one collective work on a regular basis whereas the book publisher prepares several titles working on a deadline largely imposed by himself. Accordingly, it may be said that the constraints, risks and economic opportunities present in the enterprise of the book publisher vis-à-vis the author are either absent or mitigated in the field of periodical publication. The periodical publisher risks little in the short run by including or excluding an article written by an author, since advertising for the specific issue of the publication is not generally dependent upon the authorship of articles which will appear in that issue. The subscribers or regular purchasers of the periodical have little choice in the short run in view of their commitment to purchase in rejecting specific issues of a periodical based on the authorship or subject matter of individual articles. In view of the practical differences between the two fields, which in little measure can be regarded as competitive, interpretation of ambiguous or implied periodical publishing contracts should differ from contracts respecting the publication of books.

The distribution of a periodical may occur on a daily, monthly or other

---

[3] R.S.O. 1980, c. 237; S.O. 1984, c. 11, s. 19.

[4] See Chapter 1.

regular basis through the mail, home delivery or display at retail outlets and stands. As in the book publishing field, the distribution network and set-up of the periodical publisher is well established and consolidated prior to the advent of the manuscript of the individual contributor. Furthermore, in view of the high degree of competition within the periodical publishing field, the style and format of the periodical becomes an essential ingredient in product differentiation. For these reasons, an author as contributor is given little or absolutely no right to interfere with the mode, style and distribution of the work as inserted in the periodical. To do so would entail a possible delay in the regular issuance of the publication and confuse the consistency of the content sought by the publisher in order to retain or enlarge the scope of the readership.

Unless the author is himself a joint publisher of the periodical or wishes his work to appear in the form of an advertisement, it is rare that authors contribute financially or engage in vanity publishing in periodical form. On the other hand, payment by the publisher to the author usually takes the form of a lump sum payment based on the amount of words or reputation of the author. Due to the lack of re-editions or reprinting of specific issues of a periodical on a mass basis, there is no practical reason for making the payment of royalties contingent upon the amount of copies of the periodical sold. For the most part, the circulation of a specific issue of a periodical is foreseeable as a result of past performance of previous issues. Although admittedly certain articles will cause an unforeseen run on those specific issues of the publication, it has been the general practice to reward the author for the increase in circulation by way of a larger lump sum payment than a per copy royalty.

The grant of publication rights which is usually confirmed by cross-letter rather than standard form agreement, is limited to a licence for publication in a specific issue of the periodical within a specified term. It is rare that subsidiary rights are granted to the publisher except for a right to a credit in the event of a subsequent re-publication in the form of anthology or other collective work. This however will not be the situation where the publication is a first serialization with a view to ultimate publication in book form by an enterprise affiliated with the periodical publisher.

The contract used in contemplation of the publication of works in periodicals may assume the form of a contract for services or of employment, a licence for serialization rights, or cross-letters of offer and acceptance. Simple delivery of a manuscript to the publisher may constitute an offer of a right to publish in the periodical envisaged, in consideration for payment of a reasonable sum upon ordinary terms; the publisher may proceed immediately with publication without confirmation of acceptance, the act of payment or publication in itself constituting an act of acceptance.[5] The author in such circumstances retains the

[5] Copinger and Skone James, *Copyright*, 11th ed., p. 383, para. 983 citing *Hall-Brown v. Iliffe & Sons' Ltd.*, [1929] Macg. Cop. Cas. 88.

copyright, while the publisher is entitled to a distinct right of copyright affecting the periodical as a collective work.[6]

The publisher of a periodical may on occasion publish serializations of works originally published in book form. A serialization is justified on the basis of enhancing readership especially where competing publications are involved; new readers are presumably drawn to the periodical in order to read each and every instalment of the serialized work and thereafter remain with the publication as a matter of habit. In undertaking to publish the serialization of a work, the periodical publisher relies mainly upon the representations and warranties made by the publisher of the work in book form as to the latter's right to grant a licence for publication in serial form. Unless the publisher of the work in book form is relatively unknown, the periodical publisher will rarely demand proof of authorization. Although warranty provisions in an agreement do suffice to permit an action in indemnification against the book publisher to succeed, they do not constitute a defence of any sort in an action against the periodical publisher by an author alleging infringement or unauthorized use. It has, however, been held that reliance of a newspaper publisher upon copyright notations imprinted in the work in book form does constitute evidence of error concerning the capacity of the grantor to grant, and may be sufficient to rebut an allegation of flagrancy of copyright infringement.[7]

An author chooses to contribute a work to a specific publication for various reasons including remuneration, readership and goodwill flowing from publication. If for unspecified reasons the publisher has undertaken to publish the work but later decides not to proceed, or decides to discontinue the periodical prior to publication or offers to print the article in another periodical or format, it is evident that the original expectations of the author will not have been met. In this regard, it has been held that discontinuance of the publication of a periodical or an offer to publish the contribution in another form constitutes breach of contract on the part of the publisher and the latter is bound to pay to the author a reasonable sum for the portion of the manuscript completed on a *quantum meruit* basis.[8]

In determining the quantum of damages to which an author may be entitled in the event of the failure of a publisher to proceed with publication, or in the event of the premature termination of the services of the author, the courts must determine the juridical status of the author in relationship to the publisher. An author of a series of articles appearing periodically for a specified period of time may be termed an "outside contributor", that is, one who is not to be considered as a full or part-time staff member of the publisher's enterprise. On the other hand, an author who contributes and publishes on a regular basis for an unlimited period of time may acquire the status of a part-time staff member; and

---

[6] Copyright Act, R.S.C. 1970, c. C-30, s. 3.(1)(e).

[7] *Prior v. Lansdowne Press Pty. Ltd.*, [1977] R.P.C. 511.

[8] *Planché v. Colburn* (1831), 5 C. & P. 58.

if in fact the author is given various editorial and managerial functions outside the scope of an ordinary contributor, namely the review, compilation and editing of materials to appear in a given section or supplement of the publication, the author may be said to be a sub-editor or departmental editor entitled to various legal benefits including due notice prior to termination of services and the right to compensation for unjust severance.[9]

The determination of the exact relationship between the author and publisher is also relevant in determining the ownership of copyright and standing to sue for infringement. For example, in *Beloff v. Pressdram Ltd. et al.*[10] a correspondent for a newspaper instituted proceedings for infringement of copyright against the publisher of a magazine which reproduced in its magazine an internal office memorandum written by the correspondent describing certain speculations upon the demise of a government leader. The publisher of the magazine argued that the correspondent was an employee of her newspaper publisher, and that copyright vested in the latter, which alone was entitled to bring proceedings. The document published by the magazine publisher had been previously unpublished and contained notes taken in the course of her engagement as correspondent. The evidence demonstrated that the correspondent wrote a weekly article for the newspaper publisher and took an active role in editorial responsibility for the newspaper. Notwithstanding that the correspondent did write on an incidental basis for other periodicals and appeared occasionally on television, the court found she was under a contract of service and that the newspaper publisher was the owner of the copyright to the document.[11]

It often occurs that contributors to periodicals and newspapers use a trade or pen name to designate their authorship. Where the contributions consist of a regular series of columns or features which have formed part of the periodical for some period of time, the publisher may have an interest in seeing to it that the same format and name of the author be used to identify the column or feature even following the dismissal, resignation or withdrawal of the original author. Notwithstanding that the relationship between the author and publisher may be one of employer-employee, it has been held that a right of property in the pen name vests in the author, even though the right in the published work may by force of law vest in the employer or publisher. For

---

[9] *Landa v. Greenberg* (1908), 24 T.L.R. 441, where the author's position was determined after consideration of such elements as salary, remuneration by space, responsibility for revision and compilation, and duration of services.

[10] [1973] R.P.C. 765.

[11] But see *In Re Ashley and Smith Ltd.*, [1918] Macg. Cop. Cas. 54 where the court held that two regular contributors to a newspaper were not servants of the publisher of the newspaper: they did not work at the publisher's office, were not employed exclusively by the publisher, were not under the control of the publisher, nor were they bound to render any general service except to attend sporting events and furnish a report for the newspaper upon payment of a certain amount per day for every event attended.

example, in *Landa v. Greenberg*[12] the court held that the author of a series of articles dealing with children's literature written under a pseudonym was entitled to a declaration of ownership to the name, as well as nominal damages against the publisher of the newspaper who attempted to use the name following the author's dismissal. The court held that the name constituted part of the author's stock-in-trade as a writer and had become identified with her during the course of publication of the series of articles.[13]

An author who agrees to submit an article to be credited in print to himself is entitled to write his article in his own style and express his own opinions; he is not bound to submit to have his name published as the author of an article which differs drastically from his original work. On the other hand, the publisher of the periodical is not bound to publish in the event the author has breached his warranties as to the content and rights of the article, although he is obliged to publish the article substantially as written. In *Joseph v. National Magazine Co. Ltd.*[14] an author entered into an agreement with the publisher of a periodical for publication of a full-page illustrated article dealing with jade carvings in which the author was a specialist. The author was obliged under the terms of the agreement to pay for the production of the illustrations, but was to receive no payment for the article aside from the goodwill and enhancement to reputation attached to publication under his name. Upon submission of the article, the editors of the magazine made extensive revisions; the author objected on the grounds that the article now contained several errors of fact and certain technical misdescriptions. The periodical publisher refused to publish the article without amendment; the author consequently sued for specific performance and damages.

The court held that it was justified in refusing to allow to be published the revised article under his name and as his work; there was no justification for the contention that an editor may alter the matter and style of a signed article in the way proposed, even though the article as written did not conform to the general journalistic style used consistently throughout the pages of the periodical. Nevertheless, the court refused to grant an order of specific performance for the reason that the exact contents of the article were never agreed upon between the parties and that the court would subsequently be called upon to supervise the editing of the work in order to determine which revisions could legitimately be made by the editors prior to publication. The court however did grant a nominal

---

12 (1908), 24 T.L.R. 441.

13 *Fawcett v. Modern Fiction Ltd. et al.* (1949), 66 R.P.C. 230; *Forbes v. Kemsley Newspapers Ltd.* (1951), 68 R.P.C. 180 at p. 184 where it was held that a person who writes or performs under a pseudonym is entitled to the property in that name as part of his or her stock-in-trade unless it can be shown by agreement, either express or implied, it was arranged that the name should belong to the person or company employing such writer or performer.

14 [1958] 3 All E.R. 52.

sum for damages resulting from the loss of potential goodwill and enhancement to the author's reputation as an expert on jade.

Chapter 12

Collectives

To some extent, the author may find his marketing power with a publisher increased by enrolling and remaining active in an association of writers sometimes referred to as a collective society. There are several collective societies in Canada devoted not only to the rights of authors of literary works, but as well as to those of performing artists.

The purpose in law of a collective society is to advance the rights of its members. It does so by proposing draft forms of author/publisher agreements, assisting in the negotiation of such an agreement, and instituting action if necessary against the publisher to enforce the rights of the member.

Where the collective is mainly directed toward the preservation of rights of the creator in the publishing and performance of a work, the membership of the author in the collective often provides the following conditions. The author is obliged to assign to the collective the right to licence and prohibit the reproduction of the work. The assignment is often exclusive and world-wide. The scope of reproduction includes printing and generally any material fixation of the work, including records, tapes, cassettes and any audio-visual mechanism. The collective is given the rights to collect and distribute the royalties resulting from reproduction, to monitor reproduction, to inspect the books and records of users, to negotiate any settlements arising out of conflict over the use of the work and to institute legal proceedings for the recovery of royalties or to limit use.

Furthermore, the author may bind himself contractually toward the collective to submit his author/publisher agreement to the collective for review, or at least to insist upon the inclusion in the agreement with the publisher certain clauses including the direction of payment, accounting documents and general information respecting the reproduction of the work to the office of the collective. In consideration for the services performed for the author by the collective, the author is obliged to pay a percentage of his royalties collected by the collective usually in the amount of 10%. Where legal proceedings are contemplated or instituted, the author is obliged to participate in the proceedings either by way of executing an *ad hoc* assignment of rights to the collective in order to give the latter standing to sue or to act as the named complainant or to appear as a witness and generally assist in the prosecution of the claim. The *Charter of Rights for Creators*, endorsed in this respect by the government, suggested that membership in collectives should continue to be voluntary and that authors continue to grant exclusive licences to collectives; the collective exercise of copyright has several advantages including easy access to a large volume of copyright material, a mechanism to facilitate the monitoring of the use of works and an effective administration. The Charter defines a collective as a group of copyright owners who form an association to exercise on their behalf a particular aspect of copyright. It is correctly pointed out that in practice the collectives obtain an assignment of rights from the authors which permits the collectives to negotiate with publishers on the basis of a blanket licence; at page 85:

> In return for complying with the conditions of the licence and the payment of the appropriate royalties, the purchaser of the blanket licence is at liberty to do what would otherwise be prohibited under the *Copyright Act*. From the users' point of view, lengthy searches to determine who owns the copyright are completed avoided. Drawn out negotiations to determine royalty payments for each individual use are also avoided. The societies monitor the use made of the works in their repertoires, collect and distribute royalties, and commence copyright infringement suits where necessary. This approach ensures remuneration for creators and at the same time also ensures that the public has quick access to protected works.
>
> There is a danger that the unregulated collective exercise of rights could lead to abusive practices. If the only practical access is through a collective then there is a potential that a collective, because of its dominant position, could occupy too strong a bargaining position **vis-à-vis** users. This problem was forseen by those who devised the existing copyright law. It was solved by creating a regulatory body, the copyright Appeal Board, vested with the authority to set rates after hearing the interest parties. It became impossible for collective approval. The system of regulatory approval of rates should be maintained in the revised law. The exact scope of that regulatory authority will be discussed the next section.
>
> The matter of the regulation of collectives raises a related issue concerning competition policy. Any combination of individuals who together control access to, and use of, a particular good or service are within the ambit of competition legislation because of the potential for anti-competitive behavior. It was expected that users would express concern in this regard to the Sub-Committee. They did not. In fact, quite the opposite view was expressed. Users consistently stated that the number of collectives should be kept to a minimum (the ideal situation being described as one super-collective) so that users would need to go to only one place to obtain a licence. Users do not want to have to search the repertoires of two or more societies to determine where they must obtain the necessary licence. Users, for obvious reasons, prefer the simplicity of one collective administering one particular right, trusting the Copyright Appeal Board to ensure reasonable rates.
>
> The simplicity and efficiency of one collective from a user's perspective is appreciated. However, from the perspective of competition policy, it may be that two collectives competing with each other is more desirable.

> The Sub-Committee has examined both sides of this question and is of the view that the Copyright Appeal Board provides effective protection to the public by controlling the royalty rates charged by copyright owners to users.
>
> Some critics have suggested that one problem with collective societies is that copyright owners cannot be compelled to join. Canada's obligations under the Berne Convention provide that the enjoyment and exercise of rights are not subject to the performance of formalities. Quite apart from this international commitment, the Sub-Committee is firmly opposed to any proposal which would compel creators to exercise their rights in any particular way. Copyright is a bundle of private property rights. The owners of that property can exercise their rights individually or collectively. The choice is theirs.
>
> The Sub-Committee is of the view that compelling someone to join a collective is not necessary in any event. The only practical way to administer some rights is collectively. The performing rights in music provide an excellent example. No composer has ever been forced to join a performing rights society. Yet the collective exercise of this right has worked well for decades. The reason is a practical one. If a composer wants to be compensated for the use of music he must join one of the two existing societies so that the thousands of uses of music across the country can be monitored as a basis for payment. An individual composer could attempt this monitoring and collecting, but the attempt would be unsuccessful. The payment for each use is so small that the cost of collecting would be greater than the payment. For this reason the Sub-Committee does not foresee any real problem with individual creators refusing to participate in the system, thereby exposing users to multiple infringement actions.

It would be in order at this point to review a specific case study involving the operations of a collective. In the Province of Quebec there is an organization entitled the Union des Écrivains Québécois.

The Union is said to be a syndicat professionnel governed by the Loi sur les Syndicats Professionnels. In virtue of that Act a syndicat is constituted as a corporation (section 1(4)) having various powers including:

> 9(10) Passé avec tout autre Syndicat, société, entreprise ou personne, les contrats ou conventions relatives à la poursuite de leur objet et spécialement se visant les conditions collectives du travail.
>
> 9(11) Exercé devant toute cour de justice tous les droits appartement à leur membre relativement au faits portant un préjudice direct ou indirect à l'intérêt collectif de la profession qu'il représente.

The term "conditions collectives du travail" is not defined in the Act. Neither does the Act give any specific power to the syndicat professionnel to enter into contracts which bind its members.

Under the Loi sur les Syndicats Professionnels the Union des Écrivains Québécois do not have a right to bind their individual members to any contractual arrangement unless an express and individual mandate to represent is given by each member of the Union to if for that purpose. Although the Act does permit the Union to enter into contracts respecting the "conditions collectives de travail", it cannot be said that an arrangement for payment of royalties is a "convention visant les conditions collectives de travail." Most if not all authors, for the purposes of a royalty agreement are not employed by the publishers insofar as the reproduction of books are concerned in respect of which royalties are sought. While the Act does permit the Union to take legal action invoking "tous les droits appartenant à leurs membres", there is no prohibition in the Act which would prevent the individual members from exercising their own personal rights insofar as the exercise of their profession is concerned.

It should be noted that the Statut de l'Union des Écrivains Québécois (1984), section 2.0 indicates that the objects of the Union include:

> 2.1 Représenter les écrivains;
>
> 2.2 Promouvoir leurs intérêts professionnels, moraux et économiques;
>
> 2.5 Préparer et négocier des contrats qui respectent les droits des écrivains."

The objects do not indicate that the Union has as its purpose the execution of contracts respecting the rights of authors, nor is there any indication that members by joining the Union give to it a mandate to personally represent them in the execution of contracts.

The lack of authority to act contractually in a representative capacity towards members in royalty agreements, seems to be acknowledged in the booklet "La Photocopie dans les Établissements d'Enseignement du Québec" published by l'Union des Écrivains Québécois which notes that while a contract has been entered into with respect to "reprographie d'oeuvres imprimés dans les établissements scolaires de l'ordre collegial" (Novembre 22, 1984) the full rights of authors especially insofar as reproduction beyond the maximum contractual coverage is concerned remained untouched by the agreement and must be exercised individually. As well, authors who are not inscribed in the Répertoire or roll of works protected cannot benefit from the agreement. At page 31:

> Un ouvrage qui n'est pas inscrit au Répertoire ne donne évidemment pas lieu au versement de compensations puisque l'autorisation de la reprographie n'est pas donnée. Cela n'empêche pas qu'il soit un jour inscrit pour autorisation de la reprographie soit alors donné et que par conséquent des compensations soient versées à l'auteur et à l'éditeur.

In order to bind the individual members, any agreement which the Union des Écrivains Québécois enters into must be supported by an express mandate by the individual members to the Union or by a subsequent acceptance of that agreement (specifically a "stipulation pour autrui" therein contained) by the individual members.

In virtue of a recent agreement with the Quebec government, l'Union des Écrivains Québécois and the Ministère de l'Education provided for compensation to authors for photocopying at educational institution of works listed on the Répertoire. It is evident that the individual author could not have reached without collective bargaining the valuable position attained through the efforts of a collective.

By contrast, in *Bishop v. Tele Metropole*[1] a collective society was a

---

[1] (1985), 4 C.P.R. (3d) 349 (Fed. Ct.). Compare *Durand & Cie v. La Patrie Publishing*, [1960] S.C.R. 649.

co-complainant to an action arising out of an unauthorized recording of a musical work. The collective argued standing to sue on the basis of an affiliation agreement with the author which provided (the author here being termed "Publisher"):

> 2.1
>
> Publisher hereby grants C.M.R.R.A., which grant is hereby accepted by C.M.R.R.A., the non-exclusive right as Publisher's agent during the terms of this Agreement, to administer on Publisher's behalf in Canada, and to authorize agencies outside Canada to administer, the reproductions [*sic*] rights in the Repertoire on the terms more fully set out below.
>
> 2.2 *Licensing of Mechanical and Synchronization Rights*
>
> 2.2.1 C.M.R.R.A. shall have the right to grant and authorize the granting of non-exclusive licences to produce and reproduce the Repertoire in any material form whatever including on disc, tape, film or any other audio support material, or to reproduce the Repertoire in synchronization with visual images on disc, tape, film or any other audio-visual support material, on terms which are current for the industry in Canada, or outside Canada, where such licences are granted.
>
> 2.5 *Legal and Other Action*
>
> 2.5.1 C.M.R.R.A. shall have the right to take and to authorize the taking of all action, (including the withholding of licences, to litigate, negotiate, settle, compromise, stay, terminate or abandon claims, accounts, demands, disputes and other matters relating hereto) which, in C.M.R.R.A.'s judgment, may be necessary or advisable to collect monies due Publisher and to protect and enforce Publisher's rights in the Repertoire in Canada and outside of Canada.
>
> 2.5.2 No legal action shall be commenced in Publisher's name without Publisher's prior consent.
>
> 2.5.3 All costs of such legal and other action, including lawyers fees, shall be borne by C.M.R.R.A.
>
> 4. *C.M.R.R.A. Administration Fees*
>
> 4.1 For the administration services provided by C.M.R.R.A., C.M.R.R.A. shall be entitled to retain the following fees from monies received by it:
>
> - for mechanical reproduction in North America 5%
> - for mechanical reproduction outside of North America no charge
> - for reproduction other than mechanical reproduction in North America 10%
> - for reproduction other than mechanical reproduction outside of North America no charge

The Court held that the collective did indeed have standing on the basis of the agreement, subject to some qualification as to the entitlement to relief. At pages 360-361, Strayer J. held:

> It follows from the foregoing that in so far as the statement of claims seeks remedies for infringement preceding the date of the agreement, such as damages, the plaintiff CMRRA cannot obtain such a remedy. To the extent, however, that the statement of claim seeks remedies with respect to future infringement, CMRRA can,

> in principle, partake of such remedies. It remains to be seen, of course, as to whether any or all of these remedies are available in the present case but all I am required to decide, for the purposes of determining the *locus standi* of CMRRA, is to decide whether in law such remedies could be available to it. This question I must answer in the affirmative and therefore find that CMRRA is properly a plaintiff in this action. In so far as the affiliation agreement gives it a right of action with respect to breaches of copyright arising after the date of the agreement, it cannot be regarded as a matter of maintenance or champerty because once the contract was signed CMRRA had a direct financial interest in the disposition and protection of the copyright because of the fees it stands to earn for authorized dispositions.

It is evident that collectives, in performing a role akin to labour unions, are not only necessary in certain circumstances, but also effective. It is equally apparent that publishers are not sympathetic to their strict pro-author bias except to the extent that they enforce their rights in a manner which benefits the publisher, namely in monitoring and collecting for use of published works.[2]

---

[2] Note generally, the current associations in the following fields: Société pour l'avancement des droits en audiovisuel (SADA) respecting audio-visual works; Société des auteurs et compositeurs dramatiques (SACD) respecting film works; Société des auteurs, recherchistes documentalistes et compositeurs (SARDEC), Société des gens de lettres (SGDL) et Société civile des auteurs multimedia (SCAM), Société des auteurs et compositeurs dramatiques (SACD), and Société des écrivains Canadiens de la langue française respecting literary works; Composers, Authors and Publishers Association (CAPAC), and Performing Rights Organization of Canada (PRO) respecting performing rights.

Chapter 13

Forms Of Agreement

The present chapter deals with an exposition of and commentary upon forms of agreements similar to those currently in use by commercial publishers, authors, translators and agents. The forms have been drafted following a comparative review of numerous form agreements actually in use in the publishing field, as well as those reported in the case law. The agreements presented deal with the basic relations between the author and publisher, publisher and distributor, publisher and translator, and author and agent. The paragraph headings and commentaries prefatory to each form are designed to provide a summary of the purpose and scheme of the contract in question.

As will be seen, the number of variants involved in the relationship between the parties are innumerable and some attempt has been made to provide for the more basic or recurring provisions. Standard form agreements may vary in several respects where the arrangement between the parties contemplates an assignment of copyright or a mere licence, a comprehensive grant to publish including exploitation of subsidiary rights or a mere grant to publish in book form, the publication at the entire expense of the publisher or contribution to costs by the author, single authorship or co-authorship, publication in a single or in several volumes, and royalty payments in one global advance or as a percentage of retail sales as proceeds are received. As previously suggested, the following agreements have been drafted by the present author and consequently do not reflect the contractual demands of any particular party currently engaged in the publishing field. Nevertheless, the forms do reflect actual engagements, undertakings and representations made in practice and in that respect, can be said to fairly represent real contractual situations.

1. AUTHOR-PUBLISHER AGREEMENT (SHORT FORM — NON-FICTION)

1. Undertaking to publish;
2. Mode of publication;
3. Delivery of manuscript;
4. Delivery of index;
5. Editorial assistance;
6. Page proofs;
7. Copyright;
8. Author's warranties
9. Royalties;
10. Accounting;
11. Revisions and re-editions;
12. Free copies;
13. Competing works;
14. Language requirement - Province of Quebec.

Commentary

The following form represents an author-publisher agreement in short style suitable for works of non-fiction. Although the publisher expressly undertakes to publish the work in book form, there is no obligation expressed as to the date or timing of publication. The publisher retains an absolute discretion in determining the appearance of the published work as well as the mode of distribution. On the other hand, the author is obliged to effect satisfactory delivery by a specified date and must provide sufficient editorial assistance to permit the ultimate printing of the work, in default of which he is liable to be charged for expenses. The agreement provides for an assignment of copyright for the term of the contract which is not specified; and with regard to term, reference must be made to the causes of termination at law, namely, breach of obligation, bankruptcy, exhaustion of the edition and failure to reprint. No subsidiary rights are stipulated for two reasons, the first being that the agreement effects an assignment of copyright; secondly, seeing that the agreement is directed for use where the work in question is of a non-fictional, professional or technical nature, it is rare that subsidiary rights are exercised, save for the right to reprint in cheaper editions, in the form of condensations, serializations or possibly for licence to book clubs. Where the publisher's appreciation of the market for the work as well as the author's reasonable expectations dictate that additional revenue will probably arise from sources other than publication of the work in book form, express reference to royalties for subsidiary rights is made in the longer form agreements in the present section.

The clause respecting the language of the contract is included in the event that the agreement is construed as a standard form agreement which is required by existing language legislation in the Province of Quebec to be drafted in the French language, unless the parties require that the draft be in another language.[1]

AGREEMENT made this ——— day of ———, 19— at ———.

BETWEEN: XYZ PUBLISHING COMPANY
(hereinafter called the "Publisher")

AND: MR. JOHN SMITH
(hereinafter called the "Author")

In consideration of the undertakings provided hereunder, the parties to the present Agreement declare:

1. Undertaking To Publish:

The Publisher shall publish at its own expense a work entitled ——— ("work") in book form in the style, manner and conditions more fully set out hereunder.

2. Mode Of Publication:

The Publisher shall alone determine all aspects of production, publication and distribution, including, without restriction, the quality of paper, printing and binding, the number of copies to be printed, the form and extent of advertising and marketing the price and terms of wholesale and retail sale.

3. Delivery Of Manuscript:

The Author shall deliver at the date of these presents (or by ———) a manuscript of the work in a form complete, legible and ready for printing.

4. Delivery Of Index, Etc.:

The Author shall also deliver to the Publisher tables, bibliography and other necessary supplements to the work upon request.

---

[1] Charte de la langue française, 1977 (Que.), c. 5, s. 55:
"Contracts pre-determined by one party, contracts containing printed standard clauses, and the related documents, must be drawn up in French. They may be drawn up in another language as well at the express wish of the parties."

5. Editorial Assistance:

The Publisher shall be entitled to provide all editorial assistance and work deemed necessary for the work in the event the Author is unwilling or unable to do so; and a reasonable charge for remuneration for such assistance shall be made and deducted against royalties or other payments due to the Author.

6. Page Proofs:

The Publisher shall submit page proofs of the work to the Author for revision and correction within a reasonable period of time. The cost of revisions and corrections, other than those due to printers' errors shall be deducted from royalties and other payments due to the Author where such costs exceed 15% of total printing costs.

7. Copyright:

The Author hereby assigns copyright in the work to the Publisher for the duration of this Agreement.

8. Author's Warranties:

The Author warrants to the Publisher that the work is original, does not infringe upon any existing copyright and does not contain any libellous or obscene material. The Author shall indemnify the Publisher against any claims, actions, loss or damage, including costs and expenses incurred by the Publisher as a result of any breach of the present warranty.

9. Royalties:

The Publisher shall pay to the Author a royalty of 10% of the retail sales price of the first 1000 copies of the work sold and a royalty of 15% of the retail sales price of every copy sold thereafter.

10. Accounting:

The Publisher shall render to the Author an annual account of retail sales as at February 28 in each year after the date of the first publication of the said work. The balance shown in the said account to be due to the Author shall be payable within three months after the said accounts are rendered.

11. Revisions and Re-Editions:

The Publisher shall be entitled to publish second and subsequent editions of the work under the same terms of the present Agreement. Upon the exercise of its option, the Publisher shall, in writing, require the Author to prepare such subsequent edition. In the event of the refusal of the Author to effect preparation within a reasonable delay, the Publisher may employ any other persons to prepare such subsequent edition, and the cost thereof shall be deducted from royalties and other payments due to the Author. In the event that a second or subsequent edition of the said work is prepared by a person other than the Author, the Publisher shall retain the Author's name as part of the title of the work.

12. Free Copies:

The Publisher may distribute free copies of the work for the purpose of review or advertising. The Author shall be entitled to receive ten free copies of the work and to purchase additional copies at a discount of 25% of the retail sales price.

13. Competing Works:

The Author shall not publish any work of a nature likely to compete with the work during a period of five years following publication of the first or subsequent editions of the work.

14. Language Requirement - Province of Quebec:

The parties expressly require that the present contract be drawn up and executed in the English language. Les parties ont expressément exigé que le présent contrat soit rédigé et executé en anglais.

IN WITNESS WHEREOF the parties hereto have executed this Agreement.

Publisher

Author

1.1 BASIC AUTHOR-PUBLISHER AGREEMENT

1. Undertaking to publish;
2. Delivery of the manuscript;
3. Grant to publish;
4. Author's warranty;
5. Indemnification;
6. Copyright;
7. Proofs;
8. Royalties;
9. Limitation of royalties;

10. Copies to Author;
11. Alterations;
12. Revisions and re-editions;
13. Non-liability for manuscript;
14. Accounting;
15. Discontinuance of publication;
16. Infringement;
17. Clause of non-competition;
18. Options on subsequent works;
19. Termination by default;
20. Bankruptcy;
21. Copy of the agreement;
22. Arbitration;
23. Assignment;
24. Notice;
25. Waiver;
26. Language requirement - Province of Quebec.

Commentary

The following agreement represents the basic author-publisher agreement similar to those in general use by the major publishing houses.

The publisher's undertaking to publish requires issuance of the work in printed form within 12 months following delivery of the manuscript subject to an extension due to *cas fortuit.* Notwithstanding the undertaking, the publisher retains absolute discretion in determining the nature and extent of the advertisement and distribution of the work. The author is required to deliver the manuscript if he has not already done so by the stipulated date. It is assumed that the manuscript has been accepted by the publisher for publication on the basis of a review of portions of the work or at least a detailed outline accompanied by some assurance that the manuscript as delivered will be satisfactory in content. In the event that the manuscript as delivered is unsatisfactory, the publisher has the option of termination or alteration of the manuscript at the expense of the author. The delivery provision encompasses not only questions concerning the manuscript, but as well the necessary authorizations to permit reproduction of copyright and material.

The grant to publish deals not only with the right to publish in book form , but all subsidiary rights including publication in translation, cheaper editions, serialization, condensation, dramatization and all residual rights to the work. The totality of the grant is perhaps unnecessarily confirmed by the conveyance of copyright to the publisher in the copyright clause.

The author's warranty is intended to set out all elements necessary to demonstrate at least on a *prima facie* basis that the publisher is in good faith in proceeding with publication and has no notice of defect or want in the grant accorded to the publisher by the author.

Following delivery of the manuscript, the author is under the continuing obligation to review the proofs of the work, to prepare an index which will correspond with the printed pagination, and to co-operate with the publisher in effecting registration of the copyright. The author is furthermore bound under stipulated penalty to effect revisions and prepare a re-edition, to avoid publication of competing material and to submit a certain number of subsequent works to the publisher in accordance with a right of first refusal.

The royalties provision is intended to correspond with the paragraph respecting the grant to publish. The percentage of royalties granted to the author increases as the direct involvement or risk to the publisher in exploiting the subsidiary rights to the work decreases. Nevertheless, justification for the fixing of certain percentages is based on compensation to the publisher for the risks taken at the stage of initial publication of the first edition of the work, as well as for efforts expended in negotiating the disposition of subsidiary rights on behalf of the author. Although the author is entitled to purchase copies for his own use at discount prices, no royalties are due on the basis of the sale of those copies. Although a stipulation of non-responsibility for loss or destruction of the manuscript is provided, it is assumed that the publisher does maintain insurance in this regard, especially in the event of damage or destruction due to gross negligence.

Accounting and payment of royalties are stipulated to be made on an annual basis, although projected sales may warrant the distribution of royalties on a semi-annual basis with an accounting at the year-end or year-beginning.

Although the contract does not stipulate a term or otherwise dictate a specific date for expiry, provisions for termination include discontinuance of publication, default and bankruptcy. In order to protect the right of the parties during the course of the agreement, the publisher is given exclusive rights to direct legal proceedings in the event of infringement by third parties. Where procedural requirements in certain jurisdictions require participation of the author in the suit, provision is made for the co-operation of the latter in prosecution of the claim. In view of the rights given to the publisher to initiate legal proceedings, as well as the assumption of most of the economic risks involved in the publishing process, the original of the agreement is stipulated to remain in the possession of the publisher subject to access by the author. Finally, disputes arising between the parties to the agreement are referred to binding arbitration for speedy remedy, thereby hopefully avoiding long delays ordinarily attached to the formal litigation process which may prove fatal to the publication and distribution of the work.

AGREEMENT made this ——— day of ——— 19— at ———.

BETWEEN: XYZ PUBLISHING COMPANY
(hereinafter called the "Publisher")

AND: MR. JOHN SMITH
(hereinafter called the "Author")

In consideration of the undertakings provided hereunder, the parties to the present Agreement declare:

1. Undertaking To Publish:

The Publisher shall publish a work written by the Author entitled ——— ("work") at its own expense in a style, manner and at a price which it deems in its own discretion to be most suitable for the sale of the work. The Publisher shall issue the work within twelve months from the date of the delivery of the manuscript as provided herein subject to the extension as a result of delays due to causes beyond the control of the Publisher. In no event however shall the Publisher publish the work later than twenty-four months following the date of delivery of the manuscript as provided herein;

The Publisher shall alone determine the nature and extent of distribution of the work and shall not be liable for any failure to circulate, promote or distribute the work.

2. Delivery Of The Manuscript:

The Author shall deliver to the Publisher on or before ——— one copy of the final manuscript of the work double-spaced, typewritten, satisfactory in form and content to the Publisher and ready for printing (or the Author has delivered as of the date of these presents the manuscript in final form);

The Author agrees that the minimum length of the work, inclusive of table of contents, preface and index shall exceed ——— words. The Author shall retain a copy of the manuscript for his own files.

The Publisher shall be entitled to terminate by written notice the present agreement in the event of the failure of the Author to deliver the manuscript on the date prescribed, or to deliver the same in a form satisfactory to the Publisher. In the latter event, the Publisher may choose to continue the present agreement and require the Author within sixty days of the delivery date to:

(a) retype or re-edit the manuscript in legible form;
(b) pay the cost of retyping or re-editing to be effected by the Publisher if the Author refuses or neglects to do so;
(c) deliver all tables, charts, maps, designs, drawings, photographs, illustrations, indices, appendices, forewards, glossaries, references and other inclusions necessary to complete the manuscript;
(d) pay the cost to the Publisher of supplying all inclusions mentioned above if the Author refuses or neglects to supply;
(e) furnish all written authorizations required for the reproduction of copyright material in the work;

In the event the Publisher chooses to terminate the present Agreement for failure of the Author to deliver the manuscript, the Author shall return all advances made by the Publisher.

3. Grant To Publish:

The Author hereby grants to the Publisher during the full term of copyright and all renewals thereof the exclusive right to publish the work and subsequent editions in book form in the English language in Canada and the United States of America and to:

(a) publish the work in book form in English in any other countries whether through export of bound copies or unbound sheets, or by independent manufacture;
(b) publish or entitle third parties to publish the work in any other language, and/or to arrange for the translation of the work;
(c) publish or entitle third parties to publish cheaper editions of the work;
(d) entitle book clubs to publish and distribute the work in their own editions whether by sale or lease of plates, or microfilm, or by independent manufacture;
(e) sell first serialization rights;
(f) entitle third parties to reproduce the work in the form of condensations, anthologies, selections and second serializations;
(g) entitle third parties to reproduce the work in the form of radio broadcast, television program, motion picture, live dramatization, Braille, microfilm, mechanical and electronic reproduction and recording process whatsoever;
(h) entitle third parties to exploit all forms of commercial and merchandizing uses and tie ins related to the plot, characters, title or other aspects of the work;
(i) exercise all residual rights to the work.

4. Author's Warranty:

The Author warrants to the Publisher:

(a) he is the sole author of the work;
(b) he has obtained at his own expense written authorization for use of materials from the copyright holder of or owner of rights thereto which materials form part of the work; and he shall deliver the written authorizations with the delivery of the final manuscript or upon demand;
(c) the work is original;
(d) the work has not been previously published in printed form whatever;
(e) he is the sole proprietor of all rights granted to the Publisher and has full right and power to execute the present agreement;
(f) the work and the execution of this agreement do not violate or infringe any personal, statutory or proprietary right or copyright of third parties;

(g) he has not disposed of any rights granted to the Publisher to third parties;
(h) the work is not in whole or in part libellous, obscene or otherwise unlawful;

The present warranties shall remain in force following the termination of the present agreement.

5. Indemnification:

The Author shall indemnify the Publisher against any claims, demands, legal proceedings, costs, losses and damages of any nature whatsoever arising from any alleged breach of the warranties or representations of the Author herein. The Publisher may withhold advances upon royalties or other payments due to the Author in order to permit the full exercise of the present indemnification provisions. The Publisher shall furthermore be entitled to retain counsel at its own expense and shall have the exclusive right to settle or compromise any claim, etc., brought against it.

6. Copyright:

The Publisher shall register copyright of the work in its own name as owner wherever it deems necessary. The Publisher shall be entitled to effect any renewals, extensions or continuations of copyright provided by law;

The Author shall co-operate with the Publisher in effecting registration of copyright and to that end, shall furnish all necessary documents, certificates, titles and editions relating to the work.

7. Proofs:

The Author shall review galley and page proofs of the work, which shall conform to the completed manuscript as submitted by the Author without modification whatsoever, unless with the consent of the latter. The Author shall return such proofs to the Publisher with corrections legibly inserted within one week of the receipt thereof. Where the Author has inserted modifications which are not of the nature of simple corrections of printer's errors, the Author shall bear the costs of modifications which shall form a charge against sums due to the Author hereunder.

8. Royalties:

In consideration of the fulfillment of the Author's obligations herein, the Publisher shall pay to the Author the following royalties and payments:

(a) an advance in the amount of ———— payable upon the date of delivery of the final manuscript of the work as herein provided. The stipulated advance shall constitute a charge against the total revenues of the Author arising under the present Agreement;

(b) on all copies of the regular original edition and re-edition of the work sold, less returns in Canada:
   (aa) 10% of the catalogue retail sales price on the first 5000 copies sold;
   (bb) 12 1/2% of the catalogue retail sales price of the next 2500 copies sold;
   (cc) 15% of the catalogue retail sales price on all copies sold in excess of 7500;

Where the sales price of the copies sold is discounted for sale to educational or charitable institutions, a *pro rata* reduction of royalties due on the same copies shall be made;

(c) on all copies sold in foreign countries:
   (aa) 50% of the royalties stipulated above on the regular original edition;
   (bb) 75% of the net revenues received by the Publisher on an edition in English independently manufactured and published abroad;
   (cc) 10% of the net revenues received by the Publisher on an edition manufactured abroad from the export of the Publisher of unbound sheets;

(d) on all copies of the regular edition sold directly to consumers by the Publisher by mail: 10% of the catalogue retail sales price minus shipping charges if not passed on;

(e) on all copies sold in a cheaper edition:
   (aa) 10% of the net revenues if issued by the Publisher;
   (bb) 50% of net revenues therefrom if issued by a reprint publisher;

(f) from the use of the work in first serialization: 50% of net revenues therefrom;

(g) from the use of the work by book clubs, and in the form of condensations, anthologies, selections and second serializations: 50% of net revenues therefrom;

(h) from the use of the work in translation radio broadcasts, television programs, motion pictures and live dramatizations: 75% of net revenue therefrom calculated without deduction of agent's fees;

(i) from the use of the work in all other forms including Braille, microfilm, mechanical and electronic reproduction and recording processes whatever: 50% of net revenues therefrom;

(j) from the sale of commercial rights: 50% of net revenues therefrom.

9. Limitation Of Royalties:

No royalties shall be paid to the Author for copies of the work furnished free of charge to the Author, nor to third parties for the purpose of review, marketing, promotion or distribution, nor for copies sold at less than cost, nor for copies damaged, destroyed or returned. No royalties shall be payable for copies sold to the Author at the stipulated Author's discount;

Deductions from royalties shall be made for dues or charges due to third parties for use of copyright material. Further deductions shall be made from royalties for all other charges, damages, dues and other obligations of the Author arising from the present Agreement without prejudice to all other recourses of the Publisher.

10. Copies To Author:

The Author shall be entitled to receive ten free copies of the work upon publication and shall further be entitled to buy additional copies for personal use only at a discount of 25% from the catalogue retail sale price.

11. Alterations:

The Publisher shall be entitled to alter the work for the sake of consistency of style, correction of grammar and punctuation and promotion of readability. The Publisher shall communicate with the Author prior to effecting substantial deletions, additions or other alterations, and the Author shall co-operate in making all necessary recommendations prior to printing.

12. Revisions And Re-Editions:

The Author shall prepare material for a revised edition upon the request of the Publisher. The Author shall deliver the final revised manuscript in the form and content satisfactory to the Publisher ready for printing within a reasonable period of time following the request of the Publisher. Unless otherwise provided herein, the present agreement shall apply *mutatis mutandis* to the publication of the revised edition.

In the event that the Author is unable or refuses to prepare the revised edition, to deliver the same in form and content satisfactory to the Publisher as herein provided, or in the event that the Author is deceased when the Publisher requests a revised edition, the Publisher shall be entitled to engage competent persons to prepare the revised edition and to use the names of such persons on the cover and title page of the work in conjunction with the name of the Author. The Publisher shall be entitled to deduct from royalties or other payments due to the Author the remuneration and expenses paid for the preparation of the revised edition.

13. Non-Liability For Manuscript:

The Publisher shall not be liable for any loss or damage to the manuscript delivered by the Author herein whether lost in transit or while in its possession. The Author agrees that loss of the manuscript of the work by the Publisher shall entitle him to no more than purely nominal damages and that the copy of the manuscript of the work retained by the Author shall be deemed to have a value equivalent in all respects to the manuscript delivered. For the purposes of the present paragraph, the word "manuscript" shall be deemed to include all supplemental and accessory materials including without restriction, tables, illustrations, original artworks, photographs and maps. The Author acknowledges that the manuscript of the work delivered to the Publisher may be damaged, written upon, inked and otherwise destroyed in the course of preparing the same for printing.

14. Accounting:

The Publisher shall render an account to the Author on February 28 of each year containing the statements of account, payments, charges and royalties for the preceding calendar year. Where the statement of account indicates that a sum in an amount less than $50.00 is due to the Author, no payment shall be made until the following February.

15. Discontinuance Of Publication:

The Publisher shall notify the Author in writing that the work is out of print where it determines that demand or actual sales do not warrant continued publication. Where the work is declared out of print, the Author shall be entitled within sixty days of notification to obtain the reversion of all rights and to purchase any plates, negatives or artwork of the work at cost and to acquire the existing inventory of the work at one half of the catalogue retail sales price. In the event of the failure of the Author to exercise his rights granted in the present paragraph, the Publisher may dispose of such materials in any manner it deems fit;

The work shall be deemed out of print notwithstanding that the work is on sale in the form of a cheaper edition, or that subsidiary rights continue to be exploited.

16. Infringement:

In the event a third party infringes the copyright of the work, the Publisher shall have the exclusive right to institute direct legal proceedings at the joint expense of both parties. Upon the failure or refusal of the Publisher to proceed with due diligence, the Author may institute and direct legal proceedings at his own expense and exclusively retain any recovery from settlement or satisfaction of judgment. Where the proceedings require joinder of both parties to suit, or assignment of right, the Author and Publisher shall co-operate in permitting the other to meet procedural and evidentiary requirements for due prosecution of suit.

17. Clause Of Non-Competition:

The Author shall not during the course of the present agreement publish or permit to be published any material drawn from or of a nature similar to the material contained in the work on the same subject edited or written by the Author that is likely to compete with the sale of the work.

18. Options On Subsequent Works:

The Author hereby grants to the Publisher a right of first refusal respecting his future works whether written in his name or under a pseudonym insofar as his five subsequent manuscripts suitable for publication in book form are concerned. The Publisher shall advise the Author of his decision respecting publication within thirty days following receipt of each manuscript. In the event of acceptance of such manuscript or manuscripts, the terms of publication will be subject to negotiations and mutual agreement of the parties. If within thirty days following acceptance the parties are unable to execute in good faith an agreement for publication, the Author shall be at liberty to publish his manuscript elsewhere provided that he shall not be entitled to enter into a contract for publication with any other publisher upon conditions less advantageous than those offered by the Publisher.

19. Termination By Default:

In the event of the default by the Publisher to deliver annual statements of account, or to make payment as provided herein within sixty days following written notice by registered mail of such default, the present agreement shall at the option of the Author terminate at the expiration of the delay under reserve of the rights of the Author to demand any and all sums due, and without prejudice to any other recourse available to the Author.

20. Bankruptcy:

In the event of the filing of a petition in bankruptcy against the Publisher or the filing of an assignment or proposal in bankruptcy by the Publisher, or in the event of a judgment declaring the insolvency of the Publisher by a court, or the appointment of a trustee, receiver or sequestrator of any property of the Publisher, or in the event the Publisher shall liquidate or wind up its daily operations for any cause whatsoever, the present agreement shall terminate at the option of the Author and such termination shall be effective from the date of the filing of the petition, assignment, proposal, adjudication, appointment, liquidation or winding up. In consideration of the present Agreement, the Author shall as of right acquire and be seised of all rights granted by the Author to the Publisher prior to termination. The Author shall be seised of the right to purchase the plates, bound and unbound copies of the work, although the right to purchase must be exercised not later than sixty days following the notice of the cause of termination herein described.

21. Copy Of The Agreement:

The present agreement shall be executed in one original copy only which shall remain in the possession of the Publisher. Nevertheless, the Publisher shall furnish upon request of the Author a true copy of the agreement.

22. Arbitration:

Any claim arising out of the present agreement or breach thereof shall be submitted for final and binding arbitration to any person chosen with the mutual consent of the parties. The award of the arbitrator may be submitted to a court of proper jurisdiction for confirmation or homologation.

23. Assignment:

The present Agreement shall be binding upon the assigns, heirs, executors and legal representatives of the Author and Publisher. The Publisher and Author shall not effect any assignment, transfer, sale, lease or other disposal of the rights herein contained save where otherwise stipulated without the written consent of the other. The term "Publisher" shall include any assignee, subsidiary or successor by reason of sale, consolidation, merger, exchange continuation or any other re-organization and no such re-organization shall be deemed to involve an assignment of rights necessitating the written consent of the Author.

24. Notice:

The requirements of a written notice under the present Agreement shall be deemed to have been fulfilled by delivery in person or by the sending by regular mail of the notice to the parties at the addresses hereinbefore mentioned, save in the event of the change of address following due service of notice of change of address by registered mail. The requirement of delivery of notice by registered mail shall be deemed fulfilled on the date mentioned in the postal receipt issued at the time of posting.

25. Waiver:

A waiver of any breach of this Agreement or of any of the terms or conditions by the Author or Publisher shall not be deemed a waiver of any continued or subsequent breach or in any way affect any other term of the present Agreement; no waiver shall be binding upon the Author or Publisher unless stipulated in writing and signed by the parties.

26. Language Requirement - Province of Quebec:

The parties expressly require that the present contract be drawn up and executed in the English language. Les parties ont expressément exigé que le presént contrat soit rédigé et exécuté en anglais.

IN WITNESS WHEREOF the parties hereto have duly executed the present Agreement on the date first mentioned.

____

Publisher

____

Author

1.2 ALTERNATE AND SPECIAL CLAUSES FOR THE BASIC AUTHOR-PUBLISHER AGREEMENT

1. American grant to publish;
2. Undertaking to publish a work in two or more volumes;
3. Warranty by joint authors;
4. Advances upon royalties;
5. Distribution of royalties.

1. American Grant To Publish:

The Author grants to the Publisher during the full term of copyright and all extensions thereof the exclusive right to publish and distribute the work in book form in the English language in the United States of America, the Philippine Islands and Canada, and to sell the work on a non-exclusive basis for export in all other countries, excluding Great Britain.

2. Undertaking To Publish A Work In Two Or More Volumes:

The Publisher shall publish the work at its own expense in two volumes in a style, manner and at a price which it deems in its own discretion to be suitable for the sale of the work. The Publisher shall issue the first volume of the work within twelve months from the date of the delivery of the manuscript of both volumes of the work subject to extension as a result of delays due to causes beyond the control of the Publisher. In no event, however, shall the Publisher publish the first volume of the work later than twenty-four months following the date of delivery of the manuscript as provided herein.

The Publisher shall publish the second volume of the work simultaneously with the publication of the first volume, or at its option not later than one year following the date of publication of the first volume subject to extension as a result of delays due to causes beyond the control of the Publisher.

The Publisher shall alone determine the nature and extent of distribution of the work and shall not be liable for any failure to circulate, promote or distribute the work. In particular, the Publisher may market and distribute the volumes of the work together or on a separate basis. The Publisher may furthermore choose to treat the publication of the work in separate volumes as a set, sequel or as independent books.

3. Warranty By Joint Authors:

The Authors warrant to the Publisher:

(a) They are the sole Authors of the work;
(b) They have obtained at their own expense written authorization for use of materials from the copyright holder or owner of rights thereto, which materials form part of the work; and they shall deliver the written authorizations with the delivery of the final manuscript or upon demand;
(c) The work is original;
(d) The work has not been previously published in printed form whatever;
(e) They are the sole proprietors of all rights granted to the Publisher and have full right and power to execute the present agreement;
(f) The work and the execution of this agreement do not violate or infringe any personal, statutory or proprietary right or copyright of third parties;
(g) They have not disposed of any rights granted to the Publisher to third parties;
(h) The work is not in whole or in part libellous, obscene or otherwise unlawful;

The present warranties shall remain in force following the termination of the present agreement. The Authors individually subscribe to each and everyone of the present provisions and hereby engage their joint and several liability notwithstanding that each Author is alone obliged to write or complete certain chapters or portions of the manuscript of the work.

4. Advances Upon Royalties:

The Publisher shall pay the sum of $75,000 as an advance against royalties stipulated herein which advance shall be payable in three equal instalments. The first payment shall be made upon execution of the present agreement and subsequent payments shall be made upon delivery of portions of the entirety of the manuscript in accordance with the schedule or term herein provided. Nevertheless, the Publisher shall not be obliged to make payment of the second and third instalments of the advance unless the Author demonstrates that the completion of the work may reasonably be expected by the deadline for delivery mentioned in the present agreement.

5. Distribution Of Royalties:

The Author hereby grants to the Publisher all subsidiary rights to the work, for exploitation on a worldwide basis. The Publisher distributes the net proceeds received from the exploitation of such rights on the following basis:

		Publisher	**Author**
Book club rights	:	50%	50%
Periodicals or newspaper serializations, digests, condensations, selections, abridgments	:	50%	50%
Television, radio broadcasts	:	50%	50%
Live dramatization and motion picture rights	:	20%	80%
Translation	:	20%	80%

1.3 BASIC AUTHOR-PUBLISHER AGREEMENT (AUTHOR ORIENTED)

1. Undertaking to publish;
2. Delivery of the manuscript;
3. Grant to publish;
4. Author's warranty;
5. Indemnification;
6. Copyright;
7. Proofs;
8. Royalties;
9. Limitation of royalties;
10. Copies to Author;
11. Alterations;
12. Revisions and re-editions;
13. Non-liability for manuscript;
14. Accounting;
15. Discontinuance of publication;
16. Infringement;
17. Clause of non-competition;
18. Advertising insertions;
19. Termination by default;
20. Bankruptcy;
21. Copy of the agreement;
22. Arbitration;

23. Assignment;
24. Notice;
25. Waiver;
26. Language requirement - Province of Quebec.

Commentary

The following agreement conforms to the order set out in the basic author-publisher agreement mentioned above with certain deletions and amendments to create greater rights for the benefit of the author. The undertaking to publish removes absolute discretion from the publisher to determine the style, manner and price of the work. The publisher is furthermore obliged to exercise a certain amount of diligence in promoting and distributing the work. The same element of discretion is removed from the publisher with respect to the determination of the satisfactory nature of the manuscript once delivered. Furthermore, unilateral charging against royalties by the publisher is abolished and replaced by simple obligation by the author to make full delivery.

The grant to publish is extensive in form, although all residual rights, if any, do remain under the control of the author. The grant clause may be read in conjunction with the copyright clause which vests in the author nominal copyright. The grant of subsidiary rights is made conditional upon their exercise within a stipulated period of time following the date of the execution of the agreement.

For evident reasons, the percentages and terms of the royalty schedule are more favourable than those set out in the basic author-publisher agreement. The justification for a reduction of remuneration flowing to the publisher from the exploitation of subsidiary rights is that the publisher's role is limited to printing and distributing the work and any right to additional revenues from subsidiary sources should be restricted in view of that limitation. Nevertheless, as is evident, the grant to the publisher does encompass more than simple mechanical printing and distribution of the work.

The author is given final say with respect to alterations in the manuscript and confirms his intention not to be bound by clauses of non-competition or a right of first refusal. Finally, it may be noted that the author expressly stipulates a prohibition against the insertion of advertising material in the published work, although such insertion is not common practice insofar as the publication of hard cover trade editions of a work is concerned.

AGREEMENT made this ——— day of ———, 19— at ———.

BETWEEN:	XYZ PUBLISHING COMPANY (hereinafter called the "Publisher")
AND:	MR. JOHN SMITH (hereinafter called the "Author")

In consideration of the undertakings provided hereunder, the parties to the present Agreement declare:

1. Undertaking To Publish:

The Publisher shall publish a work written by the Author entitled ——— ("work") at its own expense in a style, manner and at a price which shall be most suitable for the sale of the work. The Publisher shall issue the work within twelve months from the date of the delivery of the manuscript as provided herein subject to extension as a result of delays due to causes beyond the control of the Publisher. In no event however shall the Publisher publish the work later than twenty-four months following the date of delivery of the manuscript as provided herein;

The Publisher shall diligently determine and promote the extent of distribution of the work and shall be liable for any failure to circulate, promote or distribute the work in accordance with standard industry practice.

2. Delivery Of The Manuscript:

The Author shall deliver to the Publisher on or before ——— one copy of the final manuscript of the work double-spaced, typewritten and ready for printing (or the Author has delivered as of the date of these presents the manuscript in final form).

The Author agrees that the minimum length of the work, inclusive of table of contents, preface and index shall exceed ——— words. The Author shall retain a copy of the manuscript for his own files.

The Publisher shall be entitled to terminate by written notice the present agreement in the event of the failure of the Author to deliver the manuscript on the date prescribed.

The Author shall furthermore:

(a) deliver all tables, charts, maps, designs, drawings, photographs, illustrations, indexes, appendices, forewards, glossaries, references and other inclusions necessary to complete the manuscript;

(b) furnish all written authorizations required for the reproduction of copyright material in the work.

3. Grant To Publish:

The Author hereby grants to the Publisher during the full term of copyright and all renewals thereof the exclusive right to publish the work and subsequent editions in book form in the English language in Canada and the United States of America; and subject to the Author's right to terminate upon notice the following rights which have not been exercised within four years from the date of these presents, to:

(a) publish the work in book form (hard-cover) in English in any other countries whether through export of bound copies or unbound sheets, or by independent manufacture;
(b) publish or entitle third parties to publish the work in any other language, and/or to arrange for the translation of the work;
(c) publish or entitle third parties to publish cheaper editions of the work;
(d) entitle book clubs to publish and distribute the work in their own editions whether by sale or lease of plates, or microfilm, or by independent manufacture;
(e) sell first serialization rights;
(f) entitle third parties to reproduce the work in the form of condensations, anthologies, selections and second serializations;
(g) entitle third parties to reproduce the work in the form of radio broadcast, television program, motion picture, live dramatization, Braille, microfilm mechanical and electronic reproduction and recording processes;
(h) entitle third parties to exploit all forms of commercial and merchandising uses and tie-ins related to the plot, characters, title or other aspects of the work;

All other rights not expressly granted to the Publisher remain the exclusive rights of the Author.

4. Author's Warranty:

The Author warrants to the Publisher:

(a) he is the sole author of the work;
(b) he has obtained at his own expense written authorization for use of materials from the copyright holder of or owner of rights thereto which materials form part of the work; and he shall deliver the written authorizations with the delivery of the final manuscript or upon demand;
(c) the work is original;
(d) the work has not been previously published in printed form whatever;
(e) he is the sole proprietor of all rights granted to the Publisher and has full right and power to execute the present agreement;
(f) the work and the execution of this agreement do not violate or infringe any personal, statutory or proprietary right or copyright of third parties;
(g) he has not disposed of any rights granted to the Publisher to third parties;
(h) the work is not in whole or in part libellous, obscene or otherwise unlawful;

The present warranties shall remain in force following the termination of the present agreement.

5. Indemnification:

The Author shall indemnify the Publisher against any claims, demands, legal proceedings, costs, losses and damages of any nature whatsoever arising from any alleged breach of the warranties or representations of the Author herein. The Publisher may withhold advances upon royalties or other payments due to the Author in order to permit the full exercise of the present indemnification provisions. The Publisher shall furthermore be entitled to retain counsel at its own expense and shall have the exclusive right to settle or compromise any claim, etc., brought against it.

6. Copyright:

The Publisher shall register copyright of the work in the Author's name as owner wherever necessary. The Publisher shall be entitled to effect any renewals, extensions or continuations of copyright provided by law in order to protect the interests of the Author.

The Author shall co-operate with the Publisher in effecting registration of copyright and to that end, shall furnish all necessary documents, certificates, titles and editions relating to the work.

All editions of the work shall be duly imprinted with the copyright symbol © indicating copyright in the name of the Author.

7. Proofs:

The Author shall review galley and page proofs of the work, which shall conform to the completed manuscript as submitted by the Author without modification whatsoever, unless with the consent of the latter. The Author shall return such proofs to the Publisher with corrections legibly inserted within one week of the receipt thereof. Where the Author has inserted modifications which are not of the nature of simple corrections of printer's errors, the Author shall bear the costs of modifications which shall form a charge against sums due to the Author hereunder. The Author shall be entitled to an accounting of such charges in accordance with the provisions for accounting hereunder.

8. Royalties:

In consideration of the fulfillment of the Author's obligations herein, the Publisher shall pay to the Author the following royalties and payments:

(a) an advance in the amount of $———— payable upon the date of delivery of the final manuscript of the work as herein provided. The stipulated advance shall constitute a charge against the total revenues of the Author arising hereunder, but shall not be refunded or constitute a continuing liability on the part of the Author in the event of a breach of the present agreement by the Publisher;

(b) on all copies of the regular original edition and re-edition of the work sold, less returns in Canada:
 (aa) 10% of the catalogue retail sales price on the first 5,000 copies sold;
 (bb) 15% of the catalogue retail sales price on all copies sold in excess of 5,000;

Where the sales price of the copies sold is discounted for sale to educational or charitable institutions, a pro rata reduction of royalties due on the same copies shall be made;

(c) on all copies sold in foreign countries:
 (aa) 50% of the royalties stipulated above on the regular original edition;
 (bb) 75% of the net revenues received by the Publisher on an edition in English independently manufactured and published abroad;
 (cc) 25% of the net revenues received by the Publisher on an edition manufactured abroad from the export of the Publisher of unbound sheets;

(d) on all copies of the regular edition sold directly to consumers by the Publisher by mail: 10% of the catalogue retail sales price minus shipping charges if not passed on;

(e) on all copies sold in a cheaper edition:
 (aa) 10% of the net revenues if issued by the Publisher;
 (bb) 65% of net revenues therefrom if issued by a reprint publisher;

(f) from the use of the work in first serialization: 90% of net revenues therefrom;

(g) from the use of the work by book clubs, and in the form of translations, condensations, anthologies, selections and second serializations: 65% of net revenues therefrom;

(h) from the use of the work in radio broadcasts, television programs, motion pictures and live dramatizations: 90% of net revenues therefrom calculated without deduction of agent's fees;

(i) from the use of the work in other forms including Braille, microfilm, mechanical and electronic reproduction and recording processes: 50% of net revenues therefrom;

(j) from the sale of commercial rights: 70% of net revenues therefrom;

9. Limitation Of Royalties:

No royalties shall be paid to the Author for copies of the work furnished free of charge to the Author, nor to third parties for the purpose of review, marketing, promotion or distribution, nor for copies sold at less than cost, nor for copies damaged, destroyed or returned. No royalties shall be payable for copies sold to the Author at the stipulated Author's discount.

Deductions from royalties shall be made for dues or charges due to third parties for use of copyright material. Further deductions shall be made from royalties for all other charges, damages, dues and other obligations of the Author arising from the present Agreement without prejudice to all other recourses of the Publisher.

10. Copies To Author:

The Author shall be entitled to receive ten free copies of the work upon publication and shall further be entitled to buy additional copies for personal use only at a discount of 50% from the catalogue retail sale price.

11. Alterations:

The Publisher shall not be entitled to alter the work or title whether for the sake of consistency of style, revision of grammar and punctuation or promotion of readability without the consent of the Author.

12. Revisions And Re-Editions:

The Author shall prepare material for a revised edition upon the request of the Publisher. The Author shall deliver the final revised manuscript in the form and content satisfactory to the Publisher ready for printing within a reasonable period of time following the request of the Publisher. Unless otherwise provided herein, the present agreement shall apply *mutatis mutandis* to the publication of the revised edition.

In the event that the Author is unable or refuses to prepare and deliver the revised edition, or in the event that the Author is deceased when the Publisher requests a revised edition, the Publisher shall be entitled at its own expense to engage competent persons to prepare the revised edition and to use the names of such persons on the cover and title page of the work in conjunction with the name of the Author.

13. Non-Liability For Manuscript:

The Publisher shall not be liable for any loss or damage to the manuscript delivered by the Author herein whether lost in transit or while in its possession, save in the event of gross negligence. For the purposes of the present paragraph, the word "manuscript" shall not include any supplemental and accessory materials including without restriction, tables, illustrations, original artwork, photographs and maps. The Author shall be entitled to obtain possession of the manuscript and all supplemental and accessory materials within two months following publication of the work.

14. Accounting:

The Publisher shall render an account to the Author on February 28 and September 30 of each year containing the statements of account, payments, charges and royalties for the preceding calendar year. Where the statement of account indicates that a sum in an amount less than $50 is due to the Author, no payment shall be made until the following February.

15. Discontinuance Of Publication:

The Publisher shall notify the Author in writing that the work is out of print where it determines that demand or actual sales do not warrant continued publication. Alternatively, the Author shall be entitled by notice to require the Publisher to place the work in print failing which the work shall be deemed to be out of print. Where the work is declared or deemed to be out of print, the Author shall be entitled within sixty days of notification to obtain the reversion of all rights and to purchase any plates, negatives or artwork of the work at cost and to acquire the existing inventory of the work at one half of the catalogue retail sales price. In the event of the failure of the Author to exercise his rights granted in the present paragraph, the Publisher may dispose of such materials in any manner it deems fit;

The work shall be deemed out of print notwithstanding that the work is on sale in the form of a cheaper edition, or that subsidiary rights continue to be exploited.

16. Infringement:

In the event a third party infringes the copyright of the work, the Publisher shall have the right to institute direct legal proceedings at its own expense. Upon the failure or refusal of the Publisher to proceed with due diligence, the Author may institute and direct legal proceedings at his own expense and exclusively retain any recovery from settlement or satisfaction of judgment. Where the proceedings require joinder of both parties to suit, or assignment of right, the Author and Publisher shall co-operate in permitting the other to meet procedural and evidentiary requirements for due prosecution of suit.

17. Clause Of Non-Competition:

The Author shall be under no express or implied obligation during the course of the present agreement to refrain from publishing or permitting to be published any material drawn from or of a nature similar to the material contained in the work on the same subject edited or written by the Author that is likely to compete with the sale of the work.

18. Advertising Insertions:

No advertising material shall be inserted in the published work, whether printed on the back cover, prefatory or end papers or within the text pages without the consent of the Author. "Advertising material" shall not include lists, titles or descriptions of other works published by the Publisher printed on the back dust cover or end papers of the published work.

19. Termination By Default:

In the event of the default by the Publisher to publish the work, or to deliver annual statements of account, or to make payment as provided herein within sixty days following written notice by registered mail of such default, the present agreement shall at the option of the Author terminate at the expiration of the delay under reserve of the rights of the Author to demand any and all sums due, and without prejudice to any other recourse available to the Author. The Author shall furthermore be entitled to retain all advances made in the event of termination by reason of the default of the Publisher to publish.

20. Bankruptcy:

In the event of the filing of a petition in bankruptcy against the Publisher or the filing of an assignment or proposal in bankruptcy by the Publisher, or in the event of a judgment declaring the insolvency of the Publisher by a court, or the appointment of a trustee, receiver or sequestrator of any property of the Publisher, or in the event the Publisher shall liquidate or wind up its daily operations for any cause whatsoever, the present agreement shall terminate at the option of the Author and such termination shall be effective from the date of the filing of the petition, assignment, proposal, adjudication, appointment, liquidation or winding up. In consideration of the present Agreement, the Author shall as of right acquire and be seised of all rights granted by the Author to the Publisher prior to termination. The Author shall be seised of the right to purchase the plates, bound and unbound copies of the work, although the right to purchase must be exercised not later than sixty days following the notice of the cause of termination herein described.

21. Copy Of The Agreement:

The present agreement shall be executed in one original copy only which shall remain in the possession of the Publisher. Nevertheless, the Publisher shall furnish upon request of the Author the original or a true copy of the agreement.

22. Arbitration:

Any claim arising out of the present agreement or breach thereof shall be submitted for final and binding arbitration to any person chosen with the mutual consent of the parties. The award of the arbitrator may be submitted to a court of proper jurisdiction for confirmation or homologation.

23. Assignment:

The present Agreement shall be binding upon the assigns, heirs, executors and legal representatives of the Author and Publisher. The Publisher and Author shall not effect any assignment, transfer, sale, lease or other disposal of the rights herein contained save where otherwise stipulated without the written consent of the other. The term "Publisher" shall include any assignee, subsidiary or successor by reason of sale, consolidation, merger, exchange continuation or any other re-organization and no such re-organization shall be deemed to involve an assignment of rights necessitating the written consent of the Author.

24. Notice:

The requirements of a written notice under the present Agreement shall be deemed to have been fulfilled by delivery in person or by the sending by regular mail of the notice to the parties at the addresses hereinbefore mentioned, save in the event of the change of address following due service of notice of change of address by registered mail. The requirement of delivery of notice by registered mail shall be deemed fulfilled on the date mentioned in the postal receipt issued at the time of posting.

25. Waiver:

A waiver of any breach of this Agreement or of any of the terms or conditions by the Author or Publisher shall not be deemed a waiver of any continued or subsequent breach or in any way affect any other term of the present Agreement; no waiver shall be binding upon the Author or Publisher unless stipulated in writing and signed by the parties.

26. Language Requirement - Province Of Quebec:

The parties expressly require that the present contract be drawn up and executed in the English language. Les parties ont expressément exigé que le présent contrat soit rédigé et exécuté en anglais.

IN WITNESS WHEREOF the parties hereto have duly executed the present Agreement on the date first mentioned.

____

Publisher

____

Author

1.4 AUTHOR-PUBLISHER AGREEMENT RESPECTING FEATURES

1. Grant of publishing rights;
2. Delivery of manuscript;
3. Obligation to publish;
4. Style of publication;
5. Author's warranties;
6. Indemnification;
7. Copyright;
8. Grant to publish in other forms;
9. Royalties;
10. Loss of or damage to the features;
11. Term of agreement;
12. Assignment;
13. Notice;
14. Waiver;
15. Language requirement - Province of Quebec.

Commentary

The following agreement provides for the orderly submission of features on a periodic basis for publication at regular intervals in a magazine or newspaper. The publisher is given the right to discontinue the agreement in the event the author fails to maintain the order prescribed for submission of the work. Although not covered, the form provides a prelude to syndication of rights to the feature involving simultaneous publication in several other periodicals.

AGREEMENT made this ——— day of ———, 19— at ———.

BETWEEN: XYZ PUBLISHING COMPANY
(hereinafter called the "Publisher")

AND: MR. JOHN SMITH
(hereinafter called the "Author")

In consideration of the undertakings provided hereunder, the parties to the present agreement declare:

1. Grant Of Publishing Rights:

The Author grants to the Publisher the exclusive right to publish in its periodical entitled ——— the feature entitled "Card Games" ("Features") which consist of a grill of card symbols accompanied by a text not exceeding one hundred words in length.

2. Delivery Of Manuscript:

The Author shall deliver a new feature on a bi-weekly basis, as well as all necessary artwork in a form satisfactory to the Publisher and ready for printing during the term of the present agreement.

3. Obligation To Publish:

The Publisher shall publish the features on a bi-weekly basis in its periodical commencing two months following the delivery of the first feature by the Author. The Publisher reserves the right to refuse to publish the features for the following reasons:

(a) The feature is not technically suitable for printing;
(b) The content of the features are not novel or are redundant.

4. Style Of Publication:

The Publisher shall have the right to determine in its absolute discretion the timing, sequence and quality of production of the features. The Publisher shall furthermore have the right to make any amendments or modifications to the text or artwork of the features in order to better suit the same for publication.

5. Author's Warranties:

The Author warrants to the Publisher that he has full proprietary rights with respect to the features in that he is the sole Author, or has full power to grant and assign the exclusive right to publish; that the features are original; that the work has not been previously published in whole or in part in any other form, or edition whatever; that the work as presently constituted does not infringe upon any right of ownership under statute or common law.

6. Indemnification:

The Author shall indemnify the Publisher against any claims, damages, actions or judgments, including interest, costs and judicial and extra-judicial fees which may be sustained by or served upon the Publisher by reason of the publication of the above-mentioned features, whether or not the claim or action is founded or unfounded in law and fact. The Author shall pay any settlement deemed advisable by legal counsel subject to the Author's right of reasonable refusal. Upon full compensation and indemnification for any claims, damages or actions, as hereinbefore mentioned, the Publisher shall subrogate the Author in all its rights relating to the issues in question.

7. Copyright:

The Author shall maintain full copyright to the features and shall at his own expense secure formal copyright.

8. Grant To Publish In Other Forms:

The Author grants to the Publisher the exclusive right to reproduce the features in book form in North America provided that the same features have been published in the Publisher's periodical in accordance with the present agreement.

9. Royalties:

The Publisher shall pay to the Author the following royalties and payments: $200 per feature published in the Publisher's periodical.

Upon the publication of the features in book form as provided above, the parties shall enter into a separate agreement establishing royalty payments upon the proceeds thereof.

10. Loss Of Or Damage To The Features:

The Publisher shall not be responsible in any manner for loss of or damage to the features, and in order to minimize such loss or damage, the Author undertakes to maintain a copy of each feature delivered to the Publisher in his own files.

11. Term Of Agreement:

The term of the present agreement shall be one year following the date of its execution subject to automatic renewal for successive periods of six months unless either party gives notice of the termination within one month prior to the end of such renewal term.

The Publisher shall be entitled to terminate the agreement at any time at its option in the event that the Author fails to deliver two consecutive features provided herein.

12. Assignment:

The present agreement shall be binding upon the assigns, heirs, executors and legal representatives of the Author and Publisher. The Publisher and Author shall not effect any assignment, transfer, sale, lease or other disposal of the rights herein contained save where otherwise stipulated without the written consent of the other. The term "Publisher" shall include any assignee, subsidiary or successor by reason of sale, consolidation, merger, exchange, continuation or any other re-organization and no such re-organization shall be deemed to involve an assignment of rights necessitating the written consent of the Author.

13. Notice:

The requirements of a written notice under the present agreement shall be deemed to have been fulfilled by delivery in person or by the sending by regular mail of the notice to the parties at the addresses hereinbefore mentioned, save in the event of the change of address following due service of notice of change of address by registered mail. The requirement of delivery of notice by registered mail shall be deemed fulfilled on the date mentioned in the postal receipt issued at the time of posting.

14. Waiver:

A waiver of any breach of this agreement or of any of the terms or conditions by the Author or Publisher shall not be deemed a waiver of any continued or subsequent breach or in any way affect any other term of the present agreement; no waiver shall be binding upon the Author or Publisher unless stipulated in writing and signed by the parties.

15. Language Requirement - Province Of Quebec:

The parties expressly require that the present contract be drawn up and executed in the English language. Les parties ont expressément exigé que le présent contrat soit rédigé et exécuté en anglais.

IN WITNESS WHEREOF the parties hereto have duly executed the present Agreement on the date first mentioned.

____

Publisher

____

Author

1.5 FIRST SERIALIZATION AGREEMENT

1. Undertaking to publish;
2. Writing of the manuscript;
3. Availability of the author;
4. Drafting of the work;
5. Grant to publish;
6. Exclusivity prior to and during publication;
7. Proofs;
8. Royalties;
9. Copies of the work;
10. Competing works;
11. Waiver;
12. Notice;
13. Assignment;
14. Language requirement - Province of Quebec

Commentary

The following agreement envisages the serialization prior to publication in book form of a manuscript which is not yet written at the date of the execution of the agreement. The form is useful in dealing with an author who is incapable for various reasons of committing the text to a manuscript suitable for publication within a specified date. The agreement consequently envisages the active participation of the publisher in the writing of the manuscript subject to various controls by the author. The agreement permits the publication of the complete manuscript in serial form in several editions of the magazine or periodical and vests in the publisher all other rights including the right to publish in book form or reproduce in the subsidiary form previously mentioned. As may be seen, the publisher not only invests effort and expense in inclusion of the work in a periodical and in subsequent exploitation, but as well in the actual creation of the work; for this reason copyright is assigned to the publisher.

AGREEMENT made this ——— day of ———, 19— at ———.

BETWEEN:	XYZ PUBLISHING COMPANY (hereinafter called the "Publisher")
AND:	JOHN SMITH (hereinafter called the "Author")

In consideration of the undertaking provided herein, the parties to the present agreement declare:

1. Undertaking To Publish:

The Publisher shall publish a work to be written by the Author tentatively entitled ———— ("work") to be printed in a series of six portions as articles in a periodical published by the Publisher entitled ———— ("periodical"). The Publisher shall include the first instalment of the work in the periodical within three months following completion of the work as provided herein subject to extension as a result of delays due to causes beyond the control of the Publisher. In no event, however, shall the Publisher publish the work later than two years following the date of the completion of the manuscript.

The Author recognizes that the periodical is published on a monthly basis and generally contains articles of wide social and community concern. Nothing in the present agreement shall be deemed to grant any right to the Author to interfere in any manner with the timing of publication of the periodical, format, cover, style or other aspects related to the circulation of the periodical.

2. Writing Of The Manuscript:

The Author shall co-operate with the Publisher in preparing and writing a manuscript covering the experiences as government minister between the years 1974 to 1978, and shall to that extent:

(1) Grant interviews to designated staff of the Publisher;
(2) Disclose and refer the said staff to photographs, documentation and other materials relevant to the scope of the work;
(3) Co-operate in granting to the said staff access where possible to third persons for the purpose of interviews.

3. Availability Of Thc Author:

The Author shall make himself available to the Publisher for the purpose of creating the work at his residence for a period not exceeding three months following the date of the present agreement. During the said period, the Publisher shall at its own expense defray all costs of lodging, food and travel necessary in the opinion of the latter to obtain the presence of the Author at any given location.

4. Drafting Of The Work:

The Author shall review the work prepared for publication for the purpose of correcting substantial errors and/or omissions to the text, or for amending the same to avoid any legal prejudice. Nevertheless, the Publisher shall have the exclusive right to draft, edit and prepare the work for publication.

5. Grant To Publish:

The Author hereby grants and assigns to the Publisher the copyright to the work for the purposes of publication in serial form in the periodical in the English language. The Author furthermore grants and assigns to the Publisher the exclusive right to:

(a) Publish the work in book form in English worldwide whether through export of bound copies or unbound sheets or by independent manufacture;

(b) Publish or entitle third parties to publish in any other language and/or to arrange for the translation of the work;

(c) Publish or entitle third parties to publish cheaper editions of the work in book form;

(d) Entitle book clubs to publish and distribute the work in their own editions, whether by sale or lease of plates or microfilm or by independent manufacture;

(e) Entitle third parties to reproduce the work in the form of condensations, anthologies, selections and second serializations;

(f) Entitle third parties to reproduce the work in the form of radio broadcast, television program, motion picture, live dramatization, braille, microfilm, mechanical and electronic reproduction and recording processes;

(g) Entitle third parties to exploit all forms of commercial and merchandising uses and tie-ins related to the plot, characters, title or other aspects of the work.

6. Exclusivity Prior To And During Publication:

The Author agrees not to grant any interviews or otherwise make public in any form whatever materials, references or comments related to the content of the work prior to and during the course of serial publication in the periodical.

7. Proofs:

The Author shall not be entitled to obtain copies of or review the proofs of the work in serial form prior to insertion in the periodical. Nevertheless, the Publisher shall be entitled to request from the Author confirmation of facts contained in the work following completion of the manuscript but immediately prior to serial publication.

8. Royalties:

In consideration of the fulfillment of the Author's obligations herein, the Publisher shall pay to the Author the following royalties:

(1) A global sum of $40,000 payable in three monthly instalments commencing one month following the date of the execution of the present agreement;
(2) On all copies of the work in book form: 5% of the catalogue retail sales price of each copy sold;
(3) On all copies of the work sold in book form in a cheaper edition: 5% of the catalogue retail sales price on each copy sold;
(4) 40% of the net proceeds received by the Publisher from the use of the work by book clubs and in the form of translation, condensation, anthology, selection, second serialization, radio broadcast, television programs, motion pictures, live dramatizations and all other forms of reproduction whatever.

9. Copies Of The Work:

The Publisher shall not be obliged to give to the Author a copy of the manuscript of the work, or copies of issues of the periodicals containing the serialization.

10. Competing Works:

The Author shall not during the course of the present agreement publish or permit to be published material drawn from or of a nature similar to the material contained in the work on the same subject edited, written or indirectly created by the Author if it is likely to compete with the sale of subsidiary rights of the work mentioned herein.

11. Waiver:

A waiver of any breach of this agreement or of any of the terms or conditions by the Author or Publisher shall not be deemed a waiver of any continued or subsequent breach or in any way affect any other term of the present agreement; no waiver shall be binding upon the Author or Publisher unless stipulated in writing and signed by the parties.

12. Notice:

The requirements of a written notice under the present agreement shall be deemed to have been fulfilled by delivery in person or by the sending by regular mail of the notice to the parties at the addresses hereinbefore mentioned, save in the event of the change of address following due service of notice of change of address by registered mail. The requirement of delivery of notice by registered mail shall be deemed fulfilled on the date mentioned in the postal receipt issued at the time of posting.

13. Assignment:

The present agreement shall be binding upon the assigns, heirs, executors and legal representatives of the Author and Publisher. The Publisher and Author shall not effect any assignment, transfer, sale, lease or other disposal of the rights herein contained save where otherwise stipulated without the written consent of the other. The term "Publisher" shall include any assignee, subsidiary or successor by reason of sale, consolidation, merger, exchange, continuation or any other re-organization and no such re-organization shall be deemed to involve an assignment of rights necessitating the written consent of the Author.

14. Language Requirement - Province Of Quebec:

The parties expressly require that the present contract be drawn up and executed in the English language. Les parties ont expressément exigé que le présent contrat soit rédigé et exécuté en anglais.

IN WITNESS WHEREOF the parties hereto have duly executed the present agreement on the date first mentioned.

____

Publisher

____

Author

1.6 FOREIGN PUBLICATION IN TRANSLATION

1. Undertaking to publish;
2. Undertaking to translate;
3. Inclusions in the printed work;
4. Publication schedule;
5. Distribution;
6. Grant to publish;
7. Delivery;
8. Warranties;
9. Indemnification;
10. Copyright;
11. Proofs;
12. Royalties;
13. Grant of subsidiary rights;
14. Royalties for exercise of subsidiary rights;
15. Notice of contract for subsidiary rights;
16. Free copies to publisher;

17. Reprints and re-editions;
18. Accounting;
19. Termination by default;
20. Rights upon termination;
21. Bankruptcy;
22. Option on future work;
23. Assignment;
24. Notice;
25. Waiver;
26. Language requirement - Province of Quebec.

Commentary

The following agreement envisages the disposition of translation and foreign publication rights to the foreign publisher. The grant is limited to an exclusive right of publication and distribution in book form in the French language outside the country of original publication. The contract does not involve the sale of the translation which the publisher has commissioned; on the contrary, the foreign publisher is obliged to act as translator. The agreement furthermore assumes that the original publisher has been granted full rights to dispose of the subsidiary rights of translation and foreign publication by a prior agreement with the author. Where this has not been done, the agreement would require a stipulation to the effect that the publisher is acting in his capacity as agent for the author, if so entitled, with respect to the disposal of the rights concerned.

The foreign publisher is entitled to proceed with the exploitation of subsidiary rights only upon obtaining the prior consent of the publisher. As may be seen, the contract combines elements from both the basic author-publisher agreement and the publisher-translator agreement found in this section. It is however to be remarked that the ambiguities or express stipulations for the benefit of one party namely, the publisher, are for the most part absent from the present form of agreement seeing that both parties are publishers with possibly equal bargaining strength.

The percentages contained in the royalty schedule are remarkably less than those set out in the author-publisher agreements. The foreign publisher, of course, has increased initial costs and must distribute a portion of royalties to the translator as remuneration for his work.

AGREEMENT made this ——— day of ———, 19— at ———.

BETWEEN:	XYZ PUBLISHING COMPANY (hereinafter called the "Publisher")
AND:	ABC PUBLISHING COMPANY (hereinafter called "Foreign Publisher")

In consideration of the undertakings provided herein, the parties to the present agreement declare:

1. Undertaking To Publish:

The Foreign Publisher shall publish the work entitled ——— ("work") authored by John Smith in book form in the French language in France. The style, manner and conditions of publication including the sale price of the French language work shall be determined in the exclusive discretion of the Foreign Publisher.

2. Undertaking To Translate:

The Foreign Publisher shall translate the work in a manner and style which will not only reflect a literal transposition of English wording into the French language, but also retain the spirit and intent of the Author as conveyed in the text. The Foreign Publisher shall in no event effect a translation which abridges or edits the work, or adds a text foreign to the work or which is libellous, obscene or blasphemous, or which draws upon copyright materials for which no authorization has been obtained.

The Publisher shall not be responsible for any damages or remuneration to the translator engaged by the Foreign Publisher to effect the translation. The Foreign Publisher undertakes to obtain all necessary copyright and proprietary licences or rights from the translator in order to give full effect to the present agreement.

The Foreign Publisher shall submit a copy of the translation to the Publisher for its approval prior to publication of the work in the French language. In the event that the Publisher fails to consent or otherwise notify the Foreign Publisher within two weeks following receipt of the translation of the work, the Foreign Publisher may proceed with publication.

3. Inclusions In The Printed Work:

The Foreign Publisher shall print in the introductory pages to the published work a notation to the effect that the work was originally published in the English language by the Publisher, that the original title of the work was ——— and that the work in all forms is protected by copyright and other law.

The Foreign Publisher shall further include a notation to the effect that a published work in translation is not for sale outside France.

4. Publication Schedule:

The Foreign Publisher shall publish the work in accordance with the present agreement within two years of the date of the execution of the present agreement. In the event of delays due to causes beyond the control of the Foreign Publisher, the said delay shall be extended for a period not exceeding six months.

5. Distribution:

The Foreign Publisher shall market and distribute the work in a manner and extent to be determined in its sole discretion. The Publisher shall co-operate with the Foreign Publisher in providing all necessary information related to promoting maximum distribution of the published work in translation.

6. Grant To Publish:

The Publisher hereby grants to the Foreign Publisher the exclusive right to publish the work in book form in the French language in France, as well as the subsidiary rights hereinafter mentioned for the whole term of copyright and all subsequent renewals.

7. Delivery:

The Publisher shall deliver a copy of the work to the Foreign Publisher at the execution of this agreement. The Foreign Publisher shall not be obliged to use as the basis of its translation any other version of the work, except that delivered by the Publisher.

8. Warranties:

The Publisher warrants to the Foreign Publisher that:

(1) It has full proprietary rights with respect to the work, and/or has full power to grant and assign the exclusive right to publish the work in French translation in France; the Publisher undertakes to forward proof of such representation to the Foreign Publisher upon demand;

(2) The work is original;

(3) The work has not been previously published in whole or in part in any other form ———— in the French language in France;

(4) The work as presently constituted does not infringe upon any right of ownership under statute or common law;

(5) The work is in no way libellous, obscene or in contravention of any law whatever including criminal, penal and civil law.

9. Indemnification:

The Publisher shall indemnify the Foreign Publisher against any claims, demands, legal proceedings, costs, loss and damages of any nature whatsoever arising from any alleged breach of the warranties or representations of the Publisher herein. The Foreign Publisher may withhold advances upon royalties or other payments due to the Publisher in order to permit the full exercise of the present indemnification provisions. The Foreign Publisher shall furthermore be entitled to retain counsel at its own expense and shall have the exclusive right to settle or compromise any claim, etc., brought against it.

10. Copyright:

The Foreign Publisher shall at its own expense secure formal copyright of the translation of the work in its own name, and the Publisher shall co-operate in permitting the Foreign Publisher to effect such registration as is necessary. Nevertheless, the Publisher shall retain title to the original copyright, which shall not be affected except insofar as the present agreement provides.

11. Proofs:

The Publisher shall not be obliged in any way to review or correct galley and page proofs of the work in translation, or to submit any accessory or supplemental materials to the work including French indexes, outlines, tables of contents or bibliographies.

12. Royalties:

The Foreign Publisher shall pay to the Publisher the following sums in consideration for the rights granted herein:

(1) A non-refundable advance in the amount of $20,000;
(2) 5% of the catalogue retail price of the work on the first 10,000 copies sold;
(3) 6% of the catalogue retail price on all subsequent copies sold;
(4) No royalties shall be payable upon the copies sold at a discount to the Publisher, or upon free copies distributed for the purpose of promoting distribution.

13. Grant Of Subsidiary Rights:

The Publisher hereby grants to the Foreign Publisher the following exclusive rights in the French language only in France: reproduction in the form of reprints, anthologies, condensations, digests, abridgments, book club distribution, serializations, magazine and newspaper syndications, dramatizations, radio, television and film presentations.

14. Royalties For Exercise Of Subsidiary Rights:

The Foreign Publisher shall pay to the Publisher royalties in accordance with the present agreement on all reprints and re-editions. With respect to other subsidiary rights mentioned herein, royalties shall be paid at the rate of fifty percent of net proceeds received by the Foreign Publisher.

15. Notice Of Contract For Subsidiary Rights:

The Foreign Publisher shall notify the Publisher of any negotiations, offers and concluded contracts entered into involving any transfer, sale or licences of the rights herein. In the event that the Publisher is entitled to a portion of the revenues received or envisaged in an amount greater than $100, details of such negotiations, offers and contracts shall be presented to the Publisher upon request at the office of the Foreign Publisher, and the Publisher shall be entitled to obtain copies of all relevant documents at its own expense.

16. Free Copies To Publisher:

The Publisher shall be entitled to ten free copies of the regular edition of the work and to purchase additional copies for personal use at a discount of twenty percent from the catalogue retail sales price.

17. Reprints And Re-Editions:

The Foreign Publisher shall notify the Publisher by registered mail following the date of the depletion of stock of the work whether or not he will undertake to reprint or publish a new edition of the work. In the event that the Foreign Publisher gives affirmative notice, he shall publish the reprint or subsequent edition within six months from the date of the sending of the notice. In the event of a negative notice, or in the absence of any due notice, all rights granted in the present contract by the Publisher to the Foreign Publisher shall revert to the former at the expiry of a period of sixty days following the depletion of stock.

The stock shall not be deemed depleted if copies of the work are on sale at regular retail outlets in a cheaper edition or in any other edition, or if the Foreign Publisher is entitled hereunder or by accessory agreement to delays for publication of the work in any other edition following the depletion of stock.

18. Accounting:

The Foreign Publisher shall provide an account for royalties due to the Publisher in accordance with the present agreement on October 31 of each year, and due payment shall be made unless the sums owing are at the time less than $50 in which case payment shall be postponed until the following year.

19. Termination By Default:

In the event of the default by the Foreign Publisher to deliver annual accounts or to make payments as provided herein within sixty days following written notice by registered mail of such default, the present agreement shall at the option of the Publisher terminate at the expiration of the delay under reserve of the rights of the Publisher to demand any and all sums due and without prejudice to any other recourse available to the Publisher.

20. Rights Upon Termination:

Upon the termination of the present agreement for any cause stipulated herein or available according to law, all rights granted to the Foreign Publisher shall revert to the Publisher for his full enjoyment, possession and use. The Publisher shall be entitled to obtain possession of all manuscripts, documents and other works supplied to the Foreign Publisher and shall have the option to demand possession of the letterpress plates from the Foreign Publisher at their scrap value upon payment of all delivery and transport charges, and free of charge if type has been set in a process not involving metal plates such as offset films. The Publisher shall furthermore have the option to purchase a part or whole of the bound or unbound copies of the work at a cost not exceeding fifty percent of the printing and binding costs. The options granted to the Publisher in the present clause shall expire if not exercised within sixty days of the date of the termination of the present agreement, and the Foreign Publisher shall have the right to sell any remaining copies of the work at any price deemed suitable without payment to the Publisher of royalties.

21. Bankruptcy:

In the event of the filing of a petition in bankruptcy against the Foreign Publisher or the filing of an assignment or proposal in bankruptcy by the Foreign Publisher, or in the event of a judgment declaring the insolvency of the Foreign Publisher by a court, or the appointment of a trustee, receiver or sequestrator of any property of the Foreign Publisher, or in the event the Foreign Publisher shall liquidate or wind up its daily operations for any cause whatsoever, the present agreement shall terminate at the option of the Publisher and such termination shall be effective from the date of the filing of the petition, assignment, proposal, adjudication, appointment, liquidation or winding up. In consideration of the present agreement, the Publisher shall as of right acquire and be seised of all rights granted by the Publisher to the Foreign Publisher prior to termination. The Publisher shall be seised of the right to purchase the plates, bound and unbound copies of the work, although the right to purchase must be exercised not later than sixty days following the notice of the cause of termination herein described.

22. Option On Future Work:

The Publisher hereby grants to the Foreign Publisher the right of first refusal upon one subsequent work written by the author of the work which may constitute a sequel to, continuation or expansion of the work. The Foreign Publisher shall within thirty days of receipt of such subsequent work notify the Publisher of its acceptance or refusal, in default of which notice the Foreign Publisher shall be deemed to have refused to publish the said subsequent work.

23. Assignment:

The present agreement shall be binding upon the assigns, heirs, executors and legal representatives of the Publisher and Foreign Publisher. The Foreign Publisher and Publisher shall not effect any assignment, transfer, sale, lease or other disposal of the rights herein contained save where otherwise stipulated without the written consent of the other. The term "Foreign Publisher" shall include any assignee, subsidiary or successor by reason of sale, consolidation, merger, exchange, continuation or any other re-organization and no such re-organization shall be deemed to involve an assignment of rights necessitating the written consent of the Publisher.

24. Notice:

The requirements of a written notice under the present agreement shall be deemed to have been fulfilled by delivery in person or by the sending by regular mail of the notice to the parties at the addresses hereinbefore mentioned, save in the event of the change of address following due service of notice of change of address by registered mail. The requirement of delivery of notice by registered mail shall be deemed fulfilled on the date mentioned in the postal receipt issued at the time of posting.

25. Waiver:

A waiver of any breach of this agreement or of any of the terms or conditions by the Publisher or Foreign Publisher shall not be deemed a waiver of any continued or subsequent breach or in any way affect any other term of the present agreement; no waiver shall be binding upon the Publisher or Foreign Publisher unless stipulated in writing and signed by the parties.

26. Language Requirement - Province Of Quebec:

The parties expressly require that the present contract be drawn up and executed in the English language. Les parties ont expressément exigé que le présent contrat soit rédigé et exécuté en anglais.

IN WITNESS WHEREOF the parties hereto have duly executed the present agreement on the date first mentioned.

____

Foreign Publisher

____

Publisher

1.7 PUBLICATION IN PAPERBACK VERSION

1. Undertaking to publish;
2. Publication schedule;
3. Delivery of the work;
4. Grant of publication rights;
5. Publisher's warranties;
6. Indemnification;
7. Royalties;
8. Accounting;
9. Notice of publication;
10. Proofs;
11. Competing work;
12. Term of agreement;
13. Termination by default;
14. Bankruptcy;
15. Assignment;
16. Notice;
17. Waiver;
18. Language requirement - Province of Quebec.

Commentary

The following agreement envisages the reprinting of a published work in the form of a paperback. The delays stipulated for publication indicate that the original publisher is given a certain leeway in proceeding with issuance of the hard cover edition prior to paperback publication. Copyright is presumed to remain with the author, and subsidiary rights remain vested in the original publisher. While the grant to publish is in the form of a licence to reprint the entire work in paperback version, the publisher is under a further obligation not to exploit its subsidiary rights in such a way as to cause the issuance of the work in a cheaper edition which will compete with the product of the paperback publisher.

AGREEMENT made this ——— day of ———, 19— at ———.

BETWEEN: XYZ PUBLISHING COMPANY (hereinafter called the "Publisher")

AND: ABC PUBLISHING COMPANY (hereinafter called "Paperback Publisher")

In consideration of the undertakings provided hereunder, the parties to the present Agreement declare:

1. Undertaking To Publish:

The Paperback Publisher shall publish the work entitled ——— ("work") authored by ——— and originally published or to be published in hard cover edition by the Publisher. The work shall be published in paperback version which shall consist of a reprint of the text of the original edition in new type. The paperback version shall contain the entirety of the text of the work as originally published, although the Paperback Publisher may add an introduction, preface or index. The Paperback Publisher shall at his own discretion determine the style and nature of the paperback version and the mode of advertising, promotion and distribution of the same. The Paperback Publisher shall furthermore be entitled to determine the appearance and content of the front and back covers of the work in published form.

2. Publication Schedule:

The Paperback Publisher shall effect publication of the work within one year of the date of the execution of the present agreement, but not earlier than six months therefrom, the whole subject to delays due to causes beyond the control of the Paperback Publisher.

3. Delivery Of The Work:

The Publisher shall forward to the Paperback Publisher within twenty days of the execution of the present agreement ten free copies of the work as originally published.

4. Grant Of Publication Rights:

The Publisher grants to the Paperback Publisher the exclusive right to publish and distribute in ——— the paperback version of the work as originally published in the hard cover edition.

The Paperback Publisher shall be entitled in its sole discretion to determine the retail sales price of the paperback version of the work.

5. Publisher's Warranties:

The Publisher warrants that:

(a) It is authorized, empowered and entitled to grant the rights given herein;
(b) The said rights are not encumbered by any charge, lien or prior agreements;
(c) The Publisher is entitled to receive as principal and/or agent all sums payable in accordance with the provisions of the present agreement;
(d) The work is original;
(e) The work has been published in hard cover edition and does not infringe upon any right of copyright or ownership under statute or common law;
(f) The work is in no way libellous, obscene or in contravention of any law whatever including criminal, penal and civil law.

6. Indemnification:

The Publisher shall indemnify the Paperback Publisher against any claims, damages, actions or judgments, including interest, costs and judicial and extra-judicial fees which may be sustained by or served upon the Paperback Publisher by reason of the publication of the above-mentioned work, whether or not the claim or action is founded or unfounded in law and fact. The Publisher shall pay any settlement deemed advisable by legal counsel subject to the Publisher's right of reasonable refusal. Upon full compensation and indemnification for any claims, damages or actions, as hereinbefore mentioned, the Paperback Publisher shall subrogate the Publisher in all its rights relating to the issues in question.

7. Royalties:

The Paperback Publisher shall pay to the Publisher the following royalties and payments:

(a) The sum of $10,000 to constitute an advance upon royalties upon the sale of the first fifty thousand copies of the published work payable within ten days of the execution of the present agreement;
(b) 10% of the retail sales price of the first one hundred thousand copies sold;
(c) 15% upon all additional copies sold.

8. Accounting:

The Paperback Publisher shall render a statement of account of royalties and payments due hereunder on the last day of February and of October of each year. Nevertheless, the Publisher shall be entitled to receive bi-monthly sales reports upon giving due notice of such request.

9. Notice Of Publication:

The Paperback Publisher undertakes to print in each copy of the paperback version a notice of copyright indicating that the copyright holder is the author of the work, as well as the date of such copyright.

10. Proofs:

The Publisher shall not be entitled to receive galley or page proofs of the work to be printed in the paperback version, or to demand modifications, corrections or additions which do not appear in the work as originally published.

11. Competing Work:

The Paperback Publisher acknowledges that the Publisher is entitled to exploit all subsidiary rights respecting the work including reproduction in the form of abridgment, condensation, selections, or serialization. Nevertheless, the Publisher shall not be entitled during the course of the present agreement to exploit such subsidiary rights in a manner as to publish or allow the publication of the work in the form of a paperback version including anthologies at a retail sales price of less than $3.50.

12. Term Of Agreement:

The term of the present agreement shall be five years from the date of its execution. The agreement shall be automatically renewed for successive periods of one year, unless either party gives notice of termination sixty days prior to the end of such renewal period. Notwithstanding such termination, the Paperback Publisher shall be entitled to continue sales and distribution of all remaining stock on hand at the regular retail sales price.

13. Termination By Default:

In the event of the default by the Paperback Publisher to deliver regular statements of account, or to make payments as provided herein within sixty days following written notice of such default, the present agreement shall at the option of the Publisher terminate at the expiration of the delay under reserve of the right of the Publisher to demand any and all sums due and without prejudice to any other recourse available to the latter.

14. Bankruptcy:

In the event of the filing of a petition in bankruptcy against the Paperback Publisher or the filing of an assignment or proposal in bankruptcy by the Paperback Publisher, or in the event of a judgment declaring the insolvency of the Paperback Publisher by a court, or the appointment of a trustee, receiver or sequestrator of any property of the Paperback Publisher, or in the event the Paperback Publisher shall liquidate or wind up its daily operations for any cause whatsoever, the present agreement shall terminate at the option of the Publisher and such termination shall be effective from the date of the filing of the petition, assignment, proposal, adjudication, appointment, liquidation or winding up. In consideration of the present agreement, the Publisher shall as of right acquire and be seised of all rights granted by the Publisher to the Paperback Publisher prior to termination. The Publisher shall be seised of the right to purchase the plates, bound and unbound copies of the work, although the right to purchase must be exercised not later than sixty days following the notice of the cause of termination herein described.

15. Assignment:

The present agreement shall be binding upon the assigns, heirs, executors and legal representatives of the Publisher and Paperback Publisher. The Paperback Publisher and Publisher shall not effect any assignment, transfer, sale, lease or other disposal of the rights herein contained save where otherwise stipulated without the written consent of the other. The term "Paperback Publisher" shall include any assignee, subsidiary or successor by reason of sale, consolidation, merger, exchange, continuation or any other re-organization and no such re-organization shall be deemed to involve an assignment of rights necessitating the written consent of the Publisher.

16. Notice:

The requirements of a written notice under the present agreement shall be deemed to have been fulfilled by delivery in person or by the sending by regular mail of the notice to the parties at the addresses hereinbefore mentioned, save in the event of the change of address following due service of notice of change of address by registered mail. The requirement of delivery of notice by registered mail shall be deemed fulfilled on the date mentioned in the postal receipt issued at the time of posting.

17. Waiver:

A waiver of any breach of this agreement or of any of the terms or conditions by the Publisher or Paperback Publisher shall not be deemed a waiver of any continued or subsequent breach or in any way affect any other term of the present agreement; no waiver shall be binding upon the Publisher or Paperback Publisher unless stipulated in writing and signed by the parties.

18. Language Requirement - Province Of Quebec:

The parties expressly require that the present contract be drawn up and executed in the English language. Les parties ont expressément exigé que le présent contrat soit rédigé et exécuté en anglais.

IN WITNESS WHEREOF the parties hereto have duly executed the present agreement on the date first mentioned.

____
Publisher

____
Paperback Publisher

1.8 ANTHOLOGY-PUBLISHER AGREEMENT

1. Undertaking to publish;
2. Publication schedule;
3. Delivery of selection;
4. Grant of publication rights;
5. Publisher's warranties;
6. Alterations;
7. Royalties;
8. Free copies;
9. Credits;
10. Proofs;
11. Assignment;
12. Notice;
13. Waiver;
14. Language requirement - Province of Quebec.

AGREEMENT made this ______ day of ______, 19— at ______.

BETWEEN:	XYZ PUBLISHING COMPANY (hereinafter called the "Publisher")
AND:	ABC PUBLISHING COMPANY (hereinafter called the "Anthologizer")

In consideration of the undertakings provided hereunder, the parties to the present agreement declare:

1. Undertaking To Publish:

The Anthologizer shall publish a work entitled ——— ("Anthology") in book form in the style, manner and condition more fully set out hereunder.

2. Publication Schedule:

The Anthologizer shall effect publication of the work within a period of twelve months from the date of the execution of the present agreement.

3. Delivery Of Selection:

The Anthologizer acknowledges receipt of the work written by ———. The Anthologizer further acknowledges that the text is complete for the purposes of inclusion in the anthology.

4. Grant Of Publication Rights:

The Publisher hereby grants to the Anthologizer the exclusive right to publish the work in anthology form in the English language, in a hard cover edition upon the following conditions:

(a) The anthology contains a table of contents and introduction which makes mention of the work;
(b) The other selections in the anthology shall consist of fictional works by known authors;
(c) The present grant shall not apply to reprints, re-editions or reproduction in cheaper editions.

5. Publisher's Warranties:

The Publisher warrants to the Anthologizer that he has full proprietary rights with respect to the work of the Author and has full power and capacity to grant the rights contained herein; that the work has not been previously published in whole or in part, save in the form of a book published by the Publisher; that the work as presently constituted does not infringe upon any right of ownership under statute or common law; and the work is in no way libellous, obscene or in contravention of any law whatever including criminal, penal and civil law.

The Publisher undertakes to indemnify the Anthologizer against any claims, damages, actions or judgments, including interest, costs and judicial and extra-judicial fees which may be sustained by or served upon the Anthologizer by reason of the publication in anthology form of the work.

6. Alterations:

The Anthologizer shall publish the selection of the work as appears from the text furnished by the Publisher with these presents. The Anthologizer shall not in any way amend or alter the text without written consent of the Publisher.

7. Royalties:

The Anthologizer shall pay to the Publisher the sum of $——— payable within thirty days following publication of the anthology. The sum paid is based on the amount of words contained in the selection and is comparable to the payment made to contributors of other selections to appear in the anthology.

8. Free Copies:

The Anthologizer shall deliver to the Publisher ten free copies of the anthology within thirty days following publication and shall furnish to the author ten free copies to be delivered through the offices of the Publisher.

9. Credits:

The Anthologizer shall print in the introductory pages of the anthology an inscription noting that the selection has been taken from a work published in book form by the Publisher and stipulate the title of the book, the date and holder of the copyright, and that the selection is included in the anthology by permission of the Publisher.

10. Proofs:

The Publisher shall not be entitled to review galley or page proofs prior to the publication of the anthology.

11. Assignment:

The present agreement shall be binding upon the assigns, heirs, executors and legal representatives of the Publisher and the Anthologizer. The Anthologizer and the Publisher shall not effect any assignment, transfer, sale, lease or other disposal of the rights herein contained save where otherwise stipulated without the written consent of the other. The term "Anthologizer" shall include any assignee, subsidiary or successor by reason of sale, consolidation, merger, exchange, continuation or any other re-organization and no such re-organization shall be deemed to involve an assignment of rights necessitating the written consent of the Publisher.

12. Notice:

The requirements of a written notice under the present agreement shall be deemed to have been fulfilled by delivery in person or by the sending by regular mail of the notice to the parties at the addresses hereinbefore mentioned, save in the event of the change of address following due service of notice of change of address by registered mail. The requirement of delivery of notice by registered mail shall be deemed fulfilled on the date mentioned in the postal receipt issued at the time of posting.

13. Waiver:

A waiver of any breach of this agreement or of any of the terms or conditions by the Publisher or Anthologizer shall not be deemed a waiver of any continued or subsequent breach or in any way affect any other term of the present agreement; no waiver shall be binding upon the Publisher or Anthologizer unless stipulated in writing and signed by the parties.

14. Language Requirement - Province Of Quebec:

The parties expressly require that the present contract be drawn up and executed in the English language. Les parties ont expressément exigé que le présent contrat soit rédigé et exécuté en anglais.

IN WITNESS WHEREOF the parties hereto have duly executed the present agreement on the date first mentioned.

____

Publisher

____

Anthologizer

2. PUBLICATION WITH AUTHOR'S SUBSIDY (NO ROYALTIES)

1. Undertaking to publish;
2. Publication schedule;
3. Cost of publication;
4. Mode of payment;
5. Delivery of manuscript;
6. Printing of the work;
7. Grant of publication right;
8. Author's warranties;

9. Indemnification;
10. Copyright;
11. Publication assistance;
12. Proofs;
13. Publisher's revenues;
14. Author's copies;
15. Recovery of author's costs;
16. Storage;
17. Re-editions and subsidiary revenues;
18. Bankruptcy;
19. Assignment;
20. Notice;
21. Waiver;
22. Language requirement - Province of Quebec.

Commentary

The following agreement envisages a scheme of payment by the author to the publisher of a part or entirety of the cost of publishing the work. The role of the publisher is reduced to that of a printer with a limited function as distributor. The risks of publication reside mainly in the author who is entitled to retain all profits upon sales made by him on copies of the work, and a portion of profits upon sales made through the offices of the publisher. Copyright remains under the control of the author and the grant to publish made to the publisher does not extend to subsidiary rights.

In practice, promotion, marketing and distribution of the work in this type of vanity publishing scheme remain entirely with the author who after a period stipulated in the following agreement to be two years assumes storage costs for the inventory. Nevertheless, in the event that the book is successful in the market place, the publisher is entitled to issue subsequent editions subject to the payment of royalties thereby assuming the functions of standard commercial publishers.

AGREEMENT made this ——— day of ———, 19— at ———.

BETWEEN:	XYZ PUBLISHING COMPANY (hereinafter called the "Publisher")
AND:	MR. JOHN SMITH (hereinafter called the "Author")

In consideration of the undertakings provided hereunder, the parties to the present Agreement declare:

1. Undertaking To Publish:

The Publisher shall publish a work entitled ———— ("work") in book form in the style, manner and conditions more fully set out hereunder;

2. Publication Schedule:

The Publisher shall effect publication of the work within a period of twelve months following the delivery of the completed manuscript of the work, subject to delays beyond the control of the Publisher. The Publisher shall be deemed to have fully publicized, advertised and distributed the work by listing the title and retail sales price of the work in its annual catalogue, distributing the said catalogue to at least one hundred retail book outlets and delivering copies to purchasers in response to written purchase orders.

3. Cost Of Publication:

The Author shall pay to the Publisher the sum of $———— (or ————% of the total cost of publication of the work), including the cost of typesetting, printing, proofreading, copy editing, cover and typographic design, collating, binding and delivery. For purposes of accounting, the Author retains full rights of inspection and inquiry with respect to invoices received for services rendered and/or copies of cheques paid by the Publisher for services rendered.

4. Mode Of Payment:

The Author shall pay to the Publisher the sum of $———— (or ————% of the said total cost) in the following manner:

(a) 33% upon the execution of these presents;
(b) 33% upon delivery of the proofs;
(c) The balance upon delivery, by the Publisher to the Author or his designated agent, of 100 complimentary copies of the printed work in book form.

5. Delivery Of Manuscript:

The Author shall deliver to the Publisher a complete and legible copy of the manuscript ready for print on or before the ———— day of ————, 19—. In the event of the default of the Author to deliver, the Publisher may terminate the present Agreement by notice in writing sent by registered mail to the Author at his above-mentioned address and the date of the said notice shall be determined by the date of posting of the notice. Following a delay of one month from the date of the notice, the Publisher may institute all claims and proceedings against the Author in order to receive, as liquidated damages, 20% of the total contribution of the Author, or of the total publication cost, or the sum of $1,000, whichever is the greater.

6. Printing Of The Work:

The Publisher shall print the work in the following edition:
(a) 2,000 copies hard-bound gold-stamped, blue-red-white colour dust jacket;
(b) the book shall contain 200 pages printed on ——— paper stock in ten point ——— type.

7. Grant Of Publication Right:

The Author hereby grants to the Publisher the right to publish the work in book form.

8. Author's Warranties:

The Author warrants to the Publisher that he has full proprietary rights with respect to the manuscript and work in that he is the sole Author and/or has full power to grant and assign the exclusive right to publish; that the work is original; that the work has not been previously published in whole or in part in any other form or size whatever; that the work as presently constituted does not infringe upon any right of ownership under statute or common law; and that the work is in no way libellous, obscene or in contravention of any law whatever including criminal, penal and civil law.

9. Indemnification:

The Author shall indemnify the Publisher against any claims, damages, actions or judgments, including interest, costs and judicial and extra-judicial fees which may be sustained by or served upon the Publisher by reason of the publication of the above-mentioned work, whether or not the claim or action is founded or unfounded in law and fact. The Author shall pay any settlement deemed advisable by legal counsel subject to the Author's right of reasonable refusal. Upon full compensation and indemnification for any claims, damages or actions, as hereinbefore mentioned, the Publisher shall subrogate the Author in all its rights relating to the issues in question

10. Copyright:

The Publisher undertakes at its own expense to secure formal copyright of the work in the name of the Author and to print notice of the same in each copy of the published work. All rights of copyright, including subsidiary rights, shall remain with the Author, subject to the present Agreement.

11. Publication Assistance:

The Publisher shall assist the Author in determining the nature, quality and form of drawings, photographs, covers and other editorial matters upon request at a cost to be mutually agreed upon.

12. Proofs:

The Author upon request, shall be entitled to receive galley and page proofs of the work, which shall conform to the completed manuscript as submitted by the Author without modification whatsoever, unless with the consent of the latter. Where the Author does request the furnishing of proofs, the author shall return such proofs to the Publisher with corrections legibly inserted within one week of the receipt thereof. Where the Author has inserted modifications which are not of the nature of simple correction of printer's errors, the Author shall bear the costs of modifications which shall form a charge additional to costs of publication aforementioned.

13. Publisher's Revenues:

The Publisher shall be entitled to ———% of the catalogue price upon sales made through its offices. The catalogue price of the work shall be $———.

14. Author's Copies:

The Author shall be entitled to 500 free copies, and any further amount of copies at a discount of 50% of the catalogue price. Following the expiry of two years from the date of publication, the Author shall be entitled to take possession free of charge of any unsold copies of the first edition of the work.

15. Recovery Of Author's Costs:

Nothing in the present Agreement shall have the effect of creating a representation or warranty by the Publisher to the Author to the effect that the latter shall recoup all or any portion of his contribution to costs of publication through sales of the work or subsidiary rights;

16. Storage:

The Publisher shall "storage and warehouse" the complete or partial run of the work for a period of two years following publication date at the full expense of the Publisher. At the expiry of such period, the Publisher shall continue to "storage and warehouse" the complete or partial run of the published work at the expense of the Author, subject to notice to the contrary. The cost of storage and warehousing shall not exceed comparable commercial storage rates current at the expiry of the period mentioned.

17. Re-Editions and Subsidiary Revenues:

The Publisher shall be entitled to issue second and subsequent editions following depletion of stock, at its own expense, subject to the payment of royalties of 15% of the catalogue price to the Author on all copies sold.

The Publisher shall be entitled to publicize and distribute the second and subsequent editions in any manner it deems best. The Publisher shall furthermore be entitled to ———% of all revenues received by the Author for the disposal of subsidiary rights effected within twelve months of the date of publication of the first edition.

18. Bankruptcy:

In the event of the filing of a petition in bankruptcy against the Publisher or the filing of an assignment or proposal in bankruptcy by the Publisher, or in the event of a judgment declaring the insolvency of the Publisher by a court, or the appointment of a trustee, receiver or sequestrator of any property of the Publisher, or in the event the Publisher shall liquidate or wind up its daily operations for any cause whatsoever, the present agreement shall terminate at the option of the Author and such termination shall be effective from the date of the filing of the petition, assignment, proposal, adjudication, appointment, liquidation or winding up. In consideration of the present Agreement, the Author shall as of right acquire and be seised of all rights granted by the Author to the Publisher prior to termination. The Author shall be seised of the right to purchase the plates, bound and unbound copies of the work, although the right to purchase must be exercised not later than sixty days following the notice of the cause of termination herein described.

19. Assignment:

The present Agreement shall be binding upon the assigns, heirs, executors and legal representatives of the Author and Publisher. The Publisher and Author shall not effect any assignment, transfer, sale, lease or other disposal of the rights herein contained save where otherwise stipulated without the written consent of the other. The term "Publisher" shall include any assignee, subsidiary or successor by reason of sale, consolidation, merger, exchange, continuation or any other re-organization and no such re-organization shall be deemed to involve an assignment of rights necessitating the written consent of the Author.

20. Notice:

The requirements of a written notice under the present Agreement shall be deemed to have been fulfilled by delivery in person or by the sending by regular mail of the notice to the parties at the addresses hereinbefore mentioned, save in the event of the change of address following due service of notice of change of address by registered mail. The requirement of delivery of notice by registered mail shall be deemed fulfilled on the date mentioned in the postal receipt issued at the time of posting.

21. Waiver:

A waiver of any breach of this Agreement or of any of the terms or conditions by the Author or Publisher shall not be deemed a waiver of any continued or subsequent breach or in any way affect any other term of the present Agreement; no waiver shall be binding upon the Author or Publisher unless stipulated in writing and signed by the parties.

22. Language Requirement - Province of Quebec:

The parties expressly require that the present contract be drawn up and executed in the English language. Les parties ont expressément exigé que le présent contrat soit rédigé et exécuté en anglais.

IN WITNESS WHEREOF the parties hereto have duly executed the present Agreement on the date first mentioned.

____

Publisher

____

Author

2.1 PUBLICATION WITH AUTHOR'S SUBSIDY AND ROYALTIES

1. Undertaking to publish;
2. Publication schedule;
3. Cost of publication;
4. Mode of payment;
5. Delivery of manuscript;
6. Delivery of drawings;
7. Grant of publication rights;
8. Author's warranties;

9. Indemnification;
10. Copyright;
11. Publication assistance;
12. Proofs;
13. Royalties;
14. Limitation of royalties;
15. Recovery of author's costs;
16. Subsidiary rights;
17. Publisher's right to deal;
18. Notice of contracts for subsidiary rights;
19. Free copies to author;
20. Reprints and re-editions;
21. Termination by default;
22. Rights upon termination;
23. Bankruptcy;
24. Assignment;
25. Notice;
26. Waiver;
27. Option to publish subsequent work;
28. Language requirement - Province of Quebec.

Commentary

The following agreement does not constitute a partnership or joint venture agreement between the parties. The form of the basic author-publisher agreement has been followed with various modifications to take into account the author's obligation to contribute to the costs of the publication. The agreement obliges the author to contribute to the costs of typesetting, printing, proofreading and issuance of the work in published form, but permits him the opportunity to recoup part or all of his contribution to publication by way of royalties upon actual sales. The scheme of the agreement is designed to create an incentive to the author to subsidize the publisher. Depending on the amount of the contribution to costs by the publisher, the agreement may potentially pose a risk-free printing venture for the Publisher with an unlimited potential for profit in the rare event of success of the work in the market place. While leaving copyright nominally under the control of the author, the contract generously accords the publisher rights to participate in profits arising from the exploitation of all subsidiary rights, and to deal with the work for maximum exploitation. For evident reasons, the contract stipulates that no representation or warranty is made by the publisher to the author stipulating that the latter shall obtain a return upon his investment through sales of the work or of subsidiary rights to the work. It is further to be noted that the obligation to distribute and promote the work remains ambiguous or undefined.

AGREEMENT made this ——— day of ———, 19— at ———.

BETWEEN: XYZ PUBLISHING COMPANY
(hereinafter called the "Publisher")

AND: MR. JOHN SMITH
(hereinafter called the "Author")

In consideration of the undertakings provided hereunder, the parties to the present Agreement declare:

1. Undertaking To Publish:

The Publisher shall publish a work entitled ——— ("work") in book form in the style, manner and conditions more fully set out hereunder.

2. Publication Schedule:

The Publisher shall effect publication of the work within a period of twelve months following the delivery of the completed work, subject to delays due to causes beyond the control of the Publisher.

3. Cost of Publication:

The author shall pay to the Publisher the sum of $——— (or ———% of the total cost of publication of the work), including the cost of typesetting, printing, proofreading, copy editing, cover and typographic design, collating, binding and delivery. For purposes of accounting, the Author retains full rights of inspection and inquiry with respect to invoices received for services rendered and/or copies of cheques paid by the Publisher for services rendered.

4. Mode of Payment:

The Author shall pay to the Publisher the sum of $——— (or ———% of the said total cost) in the following manner:

(a) 33% upon the execution of these presents;
(b) 33% upon delivery of the proofs;
(c) The balance upon delivery, by the publisher to the Author or his designated agent, of twenty complimentary copies of the printed work in book form.

5. Delivery Of Manuscript:

The Author shall deliver to the Publisher a complete and legible copy of the manuscript ready for print on or before the ——— day of ———, 19—. In the event of the default of the Author to deliver, the Publisher may terminate the present Agreement by notice in writing sent by registered mail to the Author at his above-mentioned address and the date of the said notice shall be determined by the date of posting of the notice. Following a delay of one month from the date of the notice, the Publisher may institute all claims and proceedings against the Author in order to receive, as liquidated damages, 20% of the total contribution of the Author, or of the total publication cost, or the sum of $1,000, whichever is the greater.

6. Delivery Of Drawings, Etc.:

The Author shall forward to the Publisher within the same delays all drawings, charts, graphics, maps, photographs and tables, including an index and bibliography in order to complete the manuscript. In the event of the default of the Author to provide the above-mentioned supplements to the work, the Publisher may undertake to supply the said work at the full expense of the Author.

7. Grant Of Publication Rights:

The Author hereby grants to the Publisher the exclusive right to publish the work in book form in North America.

8. Author's Warranties:

The Author warrants to the Publisher that he has full proprietary rights with respect to the manuscript and work in that he is the sole Author and/or has full power to grant and assign the exclusive right to publish; that the work is original; that the work has not been previously published in whole or in part in any other form or size whatever; that the work as presently constituted does not infringe upon any right of ownership under statute or common law; and that the work is in no way libellous, obscene or in contravention of any law whatever including criminal, penal and civil law.

9. Indemnification:

The Author shall indemnify the Publisher against any claims, damages, actions or judgments, including interest, costs and judicial and extra-judicial fees which may be sustained by or served upon the Publisher by reason of the publication of the above-mentioned work, whether or not the claim or action is founded or unfounded in law and fact. The Author shall pay any settlement deemed advisable by legal counsel subject to the Author's right of reasonable refusal. Upon full compensation and indemnification for any claims, damages or actions, as hereinbefore mentioned, the Publisher shall subrogate the Author in all its rights relating to the issues in question.

10. Copyright:

The Publisher undertakes, at its own expense, to secure formal copyright of the work in the name of the Author and to print notice of copyright in each copy of the published work. In the event that the work contains portions whose copyright is subject to the rights of third parties, the Author shall, at his own expense, secure from such third parties written permission to publish such inclusion in the work and for all subsequent editions, re-prints and subsidiary rights. The Publisher reserves the right to demand receipt and delivery of such permission prior to the date of the commencement of printing of the work.

11. Publication Assistance:

The Author shall be entitled to assist the Publisher in determining the nature, quality and form of drawings, photographs, covers and all other supplements required for the publication of the work, subject to the right of the Publisher to make all final decisions. In the event the Author dissents from the Publisher's decision respecting the inclusion or form of any of the supplements, the Publisher may proceed with publication of the supplement at its own expense. Notice of such dissent shall be submitted to the Publisher in writing by registered mail and shall be deemed to be dated on the date of posting.

12. Proofs:

The Author upon request, shall be entitled to receive galley and page proofs of the work, which shall conform to the completed manuscript as submitted by the Author without modification whatsoever, unless with the consent of the latter. Where the Author does request the furnishing of proofs, the Author shall return such proofs to the Publisher with corrections legibly inserted within one week of the receipt thereof. Where the Author has inserted modifications which are not of the nature of simple correction of printer's errors, the Author shall bear the costs of modifications which shall form a charge additional to costs of publication mentioned above.

13. Royalties:

The Publisher shall remit to the Author a statement of royalties payable in the amount of 10% of the retail price of the work up to 10,000 copies sold and

12% of the retail price in excess of 10,000 copies sold. Royalty statements shall be furnished and remitted to the Author on an annual basis.

14. Limitation Of Royalties:

No royalties shall be paid with respect to copies of the work distributed on a gratuitous basis to the Author or to third parties for purposes of evaluation, review or marketing. The Publisher retains the right to set up a reserve for returns of the work in the amount of 15% of the royalties due to the Author during the period of the first year following publication.

15. Recovery Of Author's Costs:

Nothing in the present Agreement shall have the effect of creating a representation or warranty by the Publisher to the Author to the effect that the latter shall recoup all or any portion of his contribution to costs of publication through sales of the work or subsidiary rights.

16. Subsidiary Rights:

The Publisher shall pay the Author:

(a) 50% of the net revenues received by the Publisher from the following items:
- (aa) subsequent re-prints;
- (bb) anthologies;
- (cc) condensations, digests and abridgements;
- (dd) book club rights;
- (ee) serializations, magazine and newspaper syndications, film rights;
- (ff) recordings on tape and record;
- (gg) dramatic versions, including stage, film, television and radio;
- (hh) and any other type or means of reproduction whatsoever;

(b) 50% of the net revenues received by the Publisher for license of the work for translation and publication in any other language in any other country under any imprint other than that of the Publisher;

(c) 15% of the revenues received by the Publisher for bound or unbound copies sold to clubs and consumers, including book clubs, and export, but only in the event that sales of such copies are made at a discount of 50% or more from the retail price as set out herein;

(d) 7 1/2% of net revenues received by the Publisher where copies of the work are sold as "remainders" at discounts of more than 50% of the retail price.

17. Publisher's Right To Deal:

The Publisher shall maintain the exclusive right to assign, transfer, sell, lease or otherwise dispose of all subsidiary rights in the work on behalf of the Author, including the right to sell copies of the work as remainders and to otherwise promote the work with respect to its revenue producing qualities. The Author shall not in any manner whatsoever interfere with the absolute right of the Publisher to so dispose of the rights in the work, but shall in the event of such interference, indemnify the Publisher for any loss or damages incurred as a consequence of the Author's acts.

18. Notice Of Contracts For Subsidiary Rights:

The Publisher shall notify the Author of any negotiations, offers and concluded contracts entered into involving any transfer, sale or licensing of the rights herein in the event that the Author is entitled to a portion of the revenues received or envisaged in an amount greater than $100. Details of such negotiations, offers and contracts shall be presented to the Author upon request at the office of the Publisher and the Author shall be entitled to obtain copies of all relevant documents at his own expense.

19. Free Copies To Author:

The Author shall be entitled to twenty free copies of the regular edition of the work and to purchase additional copies to the extent of 300 for his personal use at a discount of 50% from the retail price.

20. Reprints And Re-Editions:

The Publisher shall notify the Author by registered mail following the date of the depletion of stock of the work whether or not he will undertake to reprint or publish a new edition of the work. In the event that the Publisher gives affirmative notice, he shall publish the reprint or subsequent edition within six months from the date of the sending of the notice. In the event of a negative notice, or in the absence of any due notice, all rights granted in the present contract by the Author to the Publisher shall revert to the former at the expiry of a period of sixty days following the depletion of stock.

The stock shall not be deemed depleted if copies of the work are on sale at regular retail outlets in a cheaper edition or in any other edition, or if the Publisher is entitled hereunder or by accessory agreement to delays for publication of the work in any other edition following the depletion of stock.

21. Termination By Default:

In the event of the default by the Publisher to deliver annual statements of account, or to make payment as provided herein within sixty days following written notice by registered mail of such default, the present agreement shall at the option of the Author terminate at the expiration of the delay under reserve of the rights of the Author to demand any and all sums due, and without prejudice to any other recourse available to the Author.

22. Rights Upon Termination:

Upon the termination of the present Agreement for any cause stipulated herein or available according to law, all rights granted to the Publisher shall revert to the Author for his full enjoyment, possession and use. The Author shall be entitled to obtain possession of all manuscripts, documents and other works supplied to the Publisher and shall have the option to demand possession of the letterpress plates from the Publisher at their scrap value upon payment of all delivery and transport charges, and free of charge if type has been set in a process not involving metal plates such as offset films. The Author shall furthermore have the option to purchase a part or whole of the bound or unbound copies of the work at a cost not exceeding 50% of the printing and binding costs. The options granted to the Author in the present clause shall expire if not exercised within sixty days of the date of the termination of the present Agreement, and the Publisher shall have the right to sell any remaining copies of the work at any price deemed suitable without payment to the Author of royalties.

23. Bankruptcy:

In the event of the filing of a petition in bankruptcy against the Publisher or the filing of an assignment or proposal in bankruptcy by the Publisher, or in the event of a judgment declaring the insolvency of the Publisher by a court, or the appointment of a trustee, receiver or sequestrator of any property of the Publisher, or in the event the Publisher shall liquidate or wind up its daily operations for any cause whatsoever, the present Agreement shall terminate at the option of the Author and such termination shall be effective from the date of the filing of the petition, assignment, proposal, adjudication, appointment, liquidation or winding up. In consideration of the present Agreement, the Author shall as of right acquire and be seised of all rights granted by the Author to the Publisher prior to termination. The Author shall be seised of the right to purchase the plates, bound and unbound copies of the work, although the right to purchase must be exercised not later than sixty days following the notice of the cause of termination herein described.

24. Assignment:

The present Agreement shall be binding upon the assigns, heirs, executors and legal representatives of the Author and Publisher. The Publisher and Author shall not effect any assignment, transfer, sale, lease or other disposal of the rights herein contained save where otherwise stipulated without the written consent of the other. The term "Publisher" shall include any assignee, subsidiary or successor by reason of sale, consolidation, merger, exchange, continuation or any other re-organization and no such re-organization shall be deemed to involve an assignment of rights necessitating the written consent of the Author.

25. Notice:

The requirements of a written notice under the present Agreement shall be deemed to have been fulfilled by delivery in person or by the sending by regular mail of the notice to the parties at the addresses hereinbefore mentioned, save in the event of the change of address following due service of notice of change of address by registered mail. The requirement of delivery of notice by registered mail shall be deemed fulfilled on the date mentioned in the postal receipt issued at the time of posting.

26. Waiver:

A waiver of any breach of this Agreement or of any of the terms or conditions by the Author or Publisher shall not be deemed a waiver of any continued or subsequent breach or in any way affect any other term of the present Agreement; no waiver shall be binding upon the Author or Publisher unless stipulated in writing and signed by the parties.

27. Option To Publish Subsequent Work:

The Publisher shall have the option to publish the subsequent work of the Author if substantially written within three years following the date of the present Agreement. Such option shall include the right of the Publisher to first reading, evaluation and priority of publication. The terms of publication envisaged under the present option shall be subject to mutual agreement.

28. Language Requirement - Province of Quebec:

The parties expressly require that the present contract be drawn up and executed in the English language. Les parties ont expressément exigé que le présent contrat soit rédigé et exécuté en anglais.

IN WITNESS WHEREOF the parties hereto have duly executed the present Agreement on the date first mentioned.

____

Publisher

____

Author

3. EXCLUSIVE AUTHOR - LITERARY AGENT AGREEMENT

1. Agency;
2. Author's duties;
3. Author's warranties;
4. Duties;
5. Prior consent;
6. Arbitration;
7. Commission;
8. Waiver;
9. Notice;
10. Death;
11. Language requirement - Province of Quebec.

Commentary

The purpose of the following agreement is to confer an exclusive agency for the benefit of the author to permit the full exploitation of the work. In many cases, the author himself acts as his own agent in attempting to solicit offers of publication for licence of subsidiary rights from third parties. As well, publishers of the original edition of the work are often conferred an agency to negotiate and contract on behalf of the author for the exploitation of subsidiary rights in the work. The literary agent is recognized in the following agreement as independent, and as the representative of other authors who may have entrusted him with competing works. Remuneration to the agent is by way of commission following actual receipt of sums by the author upon a contract for the exploitation of the work.

AGREEMENT made this ——— day of ———, 19— at ———.

BETWEEN: XYZ AGENCY LTD.
(hereinafter called "Agent")

AND: MR. JOHN SMITH
(hereinafter called "Author")

In consideration of the undertakings provided hereunder, the parties to the present Agreement declare:

1. Agency:

The Author by these presents constitutes the Agent as his sole and exclusive literary agent, for the period of ——— months respecting the transfer, lease or sale of rights of the Author for use in North America ("rights") in a work entitled ———— ("work") (or all works authored by the Author and not published as of the present date).

2. Author's Duties:

The Author shall not enter into any contract respecting the rights during the course of the present Agreement, save through the intervention of the Agent. The Author shall notify the Agent of all offers received and negotiations initiated and shall involve the Agent at an introductory stage, in all discussions with third parties respecting the rights. The Author shall accept all reasonable offers to transfer, lease or purchase the rights submitted by the Agent.

3. Author's Warranties:

The Author warrants to the Agent that he has full proprietary rights with respect to the manuscript and work in that he is the sole Author and/or has full power to grant and assign the exclusive right to publish; that the work is original; that the work has not been previously published in whole or in part in any other form whatever; that the work as presently constituted does not infringe upon any right of ownership under statute or common law; and that the work is in no way libellous, obscene or in contravention of any law whatever, including criminal, penal and civil law.

4. Duties:

The Agent shall negotiate the transfer, lease or sale of rights for the benefit and best advantage of the Author, and avoid situations involving conflict of interest in his own regard and those of his other principals; however, the Author recognizes that the Agent acts and may act on behalf of other authors whose works are of a competitive nature and that the Agent shall be at liberty to represent those other authors in negotiations to the exclusion of the Author.

5. Prior Consent:

The Agent shall not commit the Author to any obligations with a third party without having first submitted to the Author a full explanation and review of prospective contracts and received his written consent thereto.

6. Arbitration:

In the event of a dispute between the parties as to the reasonableness of any offer, the dispute shall be submitted to arbitration before any person whom the parties may deem fit and the decision of such person shall be final and binding.

7. Commission:

The Author shall pay to the Agent a commission of ten percent of all sums received by the Author under any contract for the rights negotiated pursuant to and during the course of the present Agreement, provided that the contract is executed within one year following termination. The foregoing shall not apply to any sums received or arising from contracts executed by a private company with which the Author does not deal at arm's length.

8. Waiver:

A waiver of any breach of this Agreement or of any of the terms or conditions by the Author or Agent shall not be deemed a waiver of any continued or subsequent breach or in any way affect any other term of the present Agreement; no waiver shall be binding upon the Author or Agent unless stipulated in writing and signed by the parties.

9. Notice:

The requirements of a written notice under the present Agreement shall be deemed to have been fulfilled by delivery in person or by the sending by regular mail of the notice to the parties at the addresses hereinbefore mentioned, save in the event of the change of address following due service of notice of change of address by registered mail. The requirement of delivery of notice by registered mail shall be deemed fulfilled on the date mentioned in the postal receipt issued at the time of posting.

10. Death:

The present Agreement shall enure to the benefit of and oblige the heirs, executors and administrators of the present parties.

11. Language Requirement - Province of Quebec:

The parties expressly require that the present contract be drawn up and executed in the English language. Les parties ont expréssement exigé que le présent contrat soit rédigé et exécuté en anglais.

IN WITNESS WHEREOF the parties hereto have duly executed the present Agreement on the date first mentioned.

____

Agent

____

Author

4. PUBLISHER-DISTRIBUTORSHIP AGREEMENT

1. Appointment of distributor;
2. Undertaking by the distributor;
3. Sales to the distributor;
4. Terms of payment;
5. Referrals;
6. Title to books;
7. Free copies;
8. Copyright;
9. Competing works;
10. Returns;
11. Term of contract;
12. Imprimatur;
13. Assignment;
14. Notice;
15. Waiver;
16. Language requirement - Province of Quebec.

Commentary

The following agreement envisages a conferral of exclusive distributorship upon a third party by the publisher. The agreement is, of course, unnecessary where the publisher has its own staff and facilities for distribution such as a mail order department and mailing lists of retail customers. Seeing that the obligation to distribute assumed by the publisher to the author is to be vicariously performed through the distributor, the contract imposes upon the distributor the duty to effect all necessary advertising and market contacts in order to provide adequate exposure of the published work to the public. Although the distributor is merely under the obligation to distribute only those works in book form which he has requested, it is in the latter's interest to demonstrate to the publisher his interest in promoting and distributing as many works as possible in order to prevent the lapse of the agreement at the end of the term stipulated. The distributor furthermore has a business interest in being closely identified with the publisher and to this end, requires that his name be imprinted in the book. Although the distributorship conferred is exclusive, this is not to say that the distributor is not entitled to carry only one publisher. Nevertheless, the distributor who represents more than one publisher may in certain circumstances find it difficult to please all of his principals at the same time, especially where the distribution of competing works is involved.

AGREEMENT made this ——— day of ———, 19— at ———.

BETWEEN:	XYZ PUBLISHING COMPANY (hereinafter called the "Publisher")
AND:	MR. JOHN SMITH (hereinafter called the "Distributor")

In consideration of the undertakings provided hereunder, the parties to the present Agreement declare:

1. Appointment Of Distributor:

The Publisher hereby constitutes the Distributor as his sole and exclusive distributor in ——— of all works in book form published by the Publisher with the exception of those works in translation where the original text has been initially published by a third party publisher.

2. Undertaking By The Distributor:

The Distributor accepts the present appointment and shall maintain for the due execution of the distributorship adequate staff and facilities. The Distributor shall market and sell the works in book form of the Publisher and to this end, shall effect all necessary advertising, circulate folders or catalogues, maintain continual communication with wholesalers and retail outlets, maintain an adequate inventory of the work in book form and fill all orders as placed.

3. Sales To The Distributor:

The Publisher shall sell to the Distributor all works in book form which the latter has requested. Responsibility for payment of shipping costs, fees, duties and other surcharges shall be at the entire expense of the Distributor.

4. Terms Of Payment:

The Distributor shall pay to the Publisher the catalogue retail sales price minus a discount of 50%, which sum shall be payable in American currency within one month of the receipt of delivery of stock. Alternate forms of payment, credit extension and financing arrangements are available upon discussion and mutual consent of the parties.

5. Referrals:

The Publisher shall direct all requests for orders or information concerning stock to the Distributor.

6. Title To Books:

The Distributor shall become owner of all copies of the work in book form requested from the Publisher upon delivery of the same.

7. Free Copies:

The Publisher shall give to the Distributor ten free copies of the work as well as twenty copies of each folder or poster concerning the work for the purposes of advertising and marketing. The Distributor shall in no way alter or make any material changes in the advertising material or copies of the work.

8. Copyright:

The Distributor shall take all necessary steps to avoid infringing upon or in any manner compromising the copyright of the Publisher in the works. The Distributor shall furthermore bring to the attention of the Publisher any acts of infringement or compromise committed by third parties and shall assist the Publisher in bringing all necessary legal proceedings to remedy such acts.

9. Competing Works:

The Publisher acknowledges that the Distributor may distribute works in book form or any other form of other competing publishers which works may in themselves compete with those supplied by the Publisher.

10. Returns:

The Distributor shall have the right to return to the Publisher all unsold or damaged copies of the works in book form and shall be given full credit against invoicing for stock received. Copies of works which have been on sale at retail outlets for twelve months or longer shall be presumed to be unsold and shall be returnable at the option of the Distributor to the Publisher. All returns shall be shipped at the cost of the Publisher directly to the latter or to the latter's agent.

11. Term Of Contract:

The term of the present contract shall be two years from the date of the execution of the present agreement and shall be automatically renewed for successive periods of one year unless either of the present parties gives notice of termination thirty days prior to the termination date;

The present agreement shall terminate automatically without notice or right of renewal in the event of bankruptcy, insolvency, receivership, distribution of assets generally for the benefit of the creditors or termination of business of either of the parties.

12. Imprimatur:

The Publisher shall print on the title page or following page the name and address of the distributor on each copy of the work in book form for distribution in ———.

13. Assignment:

The present agreement shall be binding upon the assigns, heirs, executors and legal representatives of the Distributor and the Publisher. The Distributor and Publisher shall not effect any assignment, transfer, sale, lease or other disposal of the rights herein contained, save where otherwise stipulated without the written consent of the other. The terms "Distributor" and "Publisher" shall include any assignee, subsidiary or successor by reason of sale, consolidation, merger, exchange, continuation or any other re-organization, and no such re-organization shall be deemed to involve an assignment of rights necessitating the written consent of the parties.

14. Notice:

The requirements of a written notice under the present agreement shall be deemed to have been fulfilled by delivery in person or by the sending by the regular mail of the notice to the parties at the addresses hereinbefore mentioned, save in the event of the change of address following due service of the notice of change of address by registered mail. The requirement of delivery of notice by registered mail shall be deemed fulfilled on the date mentioned in the postal receipt issued at the time of posting.

15. Waiver:

A waiver of any breach of this agreement or of any of the terms or conditions by the Distributor or Publisher shall not be deemed to be a waiver of any continued or subsequent breach or in any way affect any other term of the present agreement; no waiver shall be binding upon the Distributor or Publisher unless stipulated in writing and signed by the parties.

16. Language Requirement - Province Of Quebec:

The parties expressly require that the present contract be drawn up and executed in the English language. Les parties ont expressément exigé que le présent contrat soit rédigé et exécuté en anglais.

IN WITNESS WHEREOF the parties hereto have duly executed the present agreement on the date first mentioned.

____
Publisher

____
Distributor

4.1 PUBLISHER-DISTRIBUTORSHIP AGREEMENT (Long Form)

1. Appointment of distributor;
2. Undertaking by the distributor;
3. Limitation as to mode of distribution;
4. Sales to distributor;
5. Terms of payment;
6. Referrals;
7. Title to books;
8. Free copies;
9. Copyright and warranties;
10. Competing works;
11. Returns;
12. Accounting;
13. Advertising and stock;
14. Term of contract;
15. No agency;
16. Assignment;
17. Notice;
18. Waiver;
19. Language requirement - Province of Quebec.

AGREEMENT made this ——— day of ———, 19— at ———.

BETWEEN: XYZ PUBLISHING COMPANY (hereinafter called the "Publisher")

AND: ABC PUBLISHING COMPANY (hereinafter called the "Distributor")

In consideration of the undertakings provided hereunder, the parties to the present agreement declare:

1. Appointment Of Distributor:

The Publisher hereby constitutes the Distributor his sole and exclusive distributor in ——— of all works in book form published by the Publisher with the exception of the following books:

(1) Books in translation published by the Publisher where the original text has been initially published by third party publishers;
(2) Books of interest restricted to local territory;
(3) Books co-published by the Publisher;
(4) Books covered by prior distributorship agreements.

2. Undertaking By The Distributor:

The Distributor accepts the present appointment and shall maintain for the due execution of the distributorship adequate staff facilities. The Distributor shall market and sell the works in book form and to this end, shall effect all necessary advertising, circulate folders and catalogues, maintain continued communication with wholesalers and retail outlets, maintain an adequate inventory of the works in book form and fill all orders as placed.

3. Limitation As To Mode Of Distribution:

Notwithstanding the present grant, the Distributor shall not have the right to market the works in book form of the Publisher in the following manner:

(1) Bulk sales to educational institutions;
(2) Direct mail solicitation to consumers;
(3) Sales to the following retail chain systems: ———.

4. Sales To Distributor:

The Publisher shall sell to the Distributor all works in book form which the latter has requested. The Publisher shall ship to the Distributor within twenty days following receipt of written purchase orders, copies of the works ordered. In the event that the Publisher does not have sufficient stock on hand to meet the purchase orders, the Publisher shall so notify the Distributor and exercise all efforts necessary in order to obtain the stock required. Responsibility for payment of shipping costs, fees, duties and other surcharges shall be at the entire expense of the Distributor.

5. Terms Of Payment:

The Distributor shall pay to the Publisher the catalogue retail sales price minus a discount of 40% on works in book form on stock at the date of the execution of the present agreement, and with respect to such works not yet published, the Distributor shall be entitled to a discount of 40% from the catalogue retail sales price on the first 3,000 copies ordered, and 60% on all subsequent copies ordered. All payments shall be made in Canadian currency within one month of receipt of delivery of stock. Alternate forms of payment, credit extension and financing arrangements are available upon discussion and mutual consent of the parties.

Unless otherwise agreed upon, payments made following the due date shall be charged interest at the rate of one and one half percent per month.

All returns of defective or unsaleable books shall be credited but the Distributor shall not be entitled to deduct the amount of such credit from payments falling due unless returns have been made and acknowledgment of returns or credit notes have been issued.

6. Referrals:

The Publisher shall direct all requests for orders or information concerning stock to the Distributor. All catalogues or promotional materials used by the Publisher with respect to works in book form distributed by the Distributor shall make mention of the conferral of the exclusive distributorship upon the Distributor.

7. Title To Books:

The Distributor shall become owner of all copies of the work in book form requested from the Publisher upon delivery of the same to the shipping agent of the Distributor. All risks of carriage, charges for insurance and costs and losses whatever following such delivery shall be the sole responsibility of the Distributor.

8. Free Copies:

The Publisher shall give to the Distributor free of charge ten copies of each new work in book form published by the former, save those works specifically excluded from the present agreement. Free copies of the works so delivered shall be used by the Distributor solely for the purposes of evaluation and test marketing.

9. Copyright And Warranties:

The present agreement shall not be deemed in any manner to confer upon the Distributor a right of copyright or in any way derogate from the proprietary interests of the Publisher or author in the works in book form. Nevertheless, the Distributor shall take all necessary steps to avoid infringing or in any manner compromising copyright of the Publisher in the works. The Distributor shall furthermore bring to the attention of the Publisher any acts of infringement or compromise committed by third parties and shall assist the Publisher in bringing all necessary legal proceedings to remedy such acts.

The Publisher warrants that each published work to be distributed may be so distributed without violation or infringement of any rights of third parties and that such distribution where effected in accordance with standard commercial practices is otherwise lawful.

The Publisher further warrants that it is fully capable of executing the present agreement and is solely responsible for the payment of royalties or fees to third parties to permit full publication and distribution.

10. Competing Works:

The Publisher acknowledges that the Distributor may distribute works in book form or any other form of other competing publishers which works may in themselves compete with those supplied by the Publisher. The Publisher furthermore acknowledges that the Distributor is a publisher of a similar line of works in book form and effects distribution of the same.

Nevertheless, the Distributor agrees to distribute the published works of the Publisher on a basis equal to that accorded to competing published works and to this end, shall include the Publisher's published works on all catalogues, subject listings, leaflets, exhibits and representations containing a list or mention of said competing works. The Distributor shall furthermore not advertise for sale or distribute the published works of the Publisher at a price lower or higher than the catalogue retail sales price.

11. Returns:

The Distributor shall have the right to return to the Publisher all unsold or damaged copies of the works ordered and shall be credited as stipulated above. Copies of works which have been on sale at retail outlets for twelve months or longer shall be presumed to be unsold and shall be returnable at the option of the Distributor to the Publisher. All returns shall be shipped at the cost of the Publisher and directly to the latter or the latter's agent.

The Distributor shall not be entitled to sell the stock of any work in book form of the Publisher at remainder price unless with the prior consent of the Publisher. The proceeds of remaindering shall be retained by the Distributor and further credit for the difference between the invoiced price and remainder price shall be given to the Distributor.

In the event of termination of the present agreement, the Distributor shall be entitled to return all unsold copies of the published works ordered hereunder and shall be credited as if returned during the course of the agreement.

12. Accounting:

The Distributor shall furnish to the Publisher a bi-monthly report of sales of each work in book form. Nevertheless, the Publisher shall be entitled to a spot-report of the sales and inventory at earlier intervals upon the giving of due notice of such request.

13. Advertising And Stock:

The Distributor shall maintain a sufficient number of copies of each work in book form of the Publisher to permit due compliance with sales orders. In the event that sales of any specific work do not exceed two hundred copies per year, the Distributor shall at his option refuse to carry stock of that work.

All advertising and promotional materials aside from catalogues and listings created for use by the Publisher shall be subject to approval of the Publisher. In the event of the failure of the Publisher to notify the Distributor of its refusal to approve, within twenty-four hours of receipt of the advertising materials, the Distributor shall be entitled to proceed with use of the same. The Publisher shall co-operate with the Distributor in creating or supplementing advertising materials for the promotion of the works and to this end, shall furnish whatever testimonials, artwork and copy it possesses relating to the works.

14. Term Of Contract:

The term of the present agreement shall be two years from the date of the execution of the present agreement and shall be automatically renewed for successive periods of one year unless either of the present parties gives notice of termination thirty days prior to the termination date;

The present agreement shall terminate automatically without notice or right of renewal in the event of bankruptcy, insolvency, receivership, distribution of assets generally for the benefit of the creditors or termination of business of either of the parties;

In the event that the distributor fails to purchase more than $200,000 of stock of published works from the Publisher during the first year of the present agreement, either party may terminate upon the expiry of sixty days following written notice to that effect.

15. No Agency:

The present Agreement shall not be construed as creating in any manner a relationship of agency, a partnership or a joint venture between the Publisher and the Distributor.

16. Assignment:

The present Agreement shall be binding upon the assigns, heirs, executors and legal representatives of the Publisher and Distributor. The Publisher and Distributor shall not effect any assignment, transfer, sale, lease or other disposal of the rights herein contained save where otherwise stipulated without the written consent of the other. The term "Publisher" shall include any assignee, subsidiary or successor by reason of sale, consolidation, merger, exchange, continuation or any other re-organization and no such re-organization shall be deemed to involve an assignment of rights necessitating the written consent of the Distributor.

17. Notice:

The requirements of a written notice under the present Agreement shall be deemed to have been fulfilled by delivery in person or by the sending by regular mail of the notice to the parties at the addresses hereinabove mentioned, save in the event of the change of address following due service of notice of change of address by registered mail. The requirement of delivery of notice by registered mail shall be deemed fulfilled on the date mentioned in the postal receipt issued at the time of posting.

18. Waiver:

A waiver of any breach of this agreement or of any of the terms or conditions by the Distributor and Publisher shall not be deemed a waiver of any continued or subsequent breach or in any way affect any other term of the present agreement; no waiver shall be binding upon the Distributor or Publisher unless stipulated in writing and signed by the parties.

19. Language Requirement - Province Of Quebec:

The parties expressly require that the present contract be drawn up and executed in the English language. Les parties ont expressément exigé que le présent contrat soit rédigé et exécuté en anglais.

IN WITNESS WHEREOF the parties hereto have duly executed the present agreement on the date first mentioned.

____

Publisher

____

Distributor

5. TRANSLATOR-PUBLISHER AGREEMENT

1. Undertaking to translate;
2. Delivery of manuscript;
3. Translation of all aspects;
4. Quality of translation;
5. Proofs;
6. Bibliography;
7. Deadline;
8. Remuneration;
9. Credit;
10. No copyright;
11. Warranty;
12. Free copies;
13. Non-assignability;
14. Waiver;
15. Notice;
16. Language requirement - Province of Quebec.

Commentary

The need for the use of the following agreement arises where the publisher does not maintain a translator as a regular staff member.

AGREEMENT made this ——— day of ———, 19— at ———.

BETWEEN:	XYZ PUBLISHING COMPANY (hereinafter called the "Publisher")
AND:	MR. JOHN SMITH (hereinafter called the "Translator")

In consideration of the undertakings provided hereunder, the parties to the present Agreement declare:

1. Undertaking To Translate:

The Translator shall prepare and deliver to the Publisher a translation of a work in the French language originally entitled ——— ("translation") in the form, style and under the conditions set out hereunder.

2. Delivery Of Manuscript:

The Translator shall submit the translation in manuscript form, typed double spaced, legible and ready for printing. In the event that the Publisher is of the opinion that the manuscript is not in due form, the Translator shall upon notice make all necessary corrections in order to render the manuscript fit for printing.

3. Translation Of All Aspects:

The Translator shall translate each and every aspect of the original work, including the title, table of contents, preface, introduction, text, captions and index. The Translator shall create, if necessary, an original table of contents and index where the process of literal translation is insufficient to convey the sense and context thereof.

4. Quality Of Translation:

The Translator shall endeavour to adapt the original text of the work into the French language in a manner which is most in keeping with the wording, sense and spirit of the text.

5. Proofs:

The Translator shall review galley and page proofs of the work, which shall conform to the completed manuscript as submitted by the Translator without modification whatsoever, unless with the consent of the latter. The Translator shall return such proofs to the Publisher with corrections legibly inserted within one week of the receipt thereof. Where the Translator has inserted modifications which are not of the nature of simple correction of printer's errors, the Translator shall bear the costs of modifications which shall form a charge against sums due to the Translator hereunder.

6. Bibliography:

The Translator shall prepare a bibliography in French making references where possible to other works in the French language which do not appear in the bibliography in the original work.

7. Deadline:

The Translator shall deliver the manuscript in three portions on February 1, May 1 and August 1, or may as he sees fit accelerate progress on the work and remit the entirety before the last date mentioned.

8. Remuneration:

The Publisher shall pay to the Translator the sum of five thousand dollars plus one percent of the retail sales price of each copy of the translation sold. The Publisher shall advance the sum of one thousand dollars on each of the three delivery due dates mentioned above and the balance of the lump sum on the date of publication.

9. Credit:

The Publisher shall publish the translation with mention of the Translator's name on the cover and title page.

10. No Copyright:

The Translator shall not be entitled to any copyright or any other residual right whatever in the translation of the work and all such rights shall be vested in the Publisher.

11. Warranty:

The Translator warrants that:
(a) The translation is original;
(b) That he is the sole Translator of the translation;
(c) That the translation has not been effected in such manner as to contain libellous or obscene material not contained in the original work.

12. Free Copies:

The Publisher shall give to the Translator three free copies of the original work in order to proceed with the process of translation. The Publisher shall furthermore give to the Translator ten free copies of the published translation.

13. Non-Assignability:

The Translator shall not assign the present contract to any other party without the prior consent of the publisher. The Publisher nevertheless shall be entitled to assign the present agreement upon due notification to the translator.

14. Waiver:

A waiver of any breach of this Agreement or of any of the terms or conditions by the Translator or Publisher shall not be deemed a waiver of any continued or subsequent breach or in any way affect any other term of the present

Agreement; no waiver shall be binding upon the Translator or Publisher unless stipulated in writing and signed by the parties.

15. Notice:

The requirements of a written notice under the present Agreement shall be deemed to have been fulfilled by delivery in person or by the sending by regular mail of the notice to the parties at the addresses hereinbefore mentioned, save in the event of the change of address following due service of notice of change of address by registered mail. The requirement of delivery of notice by registered mail shall be deemed fulfilled on the date mentioned in the postal receipt issued at the time of posting.

16. Language Requirement - Province Of Quebec:

The parties expressly require that the present contract be drawn up and executed in the English language. Les parties ont expressément exigé que le présent contrat soit rédigé et exécuté en anglais.

IN WITNESS WHEREOF the parties hereto have duly executed the present Agreement on the date first mentioned.

____

Publisher

____

Translator

6. COLLECTIVE-AUTHOR AGREEMENT

AGREEMENT made this 10th day of June 1988

BETWEEN John Smith of Toronto, in the Province of Ontario, Canada

Hereinafter referred to as ''the Member''

-and-

THE AUTHOR'S COLLECTIVE

Hereinafter referred to as ''the Collective''

In consideration of the covenants herein contained the parties agree as follows:

DEFINITIONS

1.1 "Literary work" means any written work of whatever length, form and content, irrespective of its literary value, sue or appreciation;

1.2 "Musical work" means any musical work associated therewith including vocal and instrumental music in any mechanical reproduction;

1.3 "Dramatico-musical work" means an opera, musical play or pantomine;

1.4 "Performing right" means any right of performing a musical work in public in any part of the world or of communicating any such musical work by any means;

ASSIGNMENT

2. The Member hereby assigns all rights which he has or may have to the Collective, for all purposes. The Collective shall distribute all sums payable upon the exercise of such rights by third parties to the Member net of costs, on an annual basis.

3. The Member shall cause to be inserted in any contract he may enter into respecting present or future works he may author a clause indicating the existence of the present assignment.

4. The Member shall advise the Collective of all works he has created, and provide a written copy thereof to the Collective on a timely basis.

ROYALTIES

5. The Collective shall use its best efforts to collect all sums including royalties, respecting the rights assigned to it herein.

6. The Collective shall be entitled to institute or defend in the name of the Member any and all legal proceedings respecting the rights assigned, and shall hold the Member harmless from all expenses of such proceedings. The Member shall not be entitled to institute or defend any such proceedings with prior written consent of the Collective, and subject to the terms it shall impose.

GENERAL

7. The Member shall execute, all documents as may be reasonably necessary to give to these presents.

8. The term of the present agreement shall be five (5) years.

IN WITNESS WHEREOF the parties hereto have signed.

____

Member

____

Collective

7. PUBLISHER-CREATOR SOFTWARE AGREEMENT

AGREEMENT made this 20 day of August 198__, in the City and District of

__________________________________.

BETWEEN:

XYZ Publishers Ltd.

a corporation duly incorporated under the laws of Canada, having its principal place of business at ____ .
(hereinafter referred to as "Supplier")

AND

A corporation incorporated under the laws of Canada, having its principal place of business at ______________ . (hereinafter referred to as "Buyer")

The parties hereto in consideration of the mutual covenants and agreements herein contained mutually covenant and agree as follows:

ARTICLE 1

SUPPLIER'S DUTIES

1.1 The Supplier will perform the work described in the task order designated as Appendix A and incorporated herein as part of this Agreement for a fixed price of $30,000.

1.2 The Supplier will make available the services of its employees on a full-time basis during the term of this Agreement for the purpose of performing its obligations and executing the work pursuant to the task order.

ARTICLE 2

TERM

This Agreement shall commence on the ______ day of ________________ 19____ and shall expire on completion of the task order. It is anticipated that the task order be completed by the __________ day of ________________ 19____, at the latest.

ARTICLE 3

PRICE

In consideration for the services to be provided by the Supplier to the Buyer, the Buyer agrees to pay the Supplier the sum of $30,000, all inclusive within thirty (30) days of receipt of the invoice which shall be submitted upon completion of the task order to the satisfaction of Buyer.

ARTICLE 4

CONTRACT MANAGEMENT

4.1 The Buyer shall issue a task order containing the following minimum:

a) a unique number (for identification purposes);
b) a statement of work for that task;
c) the described start and completion date.

4.2 The Supplier agrees to complete the task order by ________________ 19____, at the latest.

ARTICLE 5

PERFORMANCE

5.1 All work to be performed by the Supplier and/or its employees hereunder will be executed in an efficient, competent, timely and professional manner and such work shall be done to the satisfaction of the Buyer.

5.2 The Supplier agrees to comply with the current Buyer's standards and guidelines applicable to the performance of work assignments and shall notify the Buyer in writing of any and all standards and guidelines to which compliance cannot be met by the Supplier or its employees prior to executing any performance of the task order.

5.3 The failure of either party at any time to require performance by the other party of any provision hereto shall in no way affect the full right to require such performance at any time thereafter, nor shall a waiver by either party of any breach of the conditions hereof be taken or held to be waiver of the provisions itself.

5.4 The Supplier will ensure that his employee(s), while on the Buyer's premises, will adhere to the general rules of conduct and dress applying to the Buyer's own employees.

ARTICLE 6

6.1 The Buyer and Supplier acknowledge and agree that the Supplier will be solely responsible for all matters relating to remuneration, discipline, withholding of income tax, unemployment insurance, workmen's compensation, leave and other matters arising between the Supplier and Supplier's employee(s) performing work for the Buyer under this Agreement.

6.2 The Buyer and Supplier acknowledge and agree that the Buyer or his representative is responsible for managing the Supplier's employees for purposes of executing the tasks outlined in Attachment A.

6.3 The Buyer may at any time request in writing the replacement of a Supplier's employee assigned to execute the task order or any part thereof. The Supplier must redress the problem or satisfy the Buyer's demands within three (3) working days after receipt of the request in writing.

ARTICLE 7

OWNERSHIP RIGHTS

7.1 The Supplier agrees that, with respect to the Supplier's work for the Buyer under the present Agreement, any developments made by the Supplier or under the Supplier's direction in connection with the Buyer's assignment shall be the sole and complete property of the Buyer and that any and all patents and copyrights shall belong to the Buyer including the right to reproduce, or distribute for sale to and use by third parties. The Supplier further agrees to sign at the Buyer's request any and all documentation required by the Supplier to give effect to such clause.

7.2 The Supplier warrants that the Supplier is free to enter into this Agreement and is not subject to any conflicting obligations or any disability which will or might prevent the Supplier from or interfere with the Supplier's execution in performance under this Agreement and that all drawings, plans, designs, documentation, flowcharts, software or programs or any other material of a similar nature will be original with the Supplier or in the public domain throughout the world and shall not infringe upon or violate any patent, copyright, or any other right of any person.

7.3 Supplier agrees that it will defend the Buyer, its affiliates, distributors, customers and users and their respective successors and assigns at Supplier's cost and expense and will indemnify and hold harmless the Buyer, its affiliates, distributors, customers and users and their respective successors and assigns from and against all suits, claims, proceedings, losses, damages, expenses and costs of any nature whatsoever arising from any actual or alleged infringement of any patent or copyright based on drawings, plans, designs, documentation, flowcharts, software or programs or any other material of a similar nature written, drawn or supplied by Supplier.

7.4 The Supplier also agrees that it will defend the Buyer and its affiliates and their respective successors and assigns, at Supplier's cost and expense and will indemnify and hold harmless the Buyer and its affiliates and their respective successors and assigns from and against all suits, claims, proceedings, losses, damages, expenses and costs of any nature whatsover arising from the Supplier or the Supplier's employees' negligence towards persons or property, in connection with the services provided by the Supplier to the Buyer under the present Agreement.

7.5 The Buyer shall give to the Supplier appropriate notice of any such claim or action upon its becoming aware of same. Furthermore, the Buyer shall, at the Supplier's cost, provide all reasonable assistance in the Supplier's defence or settlement efforts and the Supplier shall have sole authority to defend or settle such claims. Notwithstanding the Supplier's sole authority to defend or settle any such claims, the Buyer shall have, at its own expense, the right to participate in such settlement or defence.

ARTICLE 8

CONFIDENTIALITY

8.1 The Supplier acknowledges and agrees that their employee(s) will have access to confidential information regarding the affairs of the Buyer.

8.2 In order to preserve the confidentiality of such information, the Supplier agrees that it and any of its employee(s) who will perform any work under the present Agreement, will execute and be bound by the terms of the confidentiality Agreement attached hereto as Appendix C, and that the Supplier will deliver signed copies thereof to the Buyer prior to Supplier or any Supplier personnel commencing duties in performance of the present contract.

8.3 All documents and material made available to the Supplier or its employee(s) for the purpose of the Supplier's execution of its obligations pursuant to this Agreement shall be returned to the Buyer forthwith upon request and upon termination of the Agreement.

ARTICLE 9

PLACE OF WORK

9.1 All obligations of the Supplier to be performed for the Buyer pursuant to this Agreement shall be performed at the Buyer's premises in ________________ unless otherwise requested in writing in a task order, Appendix A which is incorporated into this Agreement by reference.

9.2 The Buyer's authorized representative will have full authority, and cooperation of the Supplier, in determining the status of the work to be performed by the Supplier hereunder and to review the performance of the Supplier or its employee(s).

9.3 The Buyer will provide at no cost to the Supplier office space, furniture, equipment and materials necessary for the execution of the task order at the Buyer's premises in ________________.

9.4 The Supplier and/or its employees shall exercise due care for the office environment, furniture and equipment provided for the execution of the task order.

9.5 In the event that the Buyer loans equipment to the Supplier which is to be housed at a location other than the Buyer's premises, for the performance of the task order, the Supplier agrees to insure the equipment with an insurer and for an amount to be approved in writing by the Buyer, and to hold harmless the Buyer from any damages resulting from equipment malfunctioning. The Supplier agrees to notify the Buyer of any such equipment malfunction within twenty-four (24) hours of the detection of the malfunction.

ARTICLE 10

TERMINATION

The Buyer shall be entitled to forthwith terminate this Agreement by notice in writing:

a) in the event of breach of this Agreement by the Supplier or its employee(s);

b) in the event that the Supplier's employee(s), for any reason other than the Supplier's normal holiday, are not available to perform regular obligations hereunder for a period of five (5) consecutive working days, or for a total of ten (10) business days during the term of a particular task order;

c) in the event that the Supplier or any of its employee(s) breach the terms of the confidentiality Agreement attached hereto as Appendix C incorporated in this Agreement by reference;

d) in the event of non performance.

ARTICLE 11

CHANGES

11.1 Notwithstanding the provisions of this Agreement and Appendix A hereto, the Buyer shall have the right at any time in writing to change, or add to, the work scope on any task order, and the estimated value and Appendices A and B shall be adjusted accordingly.

11.2 The Supplier has the right to reject any change of the work scope on a task order by notice in writing to that effect to Buyer within five (5) days after notification of the change. Upon failure by the Supplier to make such rejection in writing within the said period, the change shall be conclusively deemed to have been accepted by the Supplier.

ARTICLE 12

GENERAL

12.1 The Buyer agrees that it shall not knowingly hire or attempt to hire any employees of the Supplier, while so employed by the Supplier, who has done any work for the Buyer under the present Agreement, without the prior written consent of the Supplier for a period of sixty (60) days immediately after the termination of the Agreement.

12.2 No alteration, amendment, waiver, cancellation or any other change in any term or condition of this contract shall be valid or binding on either party unless the same shall have been mutually assented to in writing by both parties.

12.3 The Supplier shall apply to the Buyer for any explanation which it may require as to the meaning and intent of any clause in the specifications, terms, conditions and materials of the contract and shall be held responsible for any errors or losses consequent upon failure to request such explanation.

12.4 The failure of either party to enforce at any time any of the provisions of this Agreement, or the failure to require at any time performance by the other party of any of the provisions of this Agreement, shall in no way be construed to be a present or future waiver of such provisions, nor in any way affect the validity of either party to enforce each and every such provision thereafter. The express waiver by either party of any provision, condition or requirement of this Agreement shall not constitute a waiver of any future obligation to comply with such provision, condition or requirement.

12.5 If certain articles, in whole or in part, of this contract are considered or found to be unenforceable, this will not negate nor affect in any way the application and enforcement of the remainder of this contract.

12.6 The titles to the Articles in this contract have been inserted for convenience of reference only, do not form part of this contract, and shall not in any way affect the interpretation thereof.

ARTICLE 13

ASSIGNMENT

13.1 The Supplier shall not sub-contract any of the work assigned to it by the purchaser. In addition, the Supplier shall not assign or transfer this contract or any of its rights and obligations or any interest in the contract without the prior written consent of the Buyer. The Buyer may assign a transfer, all or any part of this Agreement, to any of its affiliates wherever located, subject to the terms and conditions herein contained.

13.2 In the performance of the work hereunder, the Supplier shall be an independent contractor of the Buyer and shall be solely responsible for the performance of all work contemplated hereunder.

ARTICLE 14

INTERPRETATION

14.1 Notwithstanding the expiration of the term of this contract or any renewal period thereof, it is acknowledged and agreed that those rights and obligations which by their nature are intended to survive such expiration or earlier termination shall survive including, without limiting the foregoing, the following provisions:

(i) all rights, duties and obligations of the parties;
(ii) Article IX;
(iii) Article X;
(iv) Article XV;
(v) the confidentiality Agreements executed pursuant to Article X.

14.2 This contract and the annexed Appendices A to D and Annexes and any documents incorporated by reference, constitute the entire Agreement between the parties hereto and supersede and cancel any and all prior representations, negotiations, undertakings, letters, acceptances, agreements, understandings and contracts whether verbal or written, between the parties hereto or their agents, with respect to or in connection with any of the matters or things to which this contract applies or refers.

14.3 In the event of any conflict or inconsistencies between the provisions of this contract and the provisions of any Appendices and Annexes attached hereto or the provisions of any documents incorporated by reference, the provisions of this contract shall prevail.

14.4 The Supplier agrees that the terms and conditions of this contract shall be treated as confidential information and that no reference to this contract or to activities pertaining thereto can be made in any form of public or commercial advertising without the prior written consent of the Buyer.

14.5 This Agreement shall be governed by and interpreted in accordance with the Laws of the Province of Quebec, Canada.

ARTICLE 15

NOTICE

Notice to either party under terms of this contract shall be given in writing by addressing the communication as below, or to such other address as shall be later given in writing:

IN WITNESS WHEREOF the parties hereto have duly executed this Agreement as of the day and year first above written.

SUPPLIER
per: ______

BUYER
per: ______

8. EXTRACTS FROM AN ACT RESPECTING COPYRIGHT R.S.C. 1970 c. C-30

As amended by 1970 (2nd Supp.), chap. 4 and chap. 10; 1974-75-76, chap. 50; 1976-77, Bill C-53 or chap. 28; 1980-81-82-83, chap. 47 and chap. 111; 1983-84, chap. 40.)

SHORT TITLE

1. This Act may be cited as the *Copyright Act*.

INTERPRETATION

2. In this Act

''book'' includes every volume, part or division of a volume, pamphlet, sheet of letterpress, sheet of music, map, chart, or plan separately published;

''cinematograph'' includes any work produced by any process analogous to cinematography;

''collective work'' means

(*a*) an encyclopaedia, dictionary, year book, or similar work,

(*b*) a newspaper, review, magazine, or similar periodical, and

(*c*) any work written in distinct parts by different authors, or in which works or parts of works of different authors are incorporated;

''delivery,'' in relation to a lecture, includes delivery by means of any mechanical instrument;

''engravings'' includes etchings, lithographs, woodcuts, prints, and other similar works, not being photographs;

''every original literary, dramatic, musical and artistic work'' includes every original production in the literary, scientific or artistic domain, whatever may be the mode or form of its expression, such as books, pamphlets, and other writings, lectures, dramatic or dramatico-musical works, musical works or compositions with or without words, illustrations, sketches, and plastic works relative to geography, topography, architecture or science;

"Her Majesty's Realms and Territories" includes any territories under Her Majesty's protection to which an order in council made under the provisions of section 28 of the *Copyright Act, 1911*, passed by the Parliament of the United Kingdom, relates;

"infringing", when applied to a copy of a work in which copyright subsists, means any copy, including any colourable imitation, made, or imported in contravention of this Act;

"lecture" includes address, speech, and sermon;

"legal representatives" includes heirs, executors, administrators, successors and assigns, or agents or attorneys who are thereunto duly authorized in writing;

"literary work" includes maps, charts, plans, tables, and compilations;

"Minister" means the Minister of Consumer and Corporate Affairs;

"musical work" means any combination of melody and harmony, or either of them, printed, reduced to writing, or otherwise graphically produced or reproduced; a representation made by means of any mechanical instrument or by radio communication;

"work" includes the title thereof when such title is original and distinctive;

"work of joint authorship" means a work produced by the collaboration of two or more authors in which the contribution of one author is not distinct from the contribution of the other author or authors;

3. (1) For the purposes of this Act, "copyright" means the sole right to produce or reproduce the work or any substantial part thereof in any material form whatever, to perform, or in the case of a lecture to deliver, the work or any substantial part thereof in public; if the work is unpublished, to publish the work or any substantial part thereof; and includes the sole right

(*a*) to produce, reproduce, perform or publish any translation of the work;

(*b*) in the case of a dramatic work, to convert it into a novel or other non-dramatic work;

(*c*) in the case of a novel or other non-dramatic work, or of an artistic work, to convert it into a dramatic work, by way of performance in public or otherwise;

(*d*) in the case of a literary, dramatic, or musical work, to make any record, perforated roll, cinematograph film, or other contrivance by means of which the work may be mechanically performed or delivered;

(*e*) in the case of any literary, dramatic, musical or artistic work, to reproduce, adapt and publicly present such work by cinematograph, if the author has given such work an original character; but if such original character is absent the cinematographic production shall be protected as a photograph;

(*f*) in case of any literary, dramatic, musical or artistic work, to communicate such work by radio communication;

and to authorize any such acts as aforesaid.

(2) For the purposes of this Act, "publication", in relation to any work, means the issue of copies of the work to the public, and does not include the performance in public of a dramatic or musical work, the delivery in public of a

lecture, the exhibition in public of an artistic work, or the construction of an architectural work of art, but for the purpose of this provision, the issue of photographs and engravings of works of sculpture and architectural works of art shall not be deemed to be publication of such works.

(3) For the purposes of this Act, other than those relating to infringement of copyright, a work shall not be deemed to be published or performed in public, and a lecture shall not be deemed to be delivered in public, if published, performed in public, or delivered in public without the consent or acquiescence of the author, his executors, administrators or assigns.

(4) For the purposes of this Act, a work shall be deemed to be first published within Her Majesty's Realms and Territories or within a foreign country to which this Act extends, notwithstanding that it has been published simultaneously in some other place; and a work shall be deemed to be published simultaneously in two places, if the time between the publication in one such place and the other place does not exceed fourteen days or such longer period as may for the time being be fixed by order in council.

(5) Where, in the case of an unpublished work, the making of the work is extended over a considerable period, the conditions of this Act conferring copyright shall be deemed to have been compiled with if the author was, during any substantial part of that period a British subject, or a subject or citizen of a foreign country to which this Act extends, or a resident within Her Majesty's Realms and Territories.

(6) For the purposes of this Act as to residence, an author of a work shall be deemed to be a resident within Her Majesty's Realms and Territories if he is domiciled within Her Majesty's Realms and Territories.

WORKS IN WHICH COPYRIGHT MAY SUBSIST

4. (1) Subject to this Act, copyright shall subsist in Canada for the term hereinafter mentioned, in every original literary, dramatic, musical and artistic work, if the author was at the date of the making of the work a British subject, a citizen or subject of a foreign country that has adhered to the Convention and the Additional Protocol thereto set out in Schedule II, or resident within Her Majesty's Realms and Territories; and if, in the case of a published work, the work was first published within Her Majesty's Realms and Territories or in such foreign country; but in no other works, except so far as the protection conferred by this Act is extended as hereinafter provided to foreign countries to which this Act does not extend.

(2) Where the Minister certifies by notice, published in the *Canada Gazette*, that any country that has not adhered to the Convention and the Additional Protocol thereto, set out in Schedule II, grants or has undertaken to grant, either by treaty, convention, agreement or law, to citizens of Canada the benefit of copyright on substantially the same basis as to its own citizens or copyright

protection substantially equal to that conferred by this Act, such country shall, for the purpose of the rights conferred by this Act, be treated as if it were a country to which this Act extends; and the Minister may give such a certificate as aforesaid, notwithstanding that the remedies for enforcing the rights, or the restrictions on the importation of copies of works, under the law of such country, differ from those in this Act.

(3) Subject to subsection (4), copyright shall subsist for the term hereinafter mentioned in records, perforated rolls, and other contrivances by means of which sounds may be mechanically reproduced, in like manner as if such contrivances were musical, literary or dramatic works.

(4) Notwithstanding subsection 3(1), for the purposes of this Act "copyright" means, in respect of any record, perforated roll or other contrivance by means of which sounds may be mechanically reproduced, the sole right to reproduce any such contrivance or any substantial part thereof in any material form.

TERM OF COPYRIGHT

5. The term for which copyright shall subsist shall, except as otherwise expressly provided by this Act, be the life of the author and a period of fifty years after his death.

6. In the case of a literary, dramatic or musical work, or an engraving, in which copyright subsists at the date of the death of the author or, in the case of a work of joint authorship, at or immediately before the date of the death of the author who dies last, but which has not been published, nor, in the case of a dramatic or musical work, been performed in public, nor, in the case of a lecture, been delivered in public before that date, copyright shall subsist until publication, or performance or delivery in public, whichever may first happen, and for a term of fifty years thereafter, and the provisions of section 7 relating to the reproduction of a published work, after the death of the author, in the case of works mentioned in this section, apply as if the author had died at the date of such publication, performance or delivery in public as aforesaid.

7. (1) After the expiration of twenty-five years, or in the case of a work in which copyright subsisted on the 4th day of June 1921, thirty years, from the death of the author of a published work, copyright in the work shall not be deemed to be infringed by the reproduction of the work for sale if the person reproducing the work proves that he has given the prescribed notice in writing of his intention to reproduce the work, and that he has paid in the prescribed manner to, or for the benefit of the owner of the copyright, royalties in respect of all copies of the work sold by him, calculated at the rate of ten per cent on the price at which he publishes the work.

(2) For the purposes of this section, the Governor in Council may make regulations prescribing the mode in which notices are to be given, and the particulars to be given in such notices, and the mode, time, and frequency of the payment of royalties, including, if he thinks fit, regulations requiring payment in advance or otherwise securing the payment of royalties.

8. (1) In the case of a work of joint authorship, copyright shall subsist during the life of the author who dies last and for a term of fifty years after his death, and references in this Act to the period after the expiration of any specified number of years from the death of the author shall be construed, as references to the period after the expiration of the like number of years from the death of the author who dies last, and in the provisions of this Act with respect to the grant of compulsory licences a reference to the date of the death of the author who dies last shall be substituted for the date of the death of the author.

(2) Authors who are nationals of any country that grants a term of protection shorter than that mentioned in subsection (1) are not entitled to claim a longer term of protection in Canada.

9. The term for which copyright shall subsist in photographs shall be fifty years from the making of the original negative from which the photograph was directly or indirectly derived, and the person who was owner of such negative at the time when such negative was made shall be deemed to be the author of the photograph so derived, and, where such owner is a body corporate, the body corporate shall be deemed for the purposes of this Act to reside within Her Majesty's Realms and Territories if it has established a place of business therein.

10. The term for which copyright shall subsist in records, perforated rolls and other contrivances by means of which sounds may be mechanically reproduced shall be fifty years from the making of the original plate from which the contrivance was directly or indirectly derived, and the person who was the owner of such original plate at the time when such plate was made shall be deemed to be the author of such contrivance, and where such owner is a body corporate, the body corporate shall be deemed for the purposes of this Act to reside within Her Majesty's Realms and Territories if it has established a place of business therein.

11. Without prejudice to any rights or privileges of the Crown, where any work is, or has been, prepared or published by or under the direction or control of Her Majesty or any government department, the copyright in the work shall, subject to any agreement with the author, belong to Her Majesty and in such case shall continue for a period of fifty years from the date of the first publication of the work.

OWNERSHIP OF COPYRIGHT

12. (1) Subject to this Act, the author of a work shall be the first owner of the copyright therein.

(2) Where, in the case of an engraving, photograph, or portrait, the plate or other original was ordered by some other person and was made for valuable consideration in pursuance of that order, then in the absence of any agreement to the contrary, the person by whom such plate or other original was ordered shall be the first owner of the copyright.

(3) Where the author was in the employment of some other person under a contract of service or apprenticeship and the work was made in the course of his employment by that person, the person by whom the author was employed shall, in the absence of any agreement to the contrary, be the first owner of the copyright; but where the work is an article or other contribution to a newspaper, magazine, or similar periodical, there shall, in the absence of any agreement to the contrary, be deemed to be reserved to the author a right to restrain the publication of the work, otherwise than as part of a newspaper, magazine, or similar periodical.

(4) The owner of the copyright in any work may assign the right, either wholly or partially, and either generally or subject to territorial limitations, and either for the whole term of the copyright or for any other part thereof, and may grant any interest in the right by licence, but no such assignment or grant is valid unless it is in writing signed by the owner of the right in respect of which the assignment or grant is made, or by his duly authorized agent.

(5) Where the author of a work is the first owner of the copyright therein, no assignment of the copyright, and no grant of any interest therein, made by him, otherwise than by will, after the 4th day of June 1921, is operative to vest in the assignee or grantee any rights with respect to the copyright in the work beyond the expiration of twenty-five years from the death of the author, and the reversionary interest in the copyright expectant on the termination of that period shall, on the death of the author, notwithstanding any agreement to the contrary, devolve on his legal representatives as part of his estate, and any agreement entered into by him as to the disposition of such reversionary interest is void; but nothing in this subsection shall be construed as applying to the assignment of the copyright in a collective work or a licence to publish a work or part of a work as part of a collective work.

(6) Where, under any partial assignment of copyright, the assignee becomes entitled to any right comprised in copyright, the assignee, as respects the rights so assigned, and the assignor, as respects the rights not assigned, shall be treated for the purposes of this Act as the owner of the copyright, and this Act has effect accordingly.

(7) Independently of the author's copyright, and even after the assignment, either wholly or partially, of the said copyright, the author has the right to claim

authorship of the work, as well as the right to restrain any distortion, mutilation or other modification of the work that would be prejudicial to his honour or reputation.

COMPULSORY LICENCES

13. Where, at any time after the death of the author of a literary, dramatic, or musical work that has been published or performed in public, a complaint is made to the Governor in Council that the owner of the copyright in the work has refused to republish or to allow the republication of the work or has refused to allow the performance in public of the work, and that by reason of such refusal the work is withheld from the public, the owner of the copyright may be ordered to grant a licence to reproduce the work or perform the work in public, as the case may be, on such terms and subject to such conditions as the Governor in Council may think fit.

LICENCES

14. (1) Any person may apply to the Minister for a licence to print and publish in Canada any book wherein copyright subsists, if at any time after publication and within the duration of the copyright the owner of the copyright fails

(*a*) to print the book or cause it to be printed in Canada, or

(*b*) to supply by means of copies so printed the reasonable demands of the Canadian market for the book.

(2) An application under subsection (1) may be in such form as may be prescribed by the regulations and shall state the proposed retail price of the edition of the book proposed to be printed.

(3) Every applicant for a licence under this section shall with his application deposit with the Minister an amount not less than ten per cent of the retail selling price of one thousand copies of the book and not less than one hundred dollars and such amount shall, if the application is unsuccessful, be returned to the applicant less such deductions for fees as may be authorized by the regulations.

(4) Notice of the application shall forthwith be communicated by the Minister to the owner of the copyright in such manner as may be prescribed by the regulations.

(5) Where the owner of the copyright does not within a delay to be fixed by the regulations after communication of the notice give an undertaking, with such security as may be prescribed by the regulations, to procure within two months after the date of such communication the printing in Canada of an edition of not less than one thousand copies of such book, the Minister in his discretion may grant to the applicant a licence to print and publish the book upon terms to be determined by the Minister after hearing the parties or affording them such opportunity to be heard as may be fixed by the regulations.

(6) Where two or more persons have applied for a licence under this section, the Minister shall award the licence to the applicant proposing the terms, in the opinion of the Minister, most advantageous to the author, and if there are two proposing terms equally advantageous to the author, to the applicant whose application was first received.

(7) Such licence when issued entitles the licensee to the sole right to print and publish such book in Canada during such term, not exceeding five years or for such edition or editions as may be fixed by the licence.

(8) Such licensee shall pay a royalty on the retail selling price of every copy of such book printed under such licence, at a rate to be determined by the Minister.

(9) The acceptance of a licence for a book shall imply an undertaking by the licensee

(*a*) to print and publish in Canada an edition of the book of not less than one thousand copies, at the price specified in the licence, and within two months from the issue of the licence, and

(*b*) to print the same from the last authorized edition of the book in such manner as may be prescribed by the Minister, in full, without abbreviation or alteration of the letterpress, and, without varying, adding to, or diminishing the main design of such of the prints, engravings, maps, charts, musical compositions, or photographs contained in the book as the licensee reproduces.

(10) Every book published under a licence under this section shall have printed or otherwise impressed upon it the words ''Printed under Canadian licence'', the calendar year of such licence and the retail selling price of such book.

(11) Where the Minister on complaint is satisfied that the licensee does not print and keep on sale in Canada a number of copies of the book sufficient to supply the reasonable demands, he shall, after giving the licensee an opportunity of being heard to show cause against the cancellation, cancel the licence.

(12) Where a book for which a licence has been issued is suppressed by the owner of the copyright, the licensee shall not print the book or any further copies thereof, but may sell any copies already printed, and may complete and sell any copies in process of being printed under his licence, but the owner of the copyright is entitled to buy all such copies at the cost of printing them.

(13) Nothing in this section authorizes the granting, without the consent of the author, of a licence to publish a second or succeeding edition of any work whereof such author has published one or more editions in Canada.

SERIAL LICENCE

15. (1) Where the publication of a book is lawfully begun as a serial elsewhere than in Her Majesty's Realms and Territories or a foreign country to which this Act applies, and the owner of the copyright has refused to grant a licence to any person in Canada, being a publisher of a periodical, to publish such book in serial form, a licence may in the discretion of the Minister be granted to any person in Canada, being the publisher of a periodical, to publish such book once in serial form in the said periodical; but a licence shall not be granted to more than one such publisher in the same city, town or place.

(2) Such licence may be issued by the Minister on application by the publisher in such form as may be prescribed by the regulations.

(3) The term "serial" under this section means and refers to any book that is first published in separate articles or as a tale or short story complete in one issue in a newspaper or periodical.

(4) The term "owner of a copyright" under this section may mean the owner of the right to publish in serial form as distinct and separate from other rights of publication.

(5) The application for a licence under this section may be in the form of a draft contract between the licensee and the owner of the copyright.

(6) Such licence may be upon the terms proposed in such draft contract, or upon terms prescribed by the regulations, but before such terms are settled the owner of the copyright is entitled to be fully heard in support of any contentions or representations he may deem it in his interests to make.

(7) The applicant for a licence under this section shall with his application deposit such amount of money as may be required by the regulations, and such money shall on the issue of the licence be paid forthwith to the owner of the copyright.

(8) Nothing in this Act prohibits the importation and circulation of newspapers, magazines and periodicals that together with foreign original matter contain serials licensed to be printed and published in Canada.

16. (1) Every licence issued under sections 13, 14 and 15 shall be deemed to constitute a contract, on the terms embodied in such licence or in this Act, between the owner of the copyright and the licensee, and the licensee is entitled to the like remedies as in the case of a contract.

(2) The licensee has the same power and right to take any action or any legal proceedings to prevent or restrain any infringement of copyright that affects the rights of such licensee or to recover compensation or damages for any such infringement that the owner of the copyright would have for an infringement of his copyright.

(3) The owner of the copyright, in addition to any other remedy in respect to such licence as a contract, is entitled, in case of default by the licensee in

observing the terms of such licence, on application to the Federal Court of Canada, to have such licence cancelled.

(4) Particulars of such cancellation may be entered on the Register of Copyrights.

(5) All moneys paid or payable by a licensee or applicant for a licence under sections 13, 14 and 15 shall be paid to the Minister.

(6) All moneys deposited by a successful applicant for a licence and all moneys due from time to time by way of royalty or otherwise from licensees shall likewise be paid to the Minister and by him paid out to the persons entitled thereto.

(7) The Minister may by regulations require every copy of a book upon which the royalty has been duly paid to be suitably stamped or marked.

(8) This section and sections 14 and 15 do not apply to any work the author of which is a British subject, other than a Canadian citizen, or the subject or citizen of a country that has adhered to the Convention and the Additional Protocol thereto set out in Schedule II.

INFRINGEMENT OF COPYRIGHT

17. (1) Copyright in a work shall be deemed to be infringed by any person who, without the consent of the owner of the copyright, does anything that, by this Act, only the owner of the copyright has the right to do.

(2) The following acts do not constitute an infringement of copyright:

(*a*) any fair dealing with any work for the purposes of private study, research, criticism, review, or newspaper summary;

(*b*) where the author of an artistic work is not the owner of the copyright therein, the use by the author of any mould, cast, sketch, plan, model, or study made by him for the purpose of the work, if he does not thereby repeat or imitate the main design of that work;

(*c*) the making or publishing of paintings, drawings, engravings, or photographs of a work of sculpture or artistic craftsmanship, if permanently situated in a public place or building, or the making or publishing of paintings, drawings, engravings, or photographs that are not in the nature of architectural drawings or plans, of any architectural work of art;

(*d*) the publication in a collection, mainly composed of non-copyright matter, *bona fide* intended for the use of schools, and so described in the title and in any advertisements issued by the publisher, of short passages from published literary works not themselves published for the use of schools in which copyright subsists, if not more than two of such passages from works by the same author are published by the same publisher within five years, and the source from which such passages are taken is acknowledged;

(*e*) the publication in a newspaper of a report of a lecture delivered in public, unless the report is prohibited by conspicuous written or printed notice affixed before and maintained during the lecture at or about the main entrance of the building in which the lecture is given, and, except while the building is being used for public worship, in a position near the lecturer; but nothing in this paragraph affects the provisions in paragraph (*a*) as to newspaper summaries;

(*f*) the reading or recitation in public by one person of any reasonable extract from any published work;

(*g*) the performance without motive of gain of any musical work at any agricultural, agricultural-industrial exhibition or fair which receives a grant from or is held under federal, provincial or municipal authority, by the directors thereof;

(*h*) the reproduction of a manuscript, original document, archive, photographic positive or negative, cinematograph film or sound recording for deposit in an institution pursuant to a direction under section 11 of the *Cultural Property Export and Import Act*;

(*i*) the disclosure, pursuant to the *Access to Information Act*, of a record within the meaning of that Act, or the disclosure, pursuant to any like Act of the legislature of a province, of like material; and

(*j*) the disclosure, pursuant to the *Privacy Act*, of personal information within the meaning of that Act, or the disclosure, pursuant to any like Act of the legislature of a province, of like information.

(3) No church, college or school and no religious, charitable or fraternal organization shall be held liable to pay any compensation to the owner of any musical work or to any person claiming through him by reason of the public performance of any musical work in furtherance of a religious, educational or charitable object.

(4) Copyright in a work shall also be deemed to be infringed by any person who

(*a*) sells or lets for hire, or by way of trade exposes or offers for sale or hire;

(*b*) distributes either for the purposes of trade, or to such an extent as to affect prejudicially the owner of the copyright;

(*c*) by way of trade exhibits in public; or

(*d*) imports for sale or hire into Canada;

any work that to his knowledge infringes copyright or would infringe copyright if it had been made within Canada.

(5) Copyright in a work shall also be deemed to be infringed by any person who for his private profit permits a theatre or other place of entertainment to be used for the performance in public of the work without the consent of the owner of the copyright, unless he was not aware, and had no reasonable ground for suspecting, that the performance would be an infringement of copyright.

(6) Nothing in paragraph 17(2)(*i*) or (*j*) authorizes any person to whom a record or information is disclosed to do anything that, by this Act, only the owner of the copyright has a right to do.

1980-81-82-83, c. 111, s. 5; 1983-84, c. 40, s. 18(1).

18. Notwithstanding anything in this Act, it shall not be an infringement of copyright in an address of a political nature delivered at a public meeting to publish a report thereof in a newspaper.

19. (1) It shall not be deemed to be an infringement of copyright in any musical, literary or dramatic work for any person to make within Canada records, perforated rolls, or other contrivances, by means of which sounds may be reproduced and by means of which the work may be mechanically performed, if such person proves

(*a*) that such contrivances have previously been made by, or with the consent or acquiescence of, the owner of the copyright in the work; and

(*b*) that he has given the prescribed notice of his intention to make the contrivances, and that there has been paid in the prescribed manner to, or for the benefit of, the owner of the copyright in the work royalties in respect of all such contrivances sold by him, as hereinafter mentioned.

(2) Nothing in subsection (1) authorizes any alterations in, or omissions from, the work reproduced, unless contrivances reproducing the work subject to similar alterations and omissions have been previously made by, or with the consent or acquiescence of, the owner of the copyright, or unless such alterations or omissions are reasonably necessary for the adaptation of the work to the contrivances in question.

(3) For the purposes of subsection (1), a musical, literary or dramatic work shall not be deemed to include a contrivance by means of which sounds may be mechanically reproduced.

(4) The making of the necessary manuscript arrangement and instrumentations of the copyrighted work, for the sole purpose of the adaptation of the work to the contrivances in question, shall not be deemed an infringement of copyright.

(5) The royalty mentioned in subsection (1) shall be two cents for each playing surface of each such record and two cents for each such perforated roll or other contrivance.

(6) Where any such contrivance is made reproducing on the same playing surface two or more different works in which copyright subsists, and the owners of the copyright therein are different persons, the sums payable by way of royalties under this section shall be apportioned among the several owners of the copyright equally.

(7) When any such contrivances by means of which a literary, dramatic or musical work may be mechanically performed have been made, then for the purposes of this section, the owner of the copyright in the work shall, in relation to any person who makes the prescribed inquiries, be deemed to have given his

consent to the making of such contrivances if he fails to reply to such inquiries within the prescribed time.

(8) For the purposes of this section, the Governor in Council may make regulations prescribing anything that under this section is to be prescribed, and prescribing the mode in which notices are to be given and the particulars to be given in such notices, and the mode, time, and frequency of the payment of royalties; and any such regulations may, if the Governor in Council thinks fit, include regulations requiring payment in advance or otherwise securing the payment of royalties.

(9) In the case of musical, literary or dramatic works published before the 1st day of January 1924, the foregoing provisions shall have effect, subject to the following modifications and additions:

(*a*) the conditions as to the previous making by, or with the consent or acquiescence of, the owner of the copyright in the work, and the restrictions as to alterations in or omissions from the work, do not apply;

(*b*) no royalties are payable in respect of contrivances lawfully made and sold by the manufacturer before the 1st day of January 1924;

(*c*) notwithstanding any assignment made before the 4th day of June 1921 of the copyright in a literary or dramatic or musical work, any rights conferred by this Act in respect of the making, or authorizing the making, of contrivances by means of which the work may be mechanically performed, shall belong to the author or his legal representatives and not to the assignee, and the royalties aforesaid shall be payable to, and for the benefit of, the author of the work or his legal representatives.

(10) Notwithstanding anything in this Act, where a record, perforated roll, or other contrivance by means of which sounds may be mechanically reproduced has been made before the 1st day of January 1924, copyright shall, as from the said date, subsist therein in like manner and for the like term as if this Act had been in force at the date of the making of the original plate from which the contrivance was directly or indirectly derived; the person who, on the 1st day of January 1924, is the owner of such original plate shall be the first owner of such copyright; and nothing in this provision shall be construed as conferring copyright in any such contrivance if the making thereof would have infringed copyright in some other such contrivance, if this provision had been in force at the time of the making of the first-mentioned contrivance.

(11) For the purposes of this section, a record, perforated roll or other contrivance by means of which sounds may be reproduced and by means of which a literary or dramatic work may be mechanically performed made within Canada with the consent or acquiescence of the owner of the copyright in the work and intended for and primarily distributed to persons unable to read print because of a physical handicap is deemed not to be a contrivance made with the consent or acquiescence of the owner of the copyright in the work.

CIVIL REMEDIES

20. (1) Where copyright in any work has been infringed, the owner of the copyright is, except as otherwise provided by this Act, entitled to all such remedies by way of injunction, damages, accounts, and otherwise, as are or may be conferred by law for the infringement of a right.

(2) The costs of all parties in any proceedings in respect of the infringement of copyright shall be in the absolute discretion of the court.

(3) In any action for infringement of copyright in any work, in which the defendant puts in issue either the existence of the copyright, or the title of the plaintiff thereto, then, in any such case,

(*a*) the work shall, unless the contrary is proved, be presumed to be a work in which copyright subsists; and

(*b*) the author of the work shall, unless the contrary is proved, be presumed to be the owner of the copyright;

and where any such question is at issue, and no grant of the copyright or of an interest in the copyright, either by assignment or licence, has been registered under this Act, then, in any such case,

(*c*) if a name purporting to be that of the author of the work is printed or otherwise indicated thereon in the usual manner, the person whose name is so printed or indicated shall, unless the contrary is proved, be presumed to be the author of the work; and

(*d*) if no name is so printed or indicated, or if the name so printed or indicated is not the author's true name or the name by which he is commonly known, and a name purporting to be that of the publisher or proprietor of the work is printed or otherwise indicated thereon in the usual manner, the person whose name is so printed, or indicated shall, unless the contrary is proved, be presumed to be the owner of the copyright in the work for the purpose of proceedings in respect of the infringement of copyright therein.

(4) Where any person infringes the copyright in any work that is protected under this Act, such person is liable to pay such damages to the owner of the right infringed as he may have suffered due to the infringement, and in addition thereto such part of the profits that the infringer has made from such infringement as the court may decide to be just and proper; and in proving profits the plaintiff shall be required to prove only receipts or revenues derived from the publication, sale or other disposition of an infringing work, or from any unauthorized performance of the work in which copyright subsists; and the defendant shall be required to prove every element of cost that he claims.

(5) The author or other owner of any copyright or any person or persons deriving any right, title or interest by assignment or grant in writing from any author or other owner as aforesaid, may each, individually for himself, in his own name as party to a suit, action, or proceeding, protect and enforce such rights as he may hold, and to the extent of his right, title, and interest is entitled to the remedies provided by this Act.

(6) The Exchequer Court of Canada shall have concurrent jurisdiction with provincial courts to hear and determine all civil actions, suits, or proceedings that may be instituted for violation of any of the provisions of this Act or to enforce the civil remedies provided by this Act.

21. All infringing copies of any work in which copyright subsists, or of any substantial part thereof, and all plates used or intended to be used for the production of such infringing copies, shall be deemed to be the property of the owner of the copyright, who accordingly may take proceedings for the recovery of the possession thereof or in respect of the conversion thereof.

22. Where proceedings are taken in respect of the infringement of the copyright in any work and the defendant in his defence alleges that he was not aware of the existence of the copyright in the work, the plaintiff is not entitled to any remedy other than an injunction in respect of the infringement if the defendant proves that at the date of the infringement he was not aware, and had no reasonable ground for suspecting that copyright subsisted in the work; but if at the date of the infringement the copyright in the work was duly registered under this Act, the defendant shall be deemed to have had reasonable ground for suspecting that copyright subsisted in the work.

23. (1) Where the construction of a building or other structure that infringes or that, if completed, would infringe the copyright in some other work has been commenced, the owner of the copyright is not entitled to obtain an injunction in respect of the construction of such building or structure or to order its demolition.

(2) The other provisions of this Act which provide that an infringing copy of a work shall be deemed to be the property of the owner of the copyright, or that impose summary penalties, do not apply in any case to which this section applies.

24. An action in respect of infringement of copyright shall not be commenced after the expiration of three years next after the infringement.

SUMMARY REMEDIES

25. (1) Where any person knowingly

(*a*) makes for sale or hire any infringing copy of a work in which copyright subsists,

(*b*) sells or lets for hire, or by way of trade exposes or offers for sale or hire any infringing copy of any such work,

(*c*) distributes infringing copies of any such work either for the purpose of trade or to such an extent as to affect prejudically the owner of the copyright,

(*d*) by way of trade exhibits in public any infringing copy of any such work, or

(*e*) imports for sale or hire into Canada any infringing copy of any such work, he is guilty of an offence under this Act and is liable on summary conviction to a fine not exceeding ten dollars for every copy dealt with in contravention of this section, but not exceeding two hundred dollars in respect of the same transaction; or in the case of a second or subsequent offence, either to such fine or to imprisonment with or without hard labour for a term not exceeding two months.

(2) Where any person knowingly makes or has in his possession any plate for the purpose of making infringing copies of any work in which copyright subsists, or knowingly and for his private profit causes any such work to be performed in public without the consent of the owner of the copyright, he is guilty of an offence under this Act, and is liable on summary conviction to a fine not exceeding two hundred dollars, or in the case of a second or subsequent offence, either to such fine or to imprisonment with or without hard labour for a term not exceeding two months.

(3) The court before which any such proceedings are taken may, whether the alleged offender is convicted or not, order that all copies of the work or all plates in the possession of the alleged offender that appear to it to be infringing copies or plates for the purpose of making infringing copies, be destroyed or delivered up to the owner of the copyright or otherwise dealt with as the court may think fit.

26. (1) Any person who, without the written consent of the owner of the copyright or of his legal representative, knowingly performs or causes to be performed in public and for private profit the whole or any part, constituting an infringement, of any dramatic or operatic work or musical composition in which copyright subsists in Canada, is guilty of an offence, and is liable on summary conviction to a fine not exceeding two hundred and fifty dollars, or in the case of a second or subsequent offence, either to such fine or to imprisonment for a term not exceeding two months, or to both.

(2) Any person who makes or causes to be made any change in or suppression of the title, or the name of the author, of any dramatic or operatic work or musical composition in which copyright subsists in Canada, or who makes or causes to be made any change in such work or composition itself without the written consent of the author or of his legal representative, in order that such work or composition may be performed in whole or in part in public for private profit, is guilty of an offence, and is liable on summary conviction to a fine not exceeding five hundred dollars, or in the case of a second or subsequent offence, either to such fine or to imprisonment for a term not exceeding four months, or to both.

IMPORTATION OF COPIES

27. Copies made out of Canada of any work in which copyright subsists that if made in Canada would infringe copyright and as to which the owner of the copyright gives notice in writing to the Department of National Revenue that he is desirous that such copies should not be so imported into Canada, shall not be so imported, and shall be deemed to be included in Schedule C to the *Customs Tariff*, and that Schedule applies accordingly.

Chapter 14

Conclusions

The publication and distribution of works are often contingent upon the execution of a formal agreement between the author and the publisher. In practice, such agreements are usually standard form containing a comprehensive treatment of the rights and obligations of the parties including the obligations of the publisher to print at its own expense and to effect distribution, as well as the obligations of the author to deliver the work, to review the proofs and to warrant the grant to publication whether in the form of assignment or licence of copyright. The contract furthermore deals extensively with the rights of the parties, including the right to royalties to exploit subsidiary rights and to reprint or issue re-editions.

Notwithstanding the currency of these agreements, the existing legislation remains for the most part silent as to the form, content and duration of such agreements.

Publishing contracts not only set out the rights of the parties with respect to the issuance of the work in book form, but also deal with the use of the work in translation, dramatization, radio and television broadcast, film and other means of reproduction. Notwithstanding the relative importance of such contracts, the courts have often been faced with ambiguities affecting even the most essential parts of the agreements namely, the conferral of copyright and the disposition of subsidiary rights. In the course of drafting and interpreting author-publisher agreements, consideration must be given to the fact that it is industry practice that the publisher undertakes the greatest economic risks concerning the publication efforts while the author risks loss of time and nominal expenses in creating the work.

In practice, author-publisher agreements may contain extensive provisions for a variety of rights and obligations; in other cases, they may be reduced to ambiguous cross-letters or implications by way of delivery. Where agreements are explicit, the contract sets out the undertaking of the publisher to publish a work in a specified form in a given territory. The publisher is furthermore obliged to effect publication of the work within a stipulated period. The cost of publication is often borne by the publisher and accordingly, the latter is given a wide discretion in determining the manner, style and conditions of publication and distribution.

The rights of the author are usually limited to the right to receive nominal royalties. It is rare that the author is given an active role in determining the essential factors such as printing, advertising, circulation and general marketing.

Although copyright is often vested in the author, the extensive nature of the license granted to the publisher reduces the value of the copyright to a nominal level.

Upon the termination of the agreement, the parties are generally free to continue their activities as author and publisher respectively save insofar as continuing liability upon warranties and rights of first refusal are concerned.

The courts are on the one hand hesitant to apply the full force of a standard form agreement to the detriment of the author, but will on the other hand refer to industry practice to determine the rights of the parties in the absence of an agreement or in the event of an ambiguity.

Appendix A

The LeSueur Case and its Sequel

The case of *Morang v. LeSueur*[1] has been referred to on several occasions in this work; the decision of the Supreme Court clarifies the law respecting the right of the author to recovery of the manuscript in the event of the failure of the publisher to proceed with publication, the right of the publisher to reject a manuscript which is not of satisfactory quality, as well as the nature of a literary manuscript in the context of a commercial sale. The rendering of the judgment by the Supreme Court however did not terminate the litigation between the parties and the dispute in issue may be said to have been resolved in a definitive way only quite recently.

In December 1905, W. D. LeSueur entered into a contract with Morang and Company Ltd. to write a biography of the late William Lyon Mackenzie for publication in the series of books issued by the publisher entitled "The Makers of Canada". Mr. LeSueur was a free-thinking intellectual and author of the time who had, even prior to his engagement and undertaking to write the biography, little of the adulation or sympathy displayed toward the subject of the work by his contemporaries. The biography was written after due research had been made by the author through letters, files and books, many of which were kept at the residence of Charles Lindsey, the son-in-law of Mackenzie.

Mr. LeSueur had been actively involved in the editorship of the Makers of Canada Series which dealt with biographies of those persons considered by historians to have contributed to the ultimate founding of the Canadian nation. The author had in fact been instrumental in having Morang and Company Ltd. reject a biography of Mackenzie written by another author on the ground that the manuscript was too favourable.

LeSueur's manuscript when completed was submitted to the publisher. The

[1] (1911), 45 S.C.R. 95.

publisher however under considerable pressure from the family of Mackenzie refused to proceed with publication of the biography on the ground that the author had been engaged to write a work of Mackenzie as a "Maker of Canada" and not as a "Puller Down" of the nation. Litigation between author and publisher consequently ensued culminating in the decision of the Supreme Court which declared the author entitled to recover the manuscripts submitted. Following the judgments, however, the son of Charles Lindsey instituted proceedings in order to prevent the author from making any further use of the manuscripts through the instrument of another publisher. Lindsey sought an order to restrain the author from making use of original papers and other materials furnished to him by Charles Lindsey. Lindsey alleged that the materials were furnished only on the assurance of the author that he was in sympathy with the character he was to depict as one of the Makers of Canada; and that he concealed his true bias.[2]

At trial on the action, Lindsey proved that LeSueur had resided in his house for several months while obtaining information and reviewing personal family papers respecting the life of Mackenzie. Although there was no direct proof respecting an agreement, Lindsey argued that by necessary implication from what took place there was an understanding that LeSueur in writing the biography would make fair use of the material he found. In 1913, Britton J. maintained the action instituted by Lindsey and ordered LeSueur to refrain from publishing or causing to be published any book which contained information obtained from the archives maintained by Lindsey respecting Mackenzie. In reviewing the evidence, the court held:[3]

> At the time of the defendant's arrangement with the plaintiff, the defendant did hold strong views against Mackenzie. At that time the defendant intended to write the life of Mackenzie on other than "conventional lines." He intended to write of Mackenzie, not as one of "The Makers of Canada," in the general acceptation of that term, but as a "puller down," as was stated during the trial.
>
> I deal with this matter simply as a matter of contract and good faith between the parties, not expressing any opinion as to whether the defendant is right or wrong in his estimate of Mackenzie. It does not, so far as it affects this case, except as a matter of good faith on the part of the defendant, make any difference whether Mackenzie was a man of high aims and unselfish purpose, contending against real wrongs permitted by bad laws and perpetrated by unjust administration, or a mere adventurer, willing to point where he would not lead, a mere inciter to rebellion against laws that were just, and administered by men able and honest.
>
> I quite recognise that the biographer should write truly of his subject. He should not, as the defendant said he would not, write any fairy tale or Jack the Giant-killer story. The defendant could write truly of the life selected, and draw such inferences as might please him from the facts; and any quarrel with his inferences would be in the nature of fair discussion. But this is a question of how the defendant came to get

---

[2] *Lindsey v. LeSueur* (1912), 1 D.L.R. 61 (Ont.).
[3] (1913), 11 D.L.R. 411 at p. 413 (Ont.).

> possession of what is now the plaintiff's property, and of the use he made of it, as distinguished from the use the plaintiff supposed the defendant would make of it, and as distinguished from the use the defendant led the plaintiff to think would be made of it, and as to the use the defendant now proposes to make of it.
>
> If the defendant obtained possession of or access to property now belonging to the plaintiff, by misrepresentation or by concealment of facts which he was bound to disclose, then he must not further use that property.
>
> I am of opinion, upon the evidence, that the defendant made use of the Mackenzie collection of books and papers otherwise than was in accord with the understanding between him and the plaintiff and Charles Lindsey.

The judgment was appealed but subsequently maintained in December 1913. The Appellate Division of the Ontario Supreme Court held[4] there was an agreement expressly made or to be implied from what took place between the parties that the author was under an obligation to depict the subject of the biography as a Maker of Canada in consideration for gaining access to the Lindsey archives. The Court held that if LeSueur was given access to the use of the documents for a particular purpose, there was an implication that they were not to be used for any other purpose. It was held that the purpose was that LeSueur should write a life of Mackenzie which would so depict him that he would rightly take a place in the publisher's series as a Maker of Canada.

Following this decision, the manuscript of the biography apparently rested with Mr. Lindsey and was eventually deposited in the Public Archives of Ontario. The manuscript was recently re-discovered and prepared for publication by an history researcher; the biography was finally published in Canada by a leading publisher in 1979.[5] It may also be noted that following the last judgment, Mr. LeSueur began to write a second biography on the subject which he felt would not be subject to injunctive recourse by Mr. Lindsey Mr. LeSueur apparently completed the second biography and had contacted another publisher who was willing to publish the same. Immediately prior to publication, the publisher indefinitely postponed the venture and the biography was consequently consigned to oblivion.[6]

---

[4] (1913), 15 D.L.R. 809.

[5] *William Lyon Mackenzie: A Re-interpretation,* MacMillan (1979).

[6] For a summary review of the publishing history of the biography, see Francis, Daniel "*King v. Revisionist*", Books in Canada, Volume 8, No. 3, March 1979, p. 4.

Appendix B

Schroeder Music Publishing Co. Ltd. v. Macaulay*

LORD REID. My Lords, the appellants are publishers of music. The respondent is a writer of songs. On 12th July 1966 they entered into a somewhat elaborate agreement under which the appellants engaged the exclusive services of the respondent for a term of five years which in a certain event was to be extended to ten years. In 1970 the respondent raised the present action claiming a declaration that the agreement is contrary to public policy and void. He also made various alternative claims which your Lordships have found it unnecessary to consider. Plowman J made the declaration claimed and his decision was affirmed by the Court of Appeal [[1974] 1 All E.R. 171].

In 1966 the respondent was aged about 21. He and a Mr McLeod had collaborated in writing a few songs, but it appears that none of them had been published. He obtained an interview with Mr Schroeder who, with Mrs Schroeder, controls an American music publishing corporation with world wide connections. The appellant company is a subsidiary of the corporation. The respondent wished to get a different kind of contract but agreed to sign this agreement which is in the appellants' standard form with a few alterations.

It is not disputed that the validity of the agreement must be determined as at the date when it was signed and it is therefore unnecessary to deal with the reasons why the respondent now wishes to be freed from it. The law with regard to the validity of agreements in restraint of trade was fully considered by this House in *Esso Petroleum Co Ltd v. Harper's Garage* [[1967] 1 All E.R. 699] and I do not intend to restate the principles there set out or to add to or modify what

* [1974] 3 All E.R. 616.

I said myself. I think that in a case like the present case two questions must be considered. Are the terms of the agreement so restrictive that either they cannot be justified at all or that they must be justified by the party seeking to enforce the agreement? Then, if there is room for justification, has that party proved justification—normally by shewing that the restrictions were no more than what was reasonably required to protect his legitimate interests. In this case evidence on the second question was scanty and I turn first to the terms of the agreement. The agreement contains 17 clauses. It must of course be read as a whole and we must consider the cumulative effect of the restrictions contained therein. I think it best to set it out in full omitting only those parts which deal with performing rights, because neither party founded on them in argument, and some formal matters. The relevant parts are as follows:

> '1. Subject as hereinafter mentioned this Agreement shall remain in force for a period of FIVE (5) years from the date hereof (hereinafter called 'the said term').
>
> '2. (a) The Publisher engages the exclusive services of the Composer and the Composer will render the same to the Publisher during the said term. (b) The Composer shall obey and comply with all lawful orders and directions in relation to his services hereunder given to him by the Publisher and shall use his best endeavours to promote the interests of the Publisher. (c) The Composer will not during the said term directly or indirectly work for, render services or be affiliated to or be interested in or connected with any person, firm or corporation engaged in the music publishing business other than the Publisher nor will he during the said term carry on or be concerned in, whether alone or in partnership, any music publishing business. (d) The Composer will not divulge to any person except as may be required by the Publisher any confidential information relating to the business of the Publisher.
>
> '3. (a) The Composer HEREBY ASSIGNS to the Publisher the full copyright for the whole world in each and every original musical composition and/or lyric including but without prejudice to the generality of the foregoing, the title words and music thereof written/or composed created or conceived by the Composer alone or in collaboration with any other person or persons and whether in his own name or under a nom-de-plume at any time during the said term or at any time prior to the date hereof insofar as such latter compositions and/or lyrics are still owned or controlled by the Composer directly or indirectly . . . (b) In this Agreement references to musical works and/or lyrics shall include the part or parts hereof (if separate and divisible) written composed created or conceived by the Composer . . .
>
> '4. Where a musical composition and/or lyric to which this Agreement applies is a "work of joint authorship" as defined by Section II of the Copyright Act 1956, the Composer will procure that his co-author or co-authors as the case may be will join with him in doing such acts and things and executing such deeds and documents as may be necessary to vest the copyright in the said work in the Publisher.
>
> '5. In respect of each work hereinbefore referred to the copyright in which has been assigned by the Composer and his collaborators (if any), the Publisher will pay to the Composer and his collaborators (if any): (a) on all piano copies sold and paid for (after the first 500 copies) in the United Kingdom of Great Britain and Northern Ireland and Eire a royalty of 10% of the marked selling price; (b) 50% of all net royalties received by the Publishers in respect of mechanical reproduction of the said

works and of all net synchronisation fees; (c) in the event of the said works being published in any country outside the United Kingdom and Eire, 50% of the net royalties received by the Publisher from persons authorised to publish the said works in such foreign territories.

'6. (a) Fees in respect of performing rights shall be divided as to 50% to the Composer and his collaborators (if any) (hereinafter referred to as "the Composer's Share") and 50% to the Publisher . . . (c) If the Composer shall be or become a member of P.R.S. and while he remains such member all performing fees shall be divided between the parties hereto in accordance with P.R.S. rules for the time being in force subject to the agreement of the parties hereinbefore contained varying the divisions as permitted by such rules so that 50% of such fees are for the Composer and his collaborators (if any) and 50% for the Publisher . . .

'8. (a) The Publisher shall pay the sum of £50 to the Composer, which shall be a general advance against royalties payable by the Publisher under this Agreement and to be recouped therefrom but in no case shall the Publisher be entitled to the return of any part of such sums. Upon the recoupment by the Publisher of said general advance payment of Fifty (£50) Pounds, the Publisher agrees to pay another Fifty (£50) Pounds, which is to be treated as a general advance as described herein. This same procedure shall continue throughout the said term hereof; i.e. as each general advance of Fifty (£50) Pounds if recouped in full by the Publisher, the Publisher shall pay to the Composer the sum of Fifty (£50) Pounds, etcetera. (b) The Publisher will render to the Composer semiannually statements showing the amount of royalties due to the Composer as at 31st December and 30th June in each year. Such statements shall be delivered within 60 days of the relevant date and shall be accompanied by a remittance for such sum (if any) as may be shown to be due to the Composer.

'9. (a) If during the said term the total of the Composer's royalties hereunder and all advances thereon (if any) shall equal or exceed £5000 then this agreement shall automatically be extended for a further period of FIVE (5) years and for the purpose of this Agreement the said period of FIVE (5) years shall be deemed to be included in and be part of the said term. (b) The Publisher may at any time during the said term terminate this Agreement by giving to the Composer one month's written notice to that effect. Such termination shall be without prejudice to the rights of the parties in respect of any antecedent breach of this Agreement and the Publisher's obligations to pay royalties hereinbefore provided for.

'10. (a) The Composer will forthwith submit to the Publisher every composition and/or lyric written and/or composed created or conceived by him alone or in collaboration. The Composer warrants to the Publisher that the copyright in all such works will pass to the Publisher free from any adverse claims or rights from any third party and that all such works submitted to the Publisher will be the original work of the Composer and his collaborators (if any). (b) The Composer will indemnify the Publisher against all claims damages and demands and against all costs incurred in the institution or defence of any actions or proceedings relating to the said works submitted to the Publisher . . .

'12. (a) The Composer will execute a standard song writer's Agreement in respect of each and every work the subject of this Agreement. Such song writer's Agreement shall be in the form annexed hereto and initialled by the parties (hereinafter referred to as "the song writer's Agreement"). (b) For the avoidance of doubt it is agreed that any assignment required under Clauses 4 or 12 hereof shall be in the form of the song writer's Agreement.

'13. In the event of any breach of the terms or conditions of this Agreement by the Composer the Publisher shall be entitled to suspend and withhold payment of royalties (including the general advances provided for in para. 8 hereinabove) until such breach has been remedied. If the Composer shall fail to remedy any such breach within One month of written notice by the Publisher requiring him so to do all royalties then or thereafter due under this Agreement shall cease to be or shall not become (as the case may be) payable . . .

'15. For the avoidance of any possible doubt and without in any way limiting the assignment hereinbefore contained it is hereby declared that the copyright hereby assigned includes: (a) the right to renew and extend the copyright and the ownership of such renewed and extended copyright. (b) the right to make and publish new adaptations and arrangements and to make such additions adaptations and alterations in and to the words and/or music as the Publisher may desire and to provide and translate the lyric thereof in any and all languages of the world.

'16. (a) The Publisher shall have the right to assign this Agreement and all rights and obligations hereunder to any person firm or corporation and shall also have the right to assign any or all rights in a particular work. (b) The Composer will not assign his rights under this Agreement without the Publisher's prior written consent.

'17. The Composer will at the Publisher's request at any time during the said term or thereafter execute any other document and do all other acts or things which may hereafter be required for vesting in the Publisher the rights and benefits hereby expressed to be assigned and conferred.'

Clauses 1 and 9(a) determine the duration of the agreement. It was to last for five years in any event and for ten years if the royalties for the first five years exceeded £5,000. There is little evidence about this extension. Five thousand pounds in five years appears to represent a very modest success, and so if the respondent's work became well known and popular he would be tied by the agreement for ten years. The duration of an agreement in restraint of trade is a factor of great importance in determining whether the restrictions in the agreement can be justified but there was no evidence as to why so long a period was necessary to protect the appellants' interests. Clause 2 requires the respondent to give the exclusive services to and obey all lawful orders of the appellants. It is not very clear what this means. Read in conjunction with cl 2(c) it probably does not prevent him from doing non-musical work so long as that does not interfere with his obligations to the appellants. I do not attach importance to this clause as being at all unduly restrictive. Clause 3 is of importance but I shall return to it later. Clauses 5 to 8 deal with remuneration. Some parts are not very clear but it was not argued that this was an unreasonable basis for the remuneration of a composer unknown when the agreement was made. Clause 9(b) entitles the appellants to terminate the agreement but there is no corresponding provision in favour of the respondent. I shall have to deal with this later. Clause 10(b) could be rather oppressive but no serious objection was taken to it and the same may be said of cl 13. Clause 16 appears to me to be important. There may sometimes be room for an argument that although on a strict literal construction restrictions could be enforced oppressively, one is entitled to have regard to the fact that a large organisation could not afford to act oppressively without damaging the goodwill of its business. But the power to assign leaves no room for that argument. We cannot assume that an assignee would always act reasonably.

The public interest requires in the interests both of the public and of the individual that everyone should be free so far as practicable to earn a livelihood and to give to the public the fruits of his particular abilities. The main question to be considered is whether and how far the operation of the terms of this agreement is likely to conflict with this objective. The respondent is bound to assign to the appellants during a long period the fruits of his musical talent. But what are the appellants bound to do with those fruits? Under the contract nothing. If they do use the songs which the respondent composes they must pay in terms of the contract. But they need not do so. As has been said they may put them in a drawer and leave them there. No doubt the expectation was that if the songs were of value they would be published to the advantage of both parties. But if for any reason the appellants chose not to publish them the respondent would get no remuneration and he could not do anything. Inevitably the respondent must take the risk of misjudgment of the merits of his work by the appellants. But that is not the only reason which might cause the appellants not to publish. There is no evidence about this so we must do the best we can with common knowledge. It does not seem fanciful and it was not argued that it is fanciful to suppose that purely commercial consideration might cause a publisher to refrain from publishing and promoting promising material. He might think it likely to be more profitable to promote work by other composers with whom he had agreements and unwise or too expensive to try to publish and popularise the respondent's work in addition. And there is always the possibility that less legitimate reasons might influence a decision not to publish the respondent's work.

It was argued that there must be read into this agreement an obligation on the publisher to act in good faith. I take that to mean that he would be in breach of contract if by reason of some oblique or malicious motive he refrained from publishing work which he would otherwise have published. I very much doubt this but even if it were so it would make little difference. Such a case would seldom occur and then would be difficult to prove.

I agree with the appellants' argument to this extent. I do not think that a publisher could reasonably be expected to enter into any positive commitment to publish future work by an unknown composer. Possibly there might be some general undertaking to use his best endeavours to promote the composer's work. But that would probably have to be in such general terms as to be of little use to the composer.

But if no satisfactory positive undertaking by the publisher can be devised, it appears to me to be an unreasonable restraint to tie the composer for this period of years so that his work will be sterilised and he can earn nothing from his abilities as a composer if the publisher chooses not to publish. If there had been in cl 9 any provision entitling the composer to terminate the agreement in such an event the case might have had a very different appearance. But as the agreement stands not only is the composer tied but he cannot recover the copyright of the work which the publisher refuses to publish.

It was strenuously argued that the agreement is in standard form, that it has stood the test of time, and that there is no indication that it ever causes injustice. Reference was made to passages in the speeches of Lord Pearce and Lord Wilberforce in the *Esso* case [[1967] 1 All E.R. 699] with which I wholly agree. Lord Pearce said [at p. 723]:

> 'It is important that the court, in weighing the question of reasonableness, should give full weight to commercial practices and to the generality of contracts made freely by parties bargaining on equal terms.'

Later Lord Wilberforce said [at pp. 729-30]:

> 'The development of the law does seem to show, however, that judges have been able to dispense from the necessity of justification under a public policy test of reasonableness such contracts or provisions of contracts as, under contemporary conditions, may be found to have passed into the accepted and normal currency of commercial or contractual or conveyancing relations. That such contracts have done so may be taken to show with at least strong prima force that, moulded under the pressures of negotiation, competition and public opinion, they have assumed a form which satisfies the test of public policy as understood by the courts at the time, or, regarding the matter from the point of view of the trade, that the trade in question has assumed such a form that for its health or expansion it requires a degree of regulation.'

But those passages refer to contracts 'made freely by parties bargaining on equal terms' or 'moulded under the pressures of negotiation, competition and public opinion'. I do not find from any evidence in this case, nor does it seem probable, that this form of contract made between a publisher and an unknown composer has been moulded by any pressure of negotiation. Indeed, it appears that established composers who can bargain on equal terms can and do make their own contracts.

Any contract by which a person engages to give his exclusive services to another for a period necessarily involves extensive restriction during that period of the common law right to exercise any lawful activity he chooses in such manner as he thinks best. Normally the doctrine of restraint of trade has no application to such restrictions: they require no justification. But if contractual restrictions appear to be unnecessary or to be reasonably capable of enforcement in an oppressive manner, then they must be justified before they can be enforced.

In the present case the respondent assigned to the appellants 'the full copyright for the whole world' in every musical composition 'composed created or conceived' by him alone or in collaboration with any other person during a period of five or it might be ten years. He received no payment (apart from an initial £50) unless his work was published and the appellants need not publish unless they chose to do so. And if they did not publish he had no right to terminate the agreement or to have any copyrights re-assigned to him. I need not consider whether in any circumstances it would be possible to justify such a one-sided agreement. It is sufficient to say that such evidence as there is falls far short of justification. It must therefore follow that the agreement so far as unperformed is unenforceable.

I would dismiss this appeal.

VISCOUNT DILHORNE. My Lords, I have had the advantage of reading the speech of my noble and learned friend, Lord Reid, in draft. I agree with it and for the reasons he gives, I, too, would dismiss this appeal.

LORD DIPLOCK. My Lords, the contract under consideration in this appeal is one whereby the respondent accepted restrictions on the way in which he would exploit his earning-power as a song-writer for the next ten years. Because this can be classified as a contract in restraint of trade the restrictions that the respondent accepted fell within one of those limited categories of contractual promises in respect of which the courts still retain the power to relieve the promisor of his legal duty to fulfil them. In order to determine whether this case is one in which that power ought to be exercised, what your Lordships have in fact been doing has been to assess the relative bargaining power of the publisher and the song-writer at the time the contract was made and to decide whether the publisher had used his superior bargaining power to exact from the song-writer promises that were unfairly onerous to him. Your Lordships have not been concerned to enquire whether the public have in fact been deprived of the fruit of the song-writer's talents by reason of the restrictions, nor to assess the likelihood that they would be so deprived in the future if the contract were permitted to run its full course.

It is, in my view, salutory to acknowledge that in refusing to enforce provisions of a contract whereby one party agrees for the benefit of the other party to exploit or to refrain from exploiting his own earning-power, the public policy which the court is implementing is not some 19th century economic theory about the benefit to the general public of freedom of trade, but the protection of those whose bargaining power is weak against being forced by those whose bargaining power is stronger to enter into bargains that are unconscionable. Under the influence of Bentham and of laissez-faire the courts in the 19th century abandoned the practice of applying the public policy against unconscionable bargains to contracts generally, as they had formerly done to any contract considered to be usurious; but the policy survived in its application to penalty clauses and to relief against forfeiture and also to the special category of contracts in restraint of trade. If one looks at the reasoning of 19th century judges in cases about contracts in restraint of trade one finds lip service paid to current economic theories but if one looks at what they said in the light of what they did, one finds that they struck down a bargain if they thought it was unconscionable as between the parties to it, and upheld it if they thought that it was not.

So I would hold that the question to be answered as respects a contract in restraint of trade of the kind with which this appeal is concerned is: was the bargain fair? The test of fairness is, no doubt, whether the restrictions are both reasonably necessary for the protection of the legitimate interests of the promisee and commensurate with the benefits secured to the promisor under the contract. For the purpose of this test all the provisions of the contract must be taken into consideration.

My Lords, the provisons of the contract have already been sufficiently stated by my noble and learned friend, Lord Reid. I agree with his analysis of them and with his conclusion that the contract is unenforceable. It does not satisfy the test of fairness as I have endeavoured to state it. I will accordingly content myself with adding some observations directed to the argument that because the contract was in a 'standard form' in common use between music publishers and song-writers, the restraints that it imposes on the song-writer's liberty to exploit his talents must be presumed to be fair and reasonable.

Appendix C

Extracts from A Charter of Rights for Creators and the Government Response

Sub-Committee's Recommendation

1. The Copyright Act should be expanded to include new property rights which reflect modern forms of creative activity and the various ways of communicating the fruits of that activity.

Government's Response

The government is strongly in favour of this objective of modernizing the existing Act and keeping it up to date in the future.

Sub-Committee's Recommendations

2. The revised law should recognize moral rights as an integral part of copyright.

3. All remedies for infringement of an economic right should be available for infringement of a moral right.

4. The term of protection for moral rights should be the same as the term of protection for economic rights.

5. The new Act should provide a moral right to authorize the use of any protected work in association with products, services, causes or institutions.

6. The revised Act should provide a moral right to prevent any modification of the original of an artistic work, including an element of a limited edition thereof, even in the absence of evidence of prejudice to the author's honour or reputation.

7. The right should be limited in order to permit the physical relocation of the work, the alteration of a structure containing the work, and legitimate restoration and preservation activities.

8. Unimpeded negotiations concerning the use and assignment of rights should be preferred whenever possible over compulsory arrangements, prohibitions and other predetermined outcomes.

Government's Response

The government agrees in principle with these recommendations.

However, recommendation 5 will not extend to works for which a blanket licence has been granted by a collective society of copyright, owners so as not to oblige users to obtain a second authorization for works that such societies have been assigned to administer.

In addition, with regard to recommendation 8, a provision will be incorporated in the Act to limit the term of licences and of the assignment of rights so as to protect creators from abuses.

WRITING AND PUBLISHING

Sub-Committee's Recommendation

18. In view of the originality involved in their preparation, editions of literary, dramatic, musical and artistic works should be protected against unauthorized reproduction for 25 years from publication. Protection should be extended on a reciprocal basis to those countries with similar protection.

Government's Response

This recommendation is accepted in principle. However, the conditions and

the procedure for the extension of the legislation to foreign editions will be defined in the Act.

Sub-Committee's Recommendations

19. Translation should be expressly included in the revised law as proper subject matter of copyright protection, without prejudice to the rights of the owner of the copyright in the underlying work.

20. Blank forms should not be specifically excluded from protection, but should be subject to the same criteria as other works.

21. Maps, charts and plans should be treated as artistic works.

Government's Response

The government accepts these recommendations.

Sub-Committee's Recommendations

22. Importation protection should be maintained for all copyright subject matter.

Government's Response

The government accepts this recommendation in principle.

Sub-Committee's Recommendations

23. A mechanism should be developed to compensate authors for the public lending of their works by libraries. The scheme should be independent of copyright law.

24. A specific right of reprographic reproduction should not be introduced.

25. No exception should be provided for reproduction by libraries.

Government's Response

The government agrees in principle with these recommendations.

Sub-Committee's Recommendations

26. The revised law should not provide for a compulsory licence to translate literary works.

27. The reproduction, public performance and printing compulsory licences should not be retained in the revised law.

Government's Response

The government accepts these recommendations.

Sub-Committee's Recommendations

28. Provision should be made in the revised law for the Copyright Appeal Board to issue non-exclusive licences where a copyright owner cannot be located.

Government's Response

The government agrees with this recommendation. Such licences will be issued subject to the conditions stated in *From Gutenberg to Telidon*, particularly the following conditions:

- **proof, to the satisfaction of the Board, that a reasonable effort has been made to locate the copyright owner;**
- **payment of royalties approximating what would be negotiated in the marketplace;**
- **proof that the work against which the licence is sought has been published.**

AUDIO-VISUAL WORKS

Sub-Committee's Recommendations

45. The new Act should provide for a distinct category of protected subject matter to be called "audio-visual works".

46. Audio-visual works should be defined to include any work in which an image appears to be in motion, with or without sound, on any material support.

47. Audio-visual works should be defined to include pre-programmed works where the movement of the picture may be the result of a player's interaction with a computer program.

48. The new Act should define the phrase "in public" as regards the right to perform in public so as to include situations where individuals share living quarters by reason of their work, education, vacation or detention.

49. "Performance in public" should be defined to include those performances effected by means of a video jukebox even where such performances can be viewed only by one person at any given time.

50. The new Act, in defining "publication", should take into account the various methods of making a work available to the public other than by issuance of copies of that work.

51. Audio-visual works should be protected for the shorter of 50 years following publication or 75 years following fixation.

Government Response

The government agrees with these recommendations in principle. The suggested definitions will be considered when developing the Act.

COMPUTERS

Sub-Committee's Recommendations

52. A new right to input any protected work into a computer should be provided in the revised law.

53. There should be no right of display in the revised law.

54. Fixation should be defined as all means capable of capturing a work, including capture in computer media, but excluding capture in a medium as volatile as a computer's main storage or display screen.

55. With respect to the right of reproduction, a material form should be one that has a certain degree of permanence.

56. Where a work created with the assistance of a computer is original the copyright in that work should be owned by the person responsible for its making and not by the owner of the copyright in the original program.

57. Ownership in compilations produced by computer data storage and retrieval systems should be vested in the individual or entity primarily responsible for the arrangements undertaken for making the compilation.

58. Computer programs should be protected by the revised law as a separate category of subject matter with the full regime of protection on the basis of reciprocity.

59. The Act should provide an exception to the right of reproduction to permit the making of a back-up copy.

60. The term of protection for computer programs should be the life of the author plus 50 years.

61. The government should study the possibility of providing an exception to permit the reproduction of a substantial part of a pre-existing program as a non-substantial part of another program.

62. Mask works fixed in semi-conductor chips should be protected by new legislation outside the *Copyright Act*.

63. The mask works to be protected are a series of related images that represent the three-dimensional pattern of circuits and components fixed in a semi-conductor chip.

Government Response

The government agrees with these recommendations in principle.

The issue of the right of display mentioned in recommendation 53, however, will be studied in further detail.

Recommendation 54 will be considered when defining the concept of fixation.

With regard to recommendation 58, the government agrees in principle that computer programs should benefit from the full regime of protection. However, it will give national treatment to foreign computer programs.

The government has studied the possibility of providing the exception suggested in recommendation 61 but has decided against it.

Finally, mask works fixed in semi-conductor chips will be protected in the Copyright Act but will be distinguished from traditional works.

Sub-Committee's Recommendations

88. The revised law should provide an exception to permit an archival institution to make a copy of a work which is not otherwise available and which is already in its collection, for the purpose of preserving the archival copy of that work.

89. An exception should be provided to permit an archival institution to make a copy of a work for another archival institution where the latter has received a request for a copy of a work from an individual researcher for the purpose of private research. The making and issuance of copies under this exception should not constitute publication.

90. The revised law should provide an exception to permit teachers and students, in the normal course of teaching activities to:

    (a) perform a work in public;

    (b) transmit and retransmit a work within the confines of a single educational institution.

91. An exception should be provided to allow for the reproduction of a work as part of questions to be asked, or answered, in an examination.

Government Response

The Government accepts these recommendations.

COLLECTIVES

Sub-Committee's Recommendations

110. The collective exercise of copyright should be encouraged.

111. The Copyright Appeal Board should be vested with the authority to regulate all collectives.

112. Membership in collectives should continue to be voluntary.

113. Creators should continue to be allowed to grant exclusive licences to collectives.

Government Response

The government agrees with these recommendations in principle.

The issue raised in recommendation 111, however, will be examined at the same time as recommendations 114 to 126 regarding the Copyright Appeal Board.

Bibliography

Copinger and Skone James, *Copyright,* 11th ed. (London: Sweet & Maxwell, 1971).

Culture Statistics, *Book Publishing and Industry Analyses,* (Ottawa: Minister of Industry, Trade and Commerce, December 1978).

Dépôt légal (Paris: Institut International de Coopération Intellectuelle, 1938).

Dryden, Jean, "Copyright in Manuscript Sources", Archivaria, Vol. 1, No. 1, Winter 1975-76.

Fox, Harold G., *Canadian Law of Copyright and Industrial Designs,* 2nd ed. (Toronto: Carswell Co. Ltd., 1967).

Grannis, C. B. (ed.), *What Happens in Book Publishing* (New York: Columbia University Press, 1957).

Graschuk, H. S., "The Professional Corporations in Alberta" (1977), 25 Can. Tax J. 109.

Jehoram, H. C., *Copyright Contracts* (1977).

Keyes, A. A. and Brunet, C., *Copyright in Canada—Proposals for a Revision of the Law* (Ottawa: Consumer and Corporate Affairs, April 1977).

Matheson, D. J., "Service Corporations" (1976), 24 Can. Tax J. 329.

Noel, W., "The Importation Provisions of the Canadian Copyright Act" (1977), 9 Ottawa L. R. 156.

Report on Copyright, Royal Commission Patents, Copyright, Trademarks and Industrial Design (Ilsley Commission) (Ottawa, 1957).

Report on Intellectual and Industrial Property (Ottawa: Economic Council of Canada, January 1971).

Report of the Royal Commission on Book Publishing (Government of Ontario, 1972).

Rothenberg, Stanley, "Oral Copyright Contracts and Statutes of Frauds" (1977), Bulletin of the Copyright Society, Vol. 25, 159.

Shapiro, Andrew, "The Standard Author Contract: A Survey of Current Draftsmanship", ASCA Copyright Law Symposium, No. 18 (New York: Columbia University Press, 1970).

Sharp, R. C., "Import Restrictions in the Canadian Copyright Act" (1975), 17 C. P. R. (2d) 20.

Spry, *Equitable Remedies* (1971).

Index